Casey Morley's *Crawl* a thriller novel: violence, demonic vill , and impossible obstacles. The tragedy and the triumph of this story are that it is not fiction–the tragedy, in the horrific abuse Morley endured as a child and later as a woman and mother. The triumph, in her unstoppable spirit and her unshakeable faith, bent on breaking the cycle of abuse. This is a vital book for anyone who suffers abuse or works with victims and for everyone intent on ending the violence.

Chuck Miceli
Author, *Amanda's Room*

No matter where I open up to, it draws me in. I have a good feeling about this, you have something good here.

Abby Beale
Creator, *Rev It Up Reading*
Author, *10 Days to Faster Reading*
The Complete Idiot's Guide® to Speed Reading

I related so well to Casey's experience because I, too, have suffered from the long-term, detrimental effects of loving and living with an alcoholic. This story brought me to a deeper awareness… I learned that I am not as far on my journey to recovery as I thought–but I'm not discouraged. I'm inspired now more than ever to continue that sometimes-very-painful path to healing. I just love a story with a happy ending!

Karen
Marketing

A quick read. Inspirational for anyone who endures or has endured abuse on any level–man, woman, or child.

Marianne
Human Resources

When Casey asked me to read this book as a favor to give her a male perspective, I did not expect I could apply any of it to myself, as I never considered myself a victim of abuse. What struck me most is how *Crawling Out* graphically illustrates the abusive nature of alcoholic relationships. Everyone around an alcoholic is affected, especially the children. This book gave me the gentle nudge I needed that Casey so often speaks about to see things in a new light. Awareness is always the first step.

Don

In *Crawling Out,* Casey Morley dares to do what each of us is called to do—to use our stories and our lives to rise from the ashes and serve a greater good. Her book is beautiful, honest, moving, close to perfection. Her courage inspires me to do the same.

Crystal
Yoga Instructor

Crawling Out

One woman's journey to an empowered life after breaking a cycle of abuse no one should have to endure.

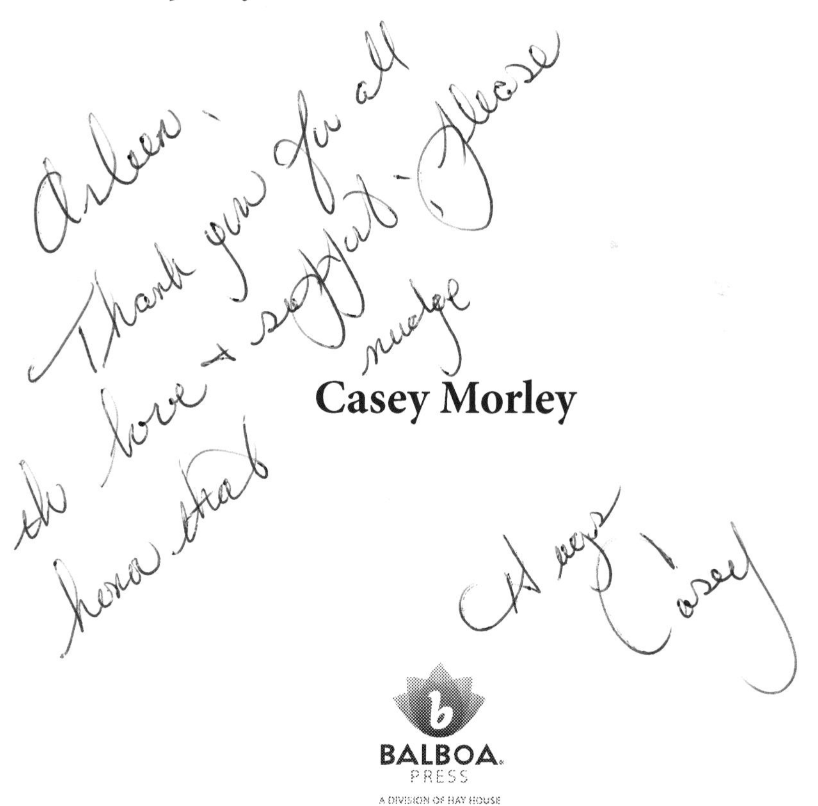

Casey Morley

BALBOA.
PRESS
A DIVISION OF HAY HOUSE

Out of respect for people's privacy, I have changed most names in this book and deleted references to specific geographical locations to protect the innocent and the anything-but-innocent.

Balboa Press books may be ordered through booksellers or by contacting:

Balboa Press
A Division of Hay House
1663 Liberty Drive
Bloomington, IN 47403
www.balboapress.com
1 (877) 407-4847

Printed in the United States of America.

ISBN: 978-1-4525-1430-7 (sc)
ISBN: 978-1-4525-1432-1 (hc)
ISBN: 978-1-4525-1431-4 (e)

Library of Congress Control Number: 2014939901

Balboa Press rev. date: 07/03/2014

Dedication

To my son Michael James, the first child I rescued from the nightmare of domestic violence and another generation of dysfunction. If it weren't for your very being, I doubt I would have had the courage or the strength to end our hell as victims. I'm so very proud of your values, morals, and strength of character. What an amazing young man you are!

To other victims of domestic violence, I hope this book inspires you to believe that you, too, have within you the strength, power, and courage to begin your own journeys of crawling out. Always remember, you don't ever have to walk alone.

To parents and future parents, I hope my story nudges you to a new awareness. Together, we can stop the cycle and end this epidemic of domestic violence, for the sake of our babies.

Contents

Author's Note

Domestic violence is on the rise in many communities, destroying families, affecting millions of our children, often leading to history repeating itself. By sharing my story, I hope to nudge you, the reader, to a new awareness, no matter where you are on your journey of life—moving you to take action and to a more peace-filled square.

Each of us can do something to help decrease domestic violence statistics. Make it personal. Think about how you can help in your neighborhood, your children's school, or your church community.

Please get involved. Learn from the many resources listed at the back of this book or visit my website, www.caseymorley.com. With awareness, as a society, we can help reduce this devastating epidemic.

Foreword

Baring your soul in public requires courage and a strong sense of self-worth.

Casey Morley had proved throughout her life that she had a deep well of the former, but she had virtually none of the latter when she began writing her story, longhand, on a yellow legal pad. What drove her to commit words to paper was determination—to heal, to break the cycle of abuse and domestic violence she had lived for fifty-plus years, and to try to make a better life for her young son, Michael.

I did not come to the process until several years later when the script on the pile of legal pads was transcribed to computer files. By that time, I'd known Casey for about twenty years and considered her a casual friend. When she asked me to edit her manuscript, all I think I asked her was, "Are you sure?" I'm known to have a heavy hand with the red pen.

I quickly realized that the red pen had very little place here. What makes this story that's so difficult to read or imagine palatable is Casey's voice, the tone with which she writes. It's as if you and she are sharing a cup of coffee and she's relating her story.

Casey and I worked for about three years polishing the book. During that time, we shed tears beyond imagination, shared her grief, bolstered each other.

I watched Casey move through the cycle of growth as she read the book to me, page by page, many times, as I edited on the computer, asked questions, brought out more stories. She progressed from barely able to speak because of the tears to anger to acceptance to moving on.

Where she initially had no self-worth, now she holds her head up high and proud. Courage is still an innate part of her. She relies on her strong spirituality and sense of right and wrong to call attention to the horrors that are abuse and domestic violence. Working to curb those horrors is her goal.

Crawling Out tells of a life no one should ever experience. Casey did. Casey survived. Casey thrives in her new life.

I'm proud to call her my dear friend, my sister.

Nancy Hooper
Hooper Editing Services
January 14, 2014

Acknowledgments

Thank you to Beth for your assistance with the outline and your labor of love typing my first handwritten draft, at the time, a task that would have taken me a lifetime to accomplish.

Sweet Brittany Knowles for your helpful, patient nature as I struggled with my limited computer skills. If it weren't for you, I would still be stuck on attach.

Karen Bernetti, my friend, client, and website designer, your work amazes me. You always remind me I have something to say.

Thank you to all my family, friends, and clients who have believed in me—supporting me, lifting me up with encouragement along the way.

Thanks, too, Sandy, Joanne, Dolores, Anne, Marcy, Deborah, Tina, Crystal, Marie, Nancy S., Marianne, Karen, and Don who read my manuscript in its various stages, taking time out of their busy lives to establish how on track this project was and give me their feedback.

My brother Bruce Morley for his ever-encouraging words and pride in the journey I have made.

My brother Keith Morley for loving and supporting me all through life and his enthusiasm and positive feedback during the days of the first handwritten rough draft.

Ruth Harris, who taught me about alcoholics and that I'm not the fool. In her words, "Alcoholics play themselves for the fools."

I cannot omit Dr. Beth Giurelli. She continually reminded me, "You must never forget what an incredibly strong woman you are." Thank you for your belief in me and knowing I had what it took to crawl out.

I especially want to thank my hardworking, sharp-eyed editor Nancy Hooper of Hooper Editing Services for her expertise, but, more important, for her nonjudgmental, unwavering, unconditional love, friendship, and support through the many grueling hours of me reading my story to her, often through tears, so she could edit my work and still keep my voice. Often encouraging me through all my fears and self-doubt. For hanging in and standing by me from start to finish. Nancy, I'm *not* incorrigible!

Finally, I would like to thank my son Michael James, my impetus for taking this journey, for his love, support, and patience through all the hours I was not present to him physically or emotionally while I worked on this project. Michael, I'm so very proud of you.

Part I

Living in Hell

The Proposal

Where is he this time? Some hole-in-the-wall I don't know about?

When I didn't hear from Tony one day after work—after a period of promises kept—I went looking for him. I found him at his favorite club. Drinks were cheaper there. He appeared fine and said he had just gotten there. He could see I was upset he was at a bar. My stomach felt sick. I thought, *Here we go again.*

He pulled a bank envelope from his flannel work shirt pocket, handed it to me, and said, "Count this for me." I assumed he was proud of his paycheck. Instead of money, inside the envelope was a diamond ring.

"Where did you get that?" I asked him incredulously. "Why do you have it? Did you find it? Whose is it?"

Tell me he hasn't done anything illegal, I thought.

Obviously annoyed with my questions and irritated, his response was, "It's yours, asshole."

Never once did I consider it was an engagement ring. And never in any of my dreams had I envisioned a proposal at a local bar. And, certainly, being called an asshole was never part of the picture.

* * *

I was twenty-eight years old when I met Tony. I had been on my own for twelve years. I had paid my way through cosmetology school, had a cute little three-room apartment, and worked hard at the salon.

Tony was tall and handsome with brown, curly hair, but his blue eyes had me—they melted me instantly. With him, I was carefree, probably for the first time in my life. I played, I danced, I sang, in a way, enjoying a childhood I never had. In hindsight, being with him helped me to begin to mourn a life unlived. I was having too much fun to notice or care about the red flags that popped up now and again.

Looking back, I now know how naïve I was. I believed in my heart that one day Tony would get tired of the bars and the late nights and would settle down with me to a life with a yard, a picket fence, and a baby or two. They'd resemble both of us—get their height, blue eyes, and curly hair from their dad and a little bit of sassiness from me. On the nights I didn't meet him at the bar, I nourished that dream as I waited for him to call or come over.

Except that most nights, he never seemed to get out of the bars and find his way to my home. After a while, we spent more time fighting than having fun.

I worked every day. He was in and out of work constantly. Money was always short. I couldn't keep up with my household expenses and, now, our social expenses. One paycheck didn't go that far.

After about five years of this, I tired of that lifestyle and began to wonder, *Have I become an alcoholic? What am I doing? This isn't working out the way I'd dreamed.*

I don't remember what part of the story I shared in my two-minute introduction at my first Alcoholics Anonymous (AA) meeting, but, oh! I was so relieved when I heard the facilitator say, "You poor thing. You need to go across the hall to Al-Anon."[1]

I tried those meetings for a while, frustrated, thinking, *He has the problem and I'm the one at the meeting*, a typical thought until you learn you can only change yourself.

I couldn't accept that, though. All my life, I'd longed to be held, wanted to be loved. I couldn't give up my dream. I couldn't give up on having a normal life, my babies. So I tried to get Tony out of the bars.

---

[1] Al-Anon, a twelve-step program based on the AA model, works to help change the attitudes and behaviors of those closest to active alcoholics, believing that alcoholism is a family disease and that when family members participate in recovery, the whole family can heal.

Often, I tried to finish work early to get to the bar and head Tony off before he got really wasted and nasty.

But, I couldn't judge whether he was drunk or not. He could change in a blink and, often, going home was not fun. He could get ugly—swear, yell. We would fight. I didn't realize at the time I was fighting for normal, but he was fighting for nothing to change.

At first, he just yelled and swore. After a while, the abuse became physical—a shove or two. I left him. I went back to him.

He was always sorry. His promises grew. He'd get a job. He'd go to the gym and work out. He'd not drink so much. And, of course, he always promised that he would never hurt me again.

Despite ample evidence to the contrary, I always believed him. Dreams die hard.

Then a shove became a punch. And one punch always followed another. One night he hurt me so badly, he drove me to the emergency room—out of town where no one would know us. He apologized all the way there. And, of course, made more promises.

On the drive to the ER, Tony convinced me to tell a story he came up with about what had happened to me. The ER staff was suspicious but I stuck to it. Unfortunately, one of the nurses recognized me, though. I was so embarrassed and scared when she asked me privately if he'd done this to me. I lied. I wanted to hide. I thought, *Just get me out of here. I'm so exhausted.*

Of course, he didn't keep his promises, and there was always a next time. I finally reached my breaking point. Thinking more clearly and more courageous, I called the police. I never realized Tony's father, who was on the police force, would or could hold up the paperwork.

While I waited for the charges to go forward, Tony worked on me constantly. For weeks on end, he made every promise in the book and kept them—trying to convince me to drop the charges.

During that time, the officer who responded to my original call came back to talk to me about the case. I remember him telling me that someone kept holding up the paperwork. He kept saying, "Don't drop the charges. I'll be there for you." He added, "I'm not like them." I wanted to trust that he would follow through, but it had gone on too long. I was exhausted and drained from the emotional strain and the promises. I just wanted it to end. After all, Tony was behaving like the kind of guy any girl would dream of. I dropped the case. Deep down, though, I worried I had blown my chance to be rescued.

Shortly after I dropped the case, Tony did get a job. I thought once again that perhaps my dreams would come true.

A Flare-Up

I didn't see Tony for three or four days. When we did meet, he apologized, telling me that he went about the proposal the wrong way. He said he'd never proposed before.

I forgave him once again and accepted the ring, believing that now that we had made the commitment, he would change, that I would have the house, the fenced back yard, the babies, the love and respect and someone to hold me. *After all,* I asked myself, *how difficult could it be for him to just go to work daily, to save money and to grow to be the best he could be?*

Just days later, I had to track him down again. When I found him, I insisted he come home with me. He did but wasn't very happy about it. He started in on me in the car, getting nastier and uglier by the minute. At one point I said, "You promised! Plus, we had such a nice week. Don't you want that kind of life?"

"I'm not drunk! I was only hanging out with my dad. There's nothing wrong with that. I'm never going to stop meeting my dad."

"All you ever do is drink with him!"

I knew that eating usually helped sober him up, so I tried to calm him down and suggested getting something to eat. But he was beyond listening to me and told me, with his typical drunken, crude language, that he wasn't effing drunk and he didn't want any effing food. He was just pissed off for having to leave the bar and that I made him angry.

Once back at my home, I decided to put a pot of water on for pasta, despite his protests that he wasn't hungry. He loved pasta and I hoped that it might soak up some of that alcohol. *Just get some food in him and our afternoon might calm down,* I thought.

While waiting for the water to boil, I decided to get comfortable in one of my favorite robes. After I had changed, I went back downstairs, and he followed me to the kitchen, attacking me verbally. He kept saying that he didn't want to effing eat. I remember telling him, "You're insufferable. Your mouth is disgusting."

His anger elevated with each moment. I certainly was paying the price for interrupting his afternoon drinking plans.

By this point, I was extremely distraught. I took off the ring and held it out to him. "I am not doing this again, and I'm not going to live this way. This is not what I want. You promised!"

He struck my hand and the ring fell into the disposal. That enraged him further, to the point that he hit the pot of boiling water, knocking it over onto me. Most of the water hit my now-exposed lower left thigh and knee, hit the floor, and splashed my ankles. The pain was instantaneous and horrific. I gasped and screamed. I literally watched my skin roll off my body. It took all of my will not to become hysterical.

I remember not wanting the neighbors to hear, thinking, *How do I bear this pain in silence?* Even though Tony and I didn't live together, the neighbors were well aware of his Dr. Jekyll and Mr. Hyde personality.

I gasped for breath and started to tremble, not knowing what to do or where to go. *Oh, God, where do I put myself? Think! Think!* I kept repeating. *Think!* The pain sent all rational thoughts—and any of what Tony might be doing—out of my brain.

Making it across the room was unbearable. My favorite soft, cozy, terrycloth robe rubbed like sandpaper against my burns and was now too much for my traumatized body to bear. I let the bathrobe fall to the floor. Each step caused increased nausea. I was weak, lightheaded, in shock.

To take the now-necessary flight up the stairs became a grueling task. I felt I would pass out after every second or third stair. I had to stop, rest, try to catch my breath, becoming more and more aware of the increasing pain.

When I finally made it to the landing, I was sweating profusely, yet I was dizzy, cold, and clammy. My hair was stuck to the back of my neck, and my scalp was so hot that it felt like bugs crawling through my hair.

My next hurdle was to walk the twelve feet from the top of the stairs to the front of my bedroom closet. I had to find something to wear.

The incident seemed to sober Tony up. He had followed me up the stairs and kept telling me, "It's bad. It's bad. It looks really bad. We have to go to the hospital."

"I just want to lie down. I'm exhausted. The pain! Oh! The pain!" I cried. I could barely move my leg. And I was so scared. I was worried that I'd be scarred; the burn covered such a big area.

I stood in front of my closet, rejecting this or that item for their textures—corduroy, flannel, wool would be intolerable against my raw leg. The strength it took to slide my clothes along the pole made me weaker and sicker by the second. The room started spinning. I was hyperventilating. I had to stop and rest. I moaned repeatedly, "I need to lie down."

Tony kept repeating, "It's bad. It's bad. We have to go."

With a shaken voice, I whimpered, "I can't do this."

My whirlwind of emotions and anguish were as overwhelming as the pain. I cried. I shook. If I had the strength, I would have screamed, "You bastard! Get away! Just get away from me!"

I don't know how much time passed. Ten or fifteen minutes, maybe. The doorbell rang. He ran to the upstairs front bedroom window. "It's the cops. Somebody called the cops," he said.

The police were at my door. I remember thinking, *I need help*. I felt sicker, more lightheaded, but also thought that I would get some help this time. Someone else had called the police. It wasn't my word against his anymore. I had to get to the door—to get myself back downstairs somehow—to let the police in. But Tony blocked me, held me back. I tried to yell for help. He put his hand over my mouth, saying, "No, no, no. Please, please don't open the door. I'll take care of you. It'll be okay. No, no. Just let them leave."

I kept struggling to get to the door. But his next words stopped me. "You'll be arrested, too."

Through the pain, I believed him. That couldn't happen. So many people would read about this, and my shame and embarrassment would be greater than the pain I was in.

The police finally left, and all I wanted to do was to lie down. "Just let me lie down. I need to rest. I'm so sick to my stomach." I felt incredibly weak and nauseous. I kept trying to convince myself, *Maybe the burn isn't that bad.*

Tony knew better. He insisted, "I'm taking you to the hospital. It looks really bad to me."

So instead of lying down, I continued to look for something to wear. I finally found a gauzy summer dress—white and clean like a gauze bandage. Maybe it wouldn't hurt.

The time spent trying to find something to wear was debilitating. The pain was so excruciating. I was ready to vomit; it was in my throat.

I trembled. I was hot. I was cold. I was frightened. I couldn't bend my leg. The room spun.

I don't remember how I made it back down the flight of stairs or how I was able to get in my car. Tony put the passenger seat all the way back so I could keep my leg extended and hold my dress away from the burn.

As soon as I arrived at another (out-of-town) emergency room, the questions started. How did this happen? Where did it happen? Was it an accident? Frightened once again but this time concerned that I would be arrested, I stayed with the accident story Tony programmed me to say during the ride.

My leg wasn't good. The ER doctor treated the burns, wrapped them up for me. He said he really couldn't do any more and that I needed to see a plastic surgeon in the morning. I was so upset. I cried and cried. This was too much for me. My leg hurt so much. I took the pain pill the ER doctor gave me, and when I got home, tried to get some sleep.

Tony didn't stay.

The Aftermath

In the morning, I tried to get ready for my doctor's appointment. Getting into the shower was horrible. When I attempted to lift or bend my leg to get it over the edge of the tub, the room instantly started to spin and I felt sick to my stomach once again. I knew I was going to pass out, going to vomit.

And the pain. I was shaking and trembling. I felt the heat rise, flushing from my feet to my face. I was sweating and clammy. I remember thinking, *I don't want to crash to the floor and crack my head open.* I knew I had to attempt to sit down and get my head between my knees, but how? Keeping my left leg straight and hanging on to the nearby vanity, I barely managed to land on the closed toilet seat and put my head between my legs as far as I could.

After a while, the room stopped spinning. Still trembling, I found another way to get into the shower, my injured leg sticking out to keep it dry, and got ready. Even though I was alone and scared, I was relieved not to have to deal with Tony and his hangover. Now I was very grateful that he went home after we returned from the hospital last evening. I had more than I could deal with for the moment.

I called a good friend who didn't hesitate when I asked for a ride to the plastic surgeon's office. Kerri-Lyn also never hesitated to speak her mind about Tony, but this time, she kept her comments to herself. The surgeon confirmed the ER doctor's assessment—first- and second-degree burns on my ankles and third-degree on my left leg. He applied Silvadene,[2] wrapped my leg up again, and told me I needed to return in four days.

I left that appointment crying; it took all my energy not to lose total control and become hysterical. Kerri-Lyn tried to console me, assuring me that I would heal and that everything would be okay, adding that the surgeon seemed like a good doctor and that he would take good care of me. I wasn't so sure of any of it. All I knew at that moment was that the entire situation, but especially the pain, was unbearable. My unspoken thought was that Tony's broken promise to never hurt me again was just as intolerable.

Once back home, Kerri-Lyn helped me get out of her car. I hugged her and thanked her for being there for me. I was exhausted, so tired, but I had to get to work. I had bills and no benefits like sick days or paid holidays. Besides, I had work responsibilities. I was the manager of ten girls. Most important to me, my clients counted on me being there as well. Responsibility was first and foremost in my world. I wanted and

---

[2] Silvadene, a topical antibacterial ointment used typically to treat severe burns as well as to eliminate any existing infections and to help prevent bacteria from entering the bloodstream.

needed people to see me as someone who had value. Still looking for some kind of approval.

The next few days were very difficult. I had trouble with the simple everyday activities of living. Sleeping was near impossible. Climbing into and out of bed was difficult. Getting in and out of the shower. Walking across a room. And, oh, those dreaded stairs! And then, getting in and out of my car.

Getting dressed was torture. I absolutely could not wear jeans. I wore dresses and leggings to keep from putting pressure on my bandages.

But the most difficult part was standing behind my styling chair all day. Every move I made was painful. Putting weight on my left leg was difficult. Dragging it around all day, unable to bend it, exhausting. But I had no choice. Nobody else would do my work for me. Not telling my clients the truth about what happened to me was emotionally draining.

The few times when Tony was around when I changed my bandages, he would comment, "Look how good you are healing."

The four days finally passed and it was time to go back to the plastic surgeon. I had to drive myself. By now, the excruciating original pain had eased up. But because I had to drive, I couldn't take a pain pill before I left.

What Tony thought was "great healing" was actually another layer of debrided skin coming up to the surface. The surgeon had to peel it off—a process called debridement[3]—that he did right there in the examining room. To this day, I believe that pain was worse than the actual burn. Without my pain pill, I thought that I would never get through the procedure. The pain was just too much. I was sick to my stomach again, weak, shaking. I just wanted it all to be over. Then, when it was done, I wondered how I would get myself onto the elevator.

---

3 Debridement is the process of removing the unhealthy, lacerated, dead, or contaminated tissue resulting from severe burns.

Or out to my car. *Thank God it's my left leg,* I thought. Trying to drive while keeping it straight had it been my right leg would have been near impossible.

I still had to get to a pharmacy to pick up Silvadene and covered spatulas and more gauze. The doctor made it very clear how important it was to keep the area as germ-free as possible to avoid infection.

I thought the hell I just lived through was over, but getting out of the car and into the pharmacy continued the torture. It had to be evident that I was in unbearable pain and distress, noticeably shaken and hurting, but the uncompassionate clerk didn't see it. She told me, "The spatulas are in the back" as she pointed to the farthest spot in the rear of the pharmacy.

That walk seemed impossible. It was one of those old-fashioned pharmacies—long and narrow—with old, uneven wooden flooring. I worried the floor would make my walk even more unsteady, inducing more pain. I also worried that I would either pass out from the pain or vomit. Even the pharmacist seemed to be unaware of my pain and distress. To make things worse, I still had to walk back through that long, narrow pharmacy to pay and then get back to my car.

Every step I took, I felt sicker. I felt the pain taking over me. I prayed, *Please, God, help. Help me. I need to get home.*

I arrived home totally exhausted. All I could think was, *I need help. I can't take another step.* I tracked Tony down at the club. I said, "I need you. I can't do this anymore by myself. I've just been through hell and back."

He said, "It's setback night. You know I play cards on Thursdays. Do you really need me?"

I was so hurt, so furious. I yelled, "Just get here!"

He arrived about ten minutes later and stayed only long enough to get me a glass of water and hand me a pain pill. Then, as quickly as he arrived, he left to get back to his cards.

Sunday finally arrived. I was grateful for the day off. Tony showed up late that morning. I expected some help from him with the everyday chores I certainly couldn't attend to, or perhaps a little pampering.

But, after he checked in on me, off he went to an annual clambake with his father. As he stood at the front door, he said, "My dad already paid for the ticket. What would I tell him?"

He walked out the door before he could hear me say, "How about the truth?"

My legs elevated, I sat there in total disbelief. He just walked out the front door as if he played no part in this nightmare.

The silence and emptiness of the house after the front door closed was heartbreaking. The tears rolled down my cheeks; I didn't think I had any tears left, but I was wrong. Again, I had been dismissed and devalued. That moment was as emotionally paralyzing to me as was the situation and the pain. In that silence, the agony of my reality overwhelmed me, pushing me deeper and deeper into despair.

Just Not Enough

Growing up in a house with five siblings—two older boys, two younger brothers, and a younger sister—wasn't easy. It was often difficult for our mother and tough on us kids. We didn't get to do much or go many places. It seems there was always "not enough." Not enough money, not enough food or clothes, not enough help. Looking back as an adult, there was not enough love, or support, and certainly not enough encouragement. *Just not enough.* When it came to our grandmothers, one said we made her too nervous, and the other said that we couldn't come for the holidays because there were too many of us.

We moved often—at least ten times—from when I was three years old to sixteen. If I had to take a guess as an adult, it was for nonpayment of rent. After she asked our father to leave, my mother had to go on state assistance until our baby brother, then only six months old, went to school. I have some memory of child support, but it was very little, something like sixty dollars a week; even in the 1960s, what could you do with that and six children to clothe and feed?

My mother worked very hard all day in a hot, steamy factory. The more Styrofoam pieces she produced, the more money she made; it was difficult for her; she was a fairly big woman. The steam and heat exhausted her, and she shifted much of what most mothers do for their families to me. I started cleaning the house when I was about eight years old, with laundry, cooking, and caring for my younger siblings added as I grew older. For years, I also had to wake my mother up in the morning, put on her socks and shoes, and do her hair. She went to work for 7:00 a.m., so I also had to get the younger kids up and fed, make their lunches before going to school myself, hoping my younger brother Ken would get them on their school bus.

Sadly, when I think of all the houses we lived in, I don't have very many happy memories; I just remember a lot of tough, miserable times.

When I was three years old, we lived in an apartment on Crown Street. One dark, rainy afternoon, we were all in the kitchen waiting for my brother Brian to get back from Crown Street market, a little corner store about five or six houses from our home, with some milk so we could eat our cereal for lunch. All of a sudden, we heard this horrible screeching. My oldest brother ran to the front living room window. He yelled, "It's a dog. A dog got hit by a car!" Seconds later, "No, Mommy, it's Brian! Mommy, it's Brian! He's lying in the road!" Brian was her second-born child. He was six years old and in the first grade.

The next thing I remember was being sent upstairs to the neighbor's with the rest of the kids—me carrying my cereal bowl, trying not to spill—while Mommy went in the ambulance with our brother.

Brian didn't come home for a very long time. The headlight of the car hit him in the face, knocking him out of his shoes. It was a very bad accident. After ten weeks in the hospital, he came home with a three-inch scar over his left eye and a three-inch scar on his left cheek. The doctors managed to stitch the little piece of his nose back on.

He was very special to our mother after that accident. It always seemed he got extra-special treatment. We kids would tease him, saying something like, "Of course. Anything for Mommy's Brian," repeating often "Mommy's Brian."

Shortly after that, we moved to Orange Street. I remember the cemetery across the street from this house. My mother would stand on the front porch to tell me when to cross and send me through the cemetery with a grocery list to give to the store owner on the next street. When I got to the other side of the cemetery, I had to cross an even bigger road all by myself. I was always scared and would run as fast as I could.

Each time my mother sent me shopping, my eye was always attracted by a box of ice cream cones with the colorful scoops of delicious-looking ice cream on top. One day I snuck the box up to the counter, hoping I had enough money. I crossed that big street as fast as I could and found a place to sit, anxious to open the box before the ice cream melted. Oh, the disappointment. The box only had boring, old cones! Luckily, my mother thought it was cute, and I didn't get into trouble for buying something not on the list.

In that house was my first memory of Daddy hurting Mommy. One afternoon after school, our parents were arguing upstairs. My father pulled my mother down the long hallway by her ponytail. Only my oldest brother crying and yelling, "Daddy, stop! Daddy, please stop!" got him to stop.

One night when I was about four, our mother wasn't home, and Daddy was supposed to get us ready for bed. It was bath night, and when it came to my turn, he said he was going to take a bath with me; he'd sit on the faucet side so I wouldn't get burned. He let me splash and play for a while. Then he showed me it, but I was too little to understand that his request was inappropriate. I do remember, though, that after this incident, whenever we kids played house, I switched from being the mommy to always being the baby.

[As I write this, I wonder if he even remembered the next morning. I wonder if he carried a heaviness in his heart and soul throughout his life. I wonder if it's what kept him from stepping up to the plate and being my daddy. I wonder if when he was on his deathbed and said, "You kids had it rough," that was some sort of apology. I wonder still.]

Another move and I was off to first grade at Catholic school with my brothers.

Down the street from our house was what we kids called "the old haunted house." Oh, we had so much fun seeing which one of us would be the bravest and go into the empty house the farthest. It usually was a brother or two and I. At first, we were so scared, we could only peak in the windows. Then we would dare each other to see who would go in first and not be frightened. The boys sent me in because they thought I was a scaredy-cat girl, and, of course, I was much braver than they were. Once I was in far enough, they followed me. Any little creak, though, we all turned around and ran out screaming, believing surely the ghost was going to get one of us. Sometimes we'd go back the next day, and sometimes we were so scared, it would take us a week to build up our courage again.

Once, when the boys went in first, I intentionally made a creepy noise, and my brothers reacted as I thought they would, scrambling and screaming like *scaredy-cat little girls,* "Let's get out of here!" running out of that old, haunted house as fast as they could. Their expressions were so funny as they turned around and saw me roaring with laughter, I had to hold my side because it hurt so much. On our way home, they said I could never go with them again. They made me promise not to tell our oldest brother how scared they were.

A new year brought a new house. In this one, Mommy seemed to be sad or upset most of the time. I was too young to understand what was going on, but I could tell she wasn't happy.

Our father was a licensed plumber. He apparently was very good at his trade but drank too much of his money away. One night he came upstairs from the cellar and told my mother his pay fell out of his work shirt pocket into the coal furnace. She yelled at him, again. She knew he'd been down there drinking.

Another payday, he arrived home with boxes of groceries, claiming that was how he was paid for the week. Mother was upset. She felt she would have gotten more for the money if she'd bought the food; she knew only too well how to stretch the dollar to be able to feed so many for a week.

If my mother didn't get mad at him, most of the time my father was a happy drunk. Sometimes he would pretend to be a long-armed tickling monster, trying to catch one of us. He would have a low growl kind of noise in his voice and would swing his arms back and forth in search of a little kid. Oh, we screeched with delight when he caught one of us! That's one of the happy memories I have of growing up.

I turned six in that house. One evening shortly after one of their money fights, I stayed up all night, sitting in our tiny living room with my mother. Even at that age, I somehow sensed she was upset. She just sat in her chair with her feet up on a hassock, starring into nowhere, tapping her hand on the arm of the chair. Every now and then, she would say, "You should go to bed," but she didn't seem to mean it. I didn't go, not until morning. I woke up around noon, and to my delight, she gave me enough money to buy a package of cupcakes for breakfast from the store across the street from that old haunted house. That was also the day I saw her and a man who wasn't my father walk to the side of the house. I peeked out our living room window, and they were kissing. I didn't know what to do or think.

That evening she went off to bingo. One of our toys got stuck up on the roof. I think it was one of those tops that when you pulled the string, the propeller would spin up and off, floating into the air. Daddy went up to get it for us but then couldn't get down. He told us, "Go get your mother."

Ken and I walked the short distance down the street to the bingo hall and peeked in the windows looking for Mommy. Once we found her, we kept calling until she heard us and turned around. Simultaneously Ken and I said, "Daddy is stuck on the roof and he can't get down." All she said was, "Let him stay there," and turned back around to play her bingo cards.

We were poor. Food was often scarce. On Thanksgiving and Christmas, our mother would get some help from the Salvation Army. They would deliver a big box of food and usually a turkey or a ham. Enough for the holiday and maybe a little left over for the next day.

While in this house, some of us kids would climb the hill at the end of our backyard to the Knights of Columbus hall. After some of the parties, they would give us the leftovers—cookies, rolls, whatever. They would actually throw the extra food down to us. My brothers would say, "They must think we are animals." We didn't care; it was extra food.

When I was in third grade, we moved again. This house was quite different. It was a multi-apartment building, three families on one side and three families on the other. We lived on the second floor on the right side of the building. On that street the ice cream truck came daily. Many of the neighborhood kids would run with their money to pick out which picture looked best on the truck. We could only get ice cream when someone else gave us the money.

My sister who's five years younger and I shared a room at the back of this house, right off the kitchen. One night I woke up smelling coffee. I could hear it percolating, and the kitchen light was on. Shortly after Daddy arrived home, Mommy and he started arguing about where he'd been, how much money he'd spent, why he hadn't come home after work. Foreshadowing my life twenty years later, in his anger, he hit the percolating coffee pot. In seconds, my mother ran out the kitchen door into the back hallway of the building, screaming, "Help me! Someone please help me!" Oh, her screams frightened me so! In a little while, a man I never saw before peeked into our bedroom to check on us, frightening me even more, so I hid under the covers alongside my little sister who slept through the whole thing.

Mommy wasn't home in the morning; it seemed like she didn't come home for a very long while. About four days went by. Daddy tried to get us all cleaned up and looking our best to go visit Mommy in the hospital. I still remember his attempt to wash my hair in the small basin of the bathroom sink. He said I kicked him in the process; he was lousy at that job.

The first thing I saw walking into my mother's hospital room was that she had a tent over her. I thought maybe we could play under it like the ones we made at home. Sometimes, Mommy let us move chairs around and drape blankets over them and use our imaginations. One day it would be our house, other times, an animal's cave. When we were wild animals, tigers, lions, and bears, we would get too loud. We would either have to take the tent down or play house more quietly.

In moments, I learned that my mother's tent wasn't for playing under. In fact, we could hardly even touch her or the bed. Mommy told us the sheet had to be like a tent because, otherwise, it would hurt her boo-boos. I walked around the bed to reach her and give her a kiss hello and at the same moment, my mom shifted her top sheet slightly. I will never forget what I saw under that sheet.

At the time, I was about the height of her hospital bed. My eye level was just right to see her burns. They looked like big cheeseburgers all over her belly. When I was a little older, I learned it was the coffee grounds. The doctors couldn't clean them out, and that caused a terrible infection. We learned we had a new baby on the way, as well. She was expecting her sixth child and fourth son, limiting what medications she could take so she wouldn't cause harm to the baby.

Baby Sammy was about eight months old when we moved to a three-family house, where we got to live on the first floor. That house had a nice backyard and behind that, a huge field for us to play in. By this time, our father no longer lived with us.

I was eight years old and making my first communion. I went shopping with my mother and grandmother, who wanted us to call her Nana. I loved this lacy, frilly dress, but Mommy wanted me to get something more on the plain side. I jumped up and down when Nana insisted that since she was paying, I got to choose. I was thrilled and felt like a princess on the morning of the ceremony in my new slip, dress, and shoes. I even got to have a donut for breakfast. That was an unusual treat, unheard of in our house.

Around this time my mother started dating, and one day she brought Teddy home. When they met, my mother started drinking. That's what they did—drink and play cards. Nana was furious one day when she stopped over and saw my mother serve Teddy steak while we kids just got cereal for dinner. My grandmother asked my mother, her daughter, "What are you doing? You can barely take care of your children."

Periodically Ken and I spent time with our aunt, our mom's sister, who had a daughter my age and a son Ken's age. We were envious of our cousins. They had everything you could think of—all the new toys, new gadgets, a nice home, a swimming pool, and Nana lived upstairs from them. They seemed so privileged.

My cousin Lilly often thought she was superior to me. One afternoon she wanted to play school. I was the student, of course. On her blackboard she wrote ten to fifteen words and with her pointer, asked me to say what they were. I hesitated when she pointed to the word "Nana." I wasn't sure, so in seconds she started pointing to the ceiling. She said, "She lives upstairs, stupid."

My eyes started to tear up; I couldn't believe she was so cruel and mean. Embarrassed and hurt, I ran out of the house, thinking, *I'm not taking this. I'm going home.* I ran right into Uncle Gordon, who also lived there. He tried to stop me but I kicked and punched him until he let me go. I didn't like him anyway; he always tried to grab my little breast when he hugged me.

I walked as fast as I could. When I reached downtown, I knew it was a straight line home from there. It was about a three-mile walk. I arrived home and just sat on the side porch under our kitchen window, scared to go in the house. I eventually worked up the courage and walked in the back door, surprising everyone. Mommy started with the questions. "What are you doing here? How did you get here? Where's your brother?"

Trembling and scared, I answered that I walked. Crying, I told her about how mean Lilly was. As I talked, Mommy picked up the phone to find out what was going on and where Ken was.

For whatever reason, my mother didn't yell at me that time. She just fed me. When I think back, what adults let a little kid walk the streets or not even care where she was?

Still Not Enough

We were still so very poor. All of us were out back one day after school, playing tag, and I was hungry. I couldn't wait until dinner, so I went looking for a snack. All I could find was the heel from a loaf of bread and some ketchup. There was literally not one other thing in the cupboards or the refrigerator.

When I entered fifth grade, we moved to a new town. That, of course, meant a new school and new friends, always difficult, even more so because it was my first time in public school. My oldest brother Danny got to stay with Nana so he wouldn't have to change schools. Our grandmother would take good care of him, especially make him delicious meals. Why him and not one of us? Didn't the rest of us matter?

Teddy lived in this town, too, making my mother happier; he was around a lot more. He would eat over, take Mommy shopping. He would buy baskets of tomatoes or peaches. We thought that was great. We usually didn't have so much of anything at one time. I often felt happy. I finally had what I thought was a daddy's attention.

One evening that summer Mommy asked him to go to the store and he asked if I wanted to go for the ride. We didn't get to go anywhere, so I was quick to say "yes" if it was okay with Mommy. On our way home from the store, he asked me if I wanted to see where he lived. As soon as we started to get close to the house, I started to think, *Maybe we could all move here.* The street was nice. All the houses looked pretty—lots of flowers along the sidewalks and plenty of children playing in their yards. We could be a real family.

Once we were inside the house, he started to show me around. I was surprised to discover there wasn't much furniture and it didn't look so pretty on the inside. He then asked if I wanted to see where his children's rooms were. The rooms were totally empty, not a trace of the children or what they liked. I remember thinking about a conversation I overheard about how when he came home from work one day, his wife, his kids were just gone. He then brought me into his bedroom and asked me to sit on his bed.

In minutes he started to touch me inappropriately. I didn't realize at the time what he was trying to do because I was only eleven. He asked me, "Do you know this is how babies are made?"

I said "yes," but I was lying. I didn't want him to think I was stupid like my cousin did.

We left shortly after that, and on the way home, he said it was going to be our secret, a daddy-daughter secret. All I thought about was I finally had a daddy like other little girls. He taught me how to plant pansies. He taught my brothers how to get a charcoal grill ready. Life went on.

Fall was right around the corner when I got my first period. I really didn't know much about it. I was not prepared and was too embarrassed to tell my mother. One day she discovered my home-made sanitary napkin and asked me, "What's this?" I lied, told her I ran into the rose bush out back playing hide and go seek with my brothers.

Shortly after that, I came down with a bad case of poison ivy. I was miserable; the itching kept me awake most of the night, and my mother kept me home from school. But, that was silly, because she still made me do her work as she directed me from her recliner. "Fold the towels, change the baby's diaper."

During Christmas vacation when I was almost twelve, a male family member visited for the week. One night I woke up, startled to see him standing over me. When he realized I saw him, he ran out of my room, only for me to discover he had been slowly tearing my panties off. They were torn in many sections. I remember being scared and upset. He left at the end of the week and I tried to forget all about it. Sadly, it took me fifty years to realize that, too, was a violation.

The winter was long. We missed playing in the woods out back, but we had a great big front lawn that had a few dips, so when the snow came, we had a blast going down it on our cardboard sleds. We would build up so much speed, we could go right across the road to the neighbor's property.

One storm that winter was more like a blizzard. Mommy sent Brian and Ken down to a mom-and-pop corner store to charge some groceries. Brian, now the oldest in the house, took Ken with him on that stormy, cold afternoon. It seemed to me a very long time had passed and they had not returned home. Eventually, Brian pulled Ken and the bag of groceries up the drive on his sled. They were tired and cold and told Mother they thought they were going to die.

We grew more and more envious of our oldest brother. He never had to do this kind of stuff living with Nana. She doted on him. Danny would come home from school to a nice warm house, the smell of something delicious for dinner, and a snack waiting for him. Nana even pressed his clothes.

When I finished sixth grade, we moved back to our hometown. This house we had to ourselves as well, and mother was happy the rooms were all on one floor. It was much easier to make friends; there were children everywhere. Teddy continued his inappropriate behavior, violating me whenever he could get me alone.

I was just starting to catch on. Daddies didn't behave this way. I was also tired of doing so much of the housework. I was tired of having nothing and doing nothing. I was sick of feeling devalued or dismissed, sick of Ted scaring me—telling me that if I said anything, I would be sent away to a bad girls' school and never see my family again. I had a lot of headaches then, to the point that one day, I didn't do my housework after school. Mother started yelling at me, asking, "What have you been doing?"

I replied, "I have a headache that's making me sick to my stomach."

Her comment: "You don't have a headache. You're just a kid. Now get your work done."

My brother Brian and I started at the junior high school that year. He was going into the eighth grade and I was entering the seventh. Even though we were not a year apart in age, we were only a year apart in school. Brian had to stay back in first grade because he was in the hospital so long from his car accident.

We enjoyed going off to school together. It was great to be back in our hometown, and we were able to connect with some of the friends we had to leave behind when we moved to Teddy's town.

Around a year after we moved back to town, we had to leave that one-story house. We started to hear scrambling inside the walls, especially the wall going down the cellar stairs. The landlord came to investigate and discovered there were rats—must have been coming from the cemetery right next door. "That's it," my mother said. She wasn't going to live like that, so off to View Street we went. This house was closer to our school and our church, and our oldest brother was able to move home and stay in the high school he started with.

All of us kids' bedrooms were upstairs, and Mommy slept downstairs. Our oldest brother had his own room over the kitchen. My sister and I had the front room right at the top of the stairs, and the other three boys' room was the room where we had a small black and white television. We would all pile on one bed after dinner and after homework to watch our favorite shows. One of my favorites was a show called *The Rifleman*, starring Chuck Connors. I especially enjoyed the combination of the theme music playing while the camera showed his authoritative walk in those cowboy boots. He always shot the rifle, and then the camera showed his face. I thought he was cute. And, in every show, he was always the good guy—and a good daddy.

We liked having our rooms upstairs. We often thought we were getting away with something when our rooms weren't picked up. Mommy didn't go up the stairs often. She always complained her legs ached. She would make us rub them for her; we always would argue whose turn it was. It was such a boring job until she started to offer us a quarter.

One night I was startled awake by someone in my room again. When I sat up, he ran out of the room, stumbling over my sister's slippers. In the morning I thought I might have had a bad dream, but her slippers were not placed neatly by the side of the bed like they usually were.

Teddy was still around the house those days, and one evening after dinner when all of us kids were upstairs, the yelling started. Mommy and Teddy had another terrible fight. They were yelling and screaming, throwing and smashing whatever they could get their hands on. Teddy was furious. He had just discovered after months of investigating that Mommy had cashed his income tax return check. He was angry because she continued to pretend she knew nothing about it. We still didn't have much and I'm sure she cashed the check in an attempt to continue to take care of us the best she could.

Once again, the bigger kids had to clean up the mess and put the house back in order. Either Mommy or Teddy had even thrown the hi-fi down the cellar stairs. How crazy was that.

That night, for the third time, I woke up with a male standing over me, and yes, my panties were half torn off. This time I told my mother. I could tell by her reaction that she didn't believe me, but she told me to sleep with her for a while. Sure enough, about a week later, I was awakened by her asking, "What are you doing in here?"

He answered, "Its cold. I was covering her up."

All she said was "Get to bed." Before I fell back to sleep, I poked her in the back, saying, "Told you."

And that was the end of it. There was never any discussion, no consoling. Just dropped as if it never happened. What does that say to a child?

Things were still financially difficult. Mom was behind on the rent and we had to move yet again. This move was very upsetting to me. I was going to have to switch junior high schools in the middle of eighth grade. "Oh please don't make me go there!" I told my mother. "It scares me."

She said, "It's only for six months and you're done with school. How hard can six months be?"

Somehow I sensed I was going to have a tough time. Most of the kids at that school lived in the projects. They wore makeup, they smoked on the corner, they acted older. They just seemed tougher to me.

My Hell Continues

Life was really getting horrible. My headaches were more frequent. I was putting on weight and felt like I was nothing but a slave around the house. And it now was very clear that the man Mom considered so wonderful was nothing but a disgusting, molesting, abusing piece of crap.

I was thrilled when I took on a Monday through Friday after-school babysitting job. The peoples' backyard met ours, so it was close and safe but, most of all, I could get away from Teddy. Unfortunately, I discovered very quickly that all my housework was still waiting when I got back home sometime between 5:00 and 6:00 p.m. Mom also took all my money. She always took our money, whether we earned it or received it as gifts. She'd say, "Let me hold it for you," but we never saw it again. If we asked for it when we got a little older, it was always, "I needed it. It's gone."

The new school was just as I expected. I didn't fit in at all. I saw teachers in the hallway with rulers, measuring the length of girls' skirts, something I'd never seen before. I didn't want to make any friends here. I just wanted the school year to be over. Just by the differences in our clothes and all the makeup the girls wore, I knew we had nothing in common. Besides, I always had to go right home after school. Certainly no after-school clubs.

One of my worst experiences during those six months was the day I wore a powder blue skirt and blouse that looked like what they wore in the 1930s that my mother brought home. When I sat at my desk, my skirt was so full it touched the floor. Just about everyone in the class was looking and laughing and pointing at me. After that day I avoided wearing that horrible outfit.

Finally, Mother noticed I wasn't wearing it and told me I had to wear it that day. So I cut it into tiny pieces. She caught me as I was going off to school in something else and sent me back to my room to change. I eventually had to tell her I couldn't change into that awful outfit because I had cut it up.

She went berserk, hitting me, slapping me across the face, pushing me, screaming that her hard-earned money paid for it.

I started to answer back, "You mean my hard-earned money."

I never got to finish my sentence. She was infuriated by my strong-willed personality—wondering where I got the nerve to stand up to her. The more she hit me, the more stubborn I became.

I finally managed to say, "It was probably my money anyway."

I didn't care at that point. I knew I would never have to wear that ugly, old-fashioned cotton thing ever again and actually felt if she killed me, I was better off. I begged her to please beat me to death and end my hell.

Days after that incident, she didn't feel well and told me I had to stay home from school to take care of her. "No!" I begged. "Please don't make me. I have perfect attendance. I want to get an award at the end of the year. Please, Mom, just once let me hear them call out my name and let me walk up on the stage and get a pat on the back." I argued, "You never let me join anything. All you say is 'Come right home.'"

She thought the whole thing was silly and made me stay home. I was despondent for weeks. It was so important to me, and she just didn't care.

Another month passed. Summer vacation was here. I had more hours at my babysitting job. It was 6:00 p.m. I just got home, and we were waiting for Brian to get home from working in the tobacco fields before sitting down to supper.

I started right in doing my chores. When I walked into the living room to put some clothes in a closet, there they were, relaxing—my mother in one chair that reclined, resting her legs, and Teddy in another with his feet up on a hassock.

I spoke up, asking, "Why am I doing all the work around here?"

I was really pissed off and sick of it all.

Mother just kept bossing me around, yelling out my chores: "Hang this up in the closet. Get the rest of the clothes off the line. Finish folding the towels."

I continued complaining, and then Teddy started in on me, telling me to listen to my mother.

With an attitude, I told him, "You're not my father. You can't tell me what to do."

I was so furious. I looked over to my mother and asked, "Do you want me to tell you what he's been doing?"

I didn't get any further. He flew off his chair and kicked me. I instantly collapsed to the floor in agony, grabbing my left leg. Moaning in pain, I dragged myself across the living room floor to the sofa. Using it for leverage, I pulled myself up, gasping for breath, screaming, "My leg, my leg." I couldn't straighten it. My mother just sat there and never said a word.

Ken finished taking the clothes off the line while I cried in my room. He kept saying, "Please don't cry. I'll help you. I'll help you." He was such a wonderful little brother.

I was grateful in the morning to leave for my babysitting job. I liked it there. It took my mind off what was going on at home, and for the first time in my life, I felt appreciated. Mrs. M. always praised me for taking such good care of her children and often paid me extra for doing so much more than what I was hired to do. Mrs. M. told me often what a pleasure it was to come home after a long day at work to find her beds made, the dishes done, and, often, her children fed and, if it was during the school year, their homework done. I never did tell her it wasn't work for me. It was an escape.

I really hated to leave their home each evening, but summer did end and I started high school with Brian. It wasn't as much fun as I thought it was going to be. Two of the eighth-grade girls who made fun of me went to school on the same bus. The two of them in their miniskirts and tons of makeup always sat in the very first seat. Every single day they made some kind of insulting comment.

I Get Even

One morning I heard, "There goes fat Morley" for the last time. I was steaming inside. I immediately started back up the bus stairs, forcing the kids behind me to back up.

Face to face with the two girls, I said, "I'd rather be fat than effing whores like you" and strutted off the bus, empowered and proud.

I only walked about ten to fifteen car lengths when Brian started yelling "Look out! Look out!" from the little bus windows.

I turned around and the two of them attacked me. I held my own. After all, I have four brothers.

In no time, Brian was on the sidelines yelling, "Come on, get 'em!" With that encouragement, I pounded the two even harder. It never entered my mind it was two against one.

The consequences never entered my mind, either. I just knew I wasn't taking it any more. Once again I was pushed to my absolute limit. A teacher walking by broke up the fight and told us to get to homeroom.

When I got to my homeroom, my friend Martha was waiting for me. She was proud of me. She had watched from the window, cheering me on, for she knew how those two girls tortured me with their inappropriate, cruel behavior. Martha also told me I had a pink slip. That meant I had to go to the office. I really didn't care at this point. I just wanted it all to stop.

My two tormentors and I had to sit and explain to the girl's principal what happened. Then the dreaded decision to call our parents. As she dialed my mother's work phone number, I was a little anxious about the call, but as she spoke in her very proper British accent, "Your daughter Kathleen was having a real free-for-all on the front lawn of the high school."

I couldn't help myself. I had to laugh. Unfortunately, it came out louder than I wanted it to.

She continued with, "And now she's laughing." I wasn't too worried until I heard her ask, "Shall I take care of the disciplinary action or shall you?"

My anxiety and worry started to skyrocket. *Oh! Please, please,* I thought, *let it be the principal.* But, no, my mother said she would.

When I arrived home after school that day, all Mother cared about was, "What did you call them?"

I kept trying to explain how they had been torturing me. No matter what I said, she just kept asking, "What. Did. You. Call. Them?" Whenever I told her, smack! One big wallop right across the mouth. She asked, "Where did you learn those words?"

I remember mumbling on my way to my room, "Why doesn't anyone care about what happens to me or how I feel? Where did I learn those words? Are you kidding me?" Ted and she screamed them at each other all the time.

I had turned fifteen, and in my second year of high school, we moved to a house up by Beaver's Pond. I thought it was so far from school, but the boys were excited, thinking they could walk down to the pond every day and go swimming. Fun for them, but for me, life was the same. Get up, take care of Mother, get the lunches made, get the younger ones up and fed, and get off to school myself. Then come home, clean the house, make dinner, do my homework, get to bed.

I worked very hard on my school work. More often than not, I was on the honor roll, no matter what it took. Sometimes it was very difficult. My parents never showed any interest in our education, neither of them ever showed up on parents' night or for school plays. No encouragement. No help. Just "do your homework."

We only saw our father once a week when he would pull up in front of our house for ten to twenty minutes. At first the five of us would run out to talk to him. Eventually, it dwindled down to the two youngest ones. By this time, our oldest brother had joined the National Guard, and for me, it wasn't worth the effort to walk to the truck. I had nothing to say to my father. He was a stranger to me, and what do you talk about with someone you don't know?

Around this time, Mr. and Mrs. B., the couple I usually babysat for on Saturdays, insisted I go see a doctor. They were concerned about my ongoing headaches and my constant complaints about my bloated body, and, once again, a very bad case of poison ivy, this time only on my hands. I had big, fluid-filled blisters from knuckle to knuckle. Mrs. B. made an appointment for me with a well-known doctor in town. On my way to the office, I was nervous, nervous about what to expect, since I couldn't remember when I'd last been to a doctor. I was scared and worried, thinking, *Will he know my secret just by looking at me and know what's wrong with me?*

I was pleased to see he was a kind-looking grandpa-type of a man. As the doctor started to examine me, I told him about my headaches. He could see my swollen, puffy body. I told him more often than not, my hands and feet swelled up so much it hurt to write my lessons at school and my shoes hurt at the end of the day. That led him to also discover that I had high blood pressure.

After the examination he told me to get my shoes on and meet him in his office. Finally, after what seemed like a very long wait, he came back to me. As he was about to sit down in his big, comfortable-looking doctor's chair, he sighed and shook his head.

My heart raced in those few seconds before he spoke. Again I thought, *Oh no! He knows. Will I really be sent away? Maybe I should run.* I sat on the edge of my chair, my leg bouncing nervously, not knowing what to expect or what I should do next.

He sighed again, still shaking his head, and said, "Young lady, I don't know why a healthy young girl like you would be having these kinds of problems. You're quite a case. Little Casey."

He stood up from his chair and said, "Let's go make you another appointment."

As we walked over to the receptionist, he put his arm around me. His gentle, grandfatherly mannerisms were very comforting to me, and for the first time in a long time, or maybe forever, I wasn't frightened of a man or on guard about what he might do next.

He turned to me, telling me not to worry, it would be okay, and asked the receptionist to give "little Casey here" another appointment.

It felt great to feel safe, even if it was only for a few minutes.

[Today, healthy and strong, I understand ever so clearly why, at the time, I was so quick to take on a nickname, a new identity. I believe it actually helped me on some level to leave the broken little girl behind along with the pain and the horrible past and start again as Casey.]

The Hiding Game

Thoughts about how unfair everything in my life was and how sick I was of it all never left me. By then it was very clear how much Teddy had wronged me. How much he scared me. How he forced himself and his very toxic world onto an innocent child. I don't know whether my mother suspected his sexual abuse, but she was very well aware of his emotional and physical abuse. Why would a mother just sit back and do nothing about what she herself witnessed over and over again. After some thought, I decided she was just as abusive to me in her demands and her hitting. But what hurt me most was that she didn't protect me. After all, isn't that a parent's most important job—to protect his or her child?

[Reflecting on this incident as I heal, I can only imagine what her story was. For a mother to act in such a manner.]

I was sure by this time that with Teddy, I wasn't the one who did wrong. Once I figured this out, I knew Teddy's threats of sending me away to "the bad girls' school" were just a bluff. The more I spoke up to him, and defended myself, the angrier he became. I didn't care. Again, I started to think, *I'd rather be dead.*

I decided I would hide from him, especially at night. I hid in closets, the front hall, or under the bed, waiting long enough for him to fall asleep. Ken, now around thirteen, started to sense my fears. One night he gave me a kitchen knife to use for protection. He told me to sleep with it under my pillow.

"If you can't use it, come get me." In a way, I felt a little better not to be so alone in the hell I was living.

One night soon after that, Mother was out playing bingo while I finished up the housework. When I was done, I went to bed thinking I was safe. *Teddy must be sleeping by now.*

I sensed he was angry because I kept hiding from him. I was startled awake by him hitting me on the head.

He woke up my sister, who cried out, "Stop hitting her!"

He ran out of the room. I sat on the side of my bed crying, trying to get all my hair rollers back in my head so I wouldn't look a mess for school the next day. Just another day (or night) in my life.

Still No Freedom

When I turned sixteen I went to work after school and during summer vacation at the same factory my mother worked at, except I worked on the fourth floor, a place with no windows, no air conditioning, on some days unbearably hot. I trimmed the edges of the Styrofoam pieces from the mold, threw them in a pile to dry and packed them up the next day for shipping.

I continued with two babysitting jobs as well; I babysat for Mr. and Mrs. B. on Saturday night and another couple who lived across the street and bowled on Sunday evenings.

I paid board to my mother and was still able to save enough money to buy my first car, a big old Buick Electra 225. One of the older men at the factory took a liking to me, so he gave me a break on it.

Oh, I was so proud that I could maneuver such a boat of a car. And proud of all my hard work to earn this privilege and some freedom. As it turned out, I didn't have any more freedom. I still had to get right home right after work or school to clean the house, do dishes, laundry, and homework.

One week I was all excited. It was football season and I asked for permission to go to a Friday night away game on the bus. My mother said yes, I could go. I tried my best all week to make sure I did everything perfectly and before she had to tell me. Friday finally arrived. The excitement and school spirit were tantalizing. I couldn't wait to get home and get ready for our first away game.

I was just about to leave for school that night when my mother changed her mind. Her reasoning: She wanted me to do her hair so she could go out later herself, but she needed to take a nap first. Not to mention, she gave my brother permission to use my car for the night, since I would be too late to get to the bus. I was so upset and angry, I didn't even want to be near her, never mind put her hair up in a French twist. It came out lousy every time, too. She kept whipping the pins out, making me start again, all the while yelling and hitting me, screaming, "Do it right!" over and over again.

When she left the house, I looked around. It was a total mess; dinner dishes piled high in the sink, laundry to come out of the dryer, more to go in. I figured, why should I always be the one to do the cleaning? I decided to do none of it and proceeded to walk to the high school.

I clearly was not thinking straight and was too upset and angry to know it. We lived five or six miles from the school, and I was about halfway there when it started to get dark.

I was especially frightened when I had to go past a park. At one point some men yelled out of their car windows, "Hey, baby!" Then I started to think about what I had done and how much danger I put myself in. I walked as fast as I could and finally arrived at school, too late. The buses had left, and there wasn't a soul around.

I don't remember how I got back home that night, but I beat my mother. I just went to bed, leaving all the mess. Maybe an hour went by before she came home. Her creep of a boyfriend couldn't wait to tell her I left, walking down the street, how long I was gone, and what time I got home. Just like a child squealing on a sibling. I thought, *You pathetic, miserable, trouble-making bastard.*

In seconds, my mother started screaming at me to get downstairs and clean up the mess. I didn't budge. She kept threatening me.

Again thinking I'd rather be dead, I yelled back, "Clean your own mess. I'm not going to be your slave anymore!"

The next thing, my sister and I heard her plodding up the stairs—boom, boom, BOOM! We looked at each other, knowing I was dead. I lay back in my bed that I shared with her, not moving a muscle.

Mother threw a load of clothes on top of me, yelling, "Now fold them!" and banged back down stairs. Five or ten minutes passed.

She yelled again, "Are you folding those clothes?"

Bravely, I yelled back, "Fold them yourself."

Well, that got me a beating and my sister folded the clothes, pretending I did them. My sister crawled back in bed, asking me if I'd gone nuts and did I want Mother to kill me.

I answered, "Yes. I'd be better off."

Speaking Up

Finally, it was Saturday again, the day to clean the whole house. I had to scrub the bathroom, vacuum, change the beds, and take care of the kids. My mother usually took all day to get the groceries, so I didn't have to rush with my work, although there was so much to do, it took all day.

I went into our living room with the vacuum. I didn't know Teddy was sitting in the chair in the corner. He looked at me. I ignored him. As I went to plug in the vacuum, he said, "Your father is a piece of shit."

I said, "You're a piece of shit."

He repeated, "Your father is a piece of shit," with a mean-spirited, angry, twisted scowl on his face.

"At least he can see his daughter. Not like you."

Teddy had no visitation rights with his youngest child, a daughter who was just one year older than I. His next child was in the service, and his first-born was married with children.

With my last comment, he jumped out of the chair and started to hit me, then took the vacuum cord and wrapped it around my neck, choking me. I was sure his anger was from me hiding from him so well and speaking up to him, telling him he's the one who was going away and he couldn't scare me anymore.

I had such rage in me for all that he had done, I felt like I was capable of really hurting him. With the cord around my neck, I grabbed the hair on top of his head and hung on as tight as I could, pulling his head toward the floor.

We created such a ruckus, Ken came running to my rescue, screaming, "Let go of her! Get off her!"

Teddy stopped immediately when he saw Ken coming at him. As I worked to calm down and catch my breath, I opened my hand and realized I held a hunk of Teddy's hair. I had pulled out enough hair to make a bald spot an inch and a half long and half inch wide right on the top of his head. I felt proud of myself, proud that I wasn't going to let him scare me or hurt me ever again.

[When I tell this story as an adult, people ask me why I seem to shrug the incident off so easily. I tell them that it wasn't anything special—it was just a typical day trying to survive.]

By this time, I'd begun confiding in Mr. and Mrs. B. Little by little, pieces of what I was living had come out. I started to feel like they were my family—the children enjoyed having me babysit for them and Mr. and Mrs. B. thought I was extremely responsible. They offered to take me in so I could get away from the hell in my own home. I didn't know at first if that was a very good idea. It scared the daylights out of me.

I babysat that evening for Mr. and Mrs. B. They could tell just by looking at me something had happened. As soon as they asked me what was wrong, I burst into tears. I told them more that evening than I ever had before. They could not believe what they heard and were shocked at what happened that afternoon, especially the fact that my mother said or did nothing about it when she arrived home.

They were going to be out very late that evening, so we had already planned that I would sleep over. Right after breakfast the next morning, we decided that I would move in with them and planned how and when I was going to leave that house of hell.

We decided that on Friday of that week, right after school, I would tell my mother. I snuck out bags of my favorite things every day, but I had to leave a lot behind, even my car.

Those five days dragged as if each were a month long. It was difficult to pretend nothing had changed. As Friday approached, I grew more and more nervous and was constantly sick to my stomach. It was horrible having to look at Teddy, the rage I felt when I had to pass by him, or to know when I did the laundry, I also did his things; when I made meals, he ate them, too. I truly don't know how I made it through those long five days.

Friday after school did finally come.

I was upset, frightened, thinking, *How will I ever get through this part?* Thoughts kept racing through my mind. *Will she hit me? Will she scream and yell or both? Will Teddy go crazy on me?* Oh! I paced the floors waiting for her to get home from work. Those thirty minutes seemed to go on forever.

I didn't waste any time. Once Mother walked in the door and sat down, I took off her wet socks and shoes and just told her what Teddy had done all those years and that I was tired of her letting him hurt me.

With my heart pounding and my hands trembling, I said, "I've moved out."

I didn't have any idea what she would do. Or what he would do. Too frightened about what would happen next, I didn't wait for any reaction. I just turned around and quickly walked out the back door.

The Transition

The door closed behind me. My hands trembled, my palms were sweaty. My heart felt like it was going to pound right out of my chest.

What will she do? I can't believe I got out the back door.

I was scared; my head felt like it was going to explode. *Will I make it down the stairs? Is she right behind me? Will she pull me back by my hair like she used to?*

Crossing the twelve or so feet from the back steps to the side of the house seemed to take forever. My legs felt like they couldn't support me. I worried, *Will they get me across the long front lawn? Will Mr. B. be there like we planned? Will I live through this?*

It seemed like hours, but I finally made it to the end of our very long driveway, and, yes, two houses down the road was Mr. B., waiting, just like he said he would, his car engine running.

I got in as fast as I could, anxious to get away from that house. I believed that if she ever caught up with me, I wouldn't live to tell about it. But Mr. B. took a moment to tell me he knew that what I just did was very difficult. He told me I was very brave and assured me I was safe and would no longer have to live like that.

He squeezed my hand and said, "Kaks (a nickname he gave me a while back), let's go home. Everyone is waiting, and I'm sure Mrs. B. has prepared a very special meal to celebrate."

I babysat so often for Mr. and Mrs. B., the transition went rather smoothly. I felt like one of the family instantly.

They had made room for my clothes in one of the double closets in the girls' room. The only sign of me being a temporary guest was my folded roll-away bed squeezed into the girls' room. Each evening I rolled it over to the end of their beds and opened it up. Every morning upon awakening, I folded it back up and moved it back out of the way so we could get ready for school.

The two girls, ages seven and nine, were delighted to have a big sister. By this time, I wasn't their babysitter. I was a loving, attentive, adopted big sister who shared their room and home. The girls were never eager to share me with their older brother. It really did feel like family.

I was always quick to help, so working alongside Mrs. B. was nice. It helped me feel I was needed and appreciated. It was a pleasant change from being expected to do it all by myself. I actually enjoyed doing my share. I felt like a team player instead of a slave. After a while, I realized that roaring, bitter anger didn't scream through my body anymore like it did when I lived at home and did my mother's work.

I learned how to make real sauce for "'ronis," a shortened word Mr. B. used for macaroni, and I often peeked over Mrs. B.'s shoulder while she sewed. She made beautiful things for her daughters. At Easter time that first year, she made them both their Easter dresses and, more impressive to me, their Easter coats. She sewed like a professional. She actually made the nicest clothes I have ever seen.

One afternoon as I stood peeking over her shoulder, she asked if I would like to try. Before I could answer, she got up from her chair and told me to sit at the sewing machine, assuring me she would watch over me. Fearful I was going to ruin her masterpiece, I started slowly. Before I knew it, the material was moving right along, and, to me, the sewing machine purred like a kitten. Then I was sewing a straight seam and making perfect darts. It was so much fun, I couldn't learn fast enough. That summer I made my first dress all by myself. Well, it was my second dress, but we won't count the dress I made in seventh grade with that horrible, cheap material.

I was so proud of myself, and Mrs. B. made it a big deal. She had the whole family sit in the family room while I modeled my first creation. As I pranced around the room trying to mimic a model's walk and stance, she described the dress. Everyone sat listening attentively with big, proud smiles on their faces. Mr. B. looked like a proud father, and every now and then, I got a wink. It was a great moment when they all applauded my accomplishment and hard work. It was the first family-oriented pat on the back I'd ever received. Seconds later, their son said, "Now let's eat." We all went to the dinner table laughing.

I started to feel like a normal teenager. I realized I no longer had those horrible headaches, and my body had lost all that water weight. My grades were better than ever, especially in accounting, where I continued to get As. I decided perhaps I'd become an accountant. I'd continue my schooling and become a CPA.

Those two years seemed to fly by, even though I missed my siblings. As my high school graduation fast approached, I learned I had to move out of Mr. and Mrs. B.'s home. Mrs. B. felt it was time for me to be on my own. That saddened and frightened me. Actually, even though I was grateful for them rescuing me, by then, I had learned that what I thought was a safe haven, in the end, had its drawbacks, and it truly was time to leave. History had started to repeat itself. Luckily, I had the summer to find a new place to live.

On graduation night, without warning, there was my mother standing in the back of the auditorium as the class of 1971 walked out. I didn't know what to say or think. After all, two years had passed since that courageous afternoon when I ran out her back door. She hadn't spoken a word to me in all that time or even attempted to make it right between us—a very awkward and uncomfortable moment. After all, what does a daughter say to a mother who didn't protect her and disowned her. And there she stood with a graduation gift, a cluster ring that lifted to expose a tiny watch. I was polite and respectful and pretended to appreciate the gift but wished it were money. I needed money much more now. I had to find a better job and get an apartment.

Scrambling for a Plan

When I learned there were no accounting schools I could walk to, I was devastated. With that dream shattered, I had to scramble for yet another plan.

That summer I worked at the factory with Mr. B. I was promoted to office work and then decided to become a cosmetologist at a local hairdressing school. Between my babysitting money and my pay, I was able to save enough money to pay for school and my first few weeks' rent. I found a small walk-up apartment about five blocks from school for twenty-seven dollars a week, everything included. I went to school full time, Tuesday through Saturday, 8:00 a.m. to 5:00 p.m.

Because my car was in my mother's name, I had to leave it at her house when I left home. When I lived with Mr. and Mrs. B., it wasn't an issue, because Mr. B. would either drive me or lend me his car. Now, though, I had to walk everywhere, so, after school, I walked about four blocks further to my part-time job at W. T. Grants. Some days I was lucky, and my teacher, Miss Deb, would let me leave a few minutes early. She knew I was on my own and that every penny counted. The quicker I punched in, the easier it was for me. I would punch out at 9:00 p.m. and walk back through town to my little apartment. I didn't really mind the walk, but on some nights, I had to pass people hanging around on the street who made me feel unsafe or, at times, a drunk lying in a store entryway. Those types of surprises really shook me.

Once I was home, I had a bowl of cereal for dinner. It was cheap back then. After dinner, I studied and went to bed.

I did very well at school; my grades often amazed my teachers, and I was quickly put on the floor (an expression the teachers used when they wanted you to go downstairs and take care of the clients). I think I worked downstairs for only six weeks or so when I was put in charge of opening up on Saturday mornings. I was honored. Another needed pat on the back.

I used my tips to buy my food. The women tipped a quarter or two back then. I cleared twenty-one dollars a week from my job at Grants, so on Mondays I cleaned for Mr. B.'s mother. She had me washing walls, bed frames, and a lot of heavy work for six dollars and lunch. I had no choice—I needed the money to make my rent. Six dollars for eight hours of work. I shake my head at this memory.

Work after school was just okay; I did what I needed to do. After a few months, I allowed the girl who worked in another department there to move in with me. I only thought about how it would help financially; never did I ever expect her to be promiscuous. The uncomfortable times when she had her male friends over seemed endless. They didn't seem to care that I could see and hear them as they were intimate.

When I couldn't live like that another minute, I decided to leave my own apartment and moved over to the next street on the second floor. The owner of the house was a sweet old woman. Surely I would be safe.

I spent one whole Friday getting my things moved. I felt everything was going to be fine.

Around midnight, I was attempting to get my kitchen together enough to have a coffee before opening the school in the morning. The coffee can dropped out of my hand and crashed onto the top of the stove. An army of bugs scrambled from every nook and cranny of that appliance. I think they were cockroaches.

"Oooohhhh!" I screeched.

I was so upset!

I had heard they only come out in the dark. I turned every light on in the apartment and sat on a wooden kitchen chair on top of the bed all night long, constantly scoping the bed to make sure they hadn't crawled up to join me. In the early morning, I emptied all my packed boxes on the front lawn and shook everything out to be sure to not take any of those bugs with me.

I was grateful once I opened up school and had the place running smoothly; Miss Deb let me leave to find another place to live. Life was taxing for the next forty-eight hours. I was very upset, out of the money for my two weeks' rent, and exhausted. But, life had to go on. What choice did I have?

I was diligent about getting my time in and completed my 2,000 hours in one year. It seemed to take a lifetime to hear from the state about whether I passed my cosmetology exam.

While waiting to hear, I received a phone call from a local salon owner who asked me to come in for an interview. Her salon was located only two blocks past my part-time job. She shared that she received my phone number from Miss Deb, who had recommended me highly.

I was so thrilled; I put on the only 45 record I owned, a song I played almost daily to keep my spirits up, "I'm the Happiest Girl in the Whole USA." I turned it up as loud as it would go on my kid-style record player that played only one record at a time.

My landlady came upstairs, knocking on the door to see what was going on. Jumping up and down, I told her about the phone call. Yippee!

My interview went very well. I was hired. All I had to do now was wait to see when or if I received my state license in the mail.

The days seemed to drag after the morning I took my exam. I worried, *Maybe I failed.* I did finish way before many of the other students. One afternoon about a month later, there it was. My license had arrived. Once again, I played my "Happiest Girl" song as I danced in my tiny kitchen, trying to collect myself to call my new boss.

She said, "Congratulations! When can you start?"

I worked long and hard at the salon, saved my money, and eventually had enough to put down on a used car. Right across the street from my job was an insurance company. I was thrilled to learn I could receive a discounted price on car insurance because of my good grades.

I was on top of the world, excited by that break. I went looking for a car I could afford. I was discouraged when all the car dealerships asked for a cosigner, since I was too young to have any established credit history.

I gathered up my courage and asked my oldest brother, believing that I had surely proved that I was a responsible young woman.

All he said was, "NO!"

There was no, "How are you doing?" Or, "How is work going?" Just one big "NO!" Those words devastated me. I cried all night, hurt and worried about how I would ever be able to buy a car now.

Resigning myself to walking a little longer while I built a credit history, that next weekend I talked to a friend of my mother's about what a struggle it was to buy anything with no credit. He offered to drive me to the dealership and to cosign.

All I could think of was, *This is a miracle.* I never picked up on the fact that he had a little crush on me and hoped that we'd spend some time together. He was old enough to be my grandfather! I remained respectful and grateful when I ran into him after that and treated him as if he were, indeed, my grandfather.

I worked hard to build up my savings and finally could afford a bigger place. I found a three-room apartment on the third floor in a house across town. It was wonderful having more space. I had nice neighbors, but most of all, I felt safer. Life finally seemed to be going in the right direction.

James vs. Boston

One evening after dinner, I decided to relax on the sofa. It was so old, I had stuffed magazines under the cushions to raise them. They were higher but so uncomfortable, I stretched out on the floor on my stomach in front of my little black-and-white television.

After a while, I wanted to change the channel. Leaning on my right elbow, I reached up for the knob with my left hand, heard a "pop," and instantly felt pain in my right arm. The pain seemed to let up a bit after I took some ibuprofen, so I went to bed.

About six months later, I moved out of my hot third-floor apartment to a beautiful brick building right next door with only three other apartments and a locked front entryway. It was an easy move because I had the same landlord. My new apartment had four rooms; was clean, light, and spacious; and had a laundry room in the basement. That in itself was a wonderful improvement. Definitely a step up.

I was extremely busy at the salon, working forty-plus hours and definitely getting my bills paid but not saving enough. I decided to try out bartending.

I thought, *My mom is doing it. My brother is doing it. I'm going to try it.* I walked into a local corner bar and said, "I would like to apply for a bartending job. Do you need any help?"

Their first question, "Have you ever tended bar before?"

No, but I filled out an application anyway and was hired on the spot for four nights a week.

Wow, I thought. *That was easy.* I was very excited and never thought about how much more work I was really taking on.

One night on my way into work, there at the bar with his back to me was a man with the biggest, strongest-looking back and shoulders I'd ever seen. He was dressed in a black silk shirt and white jeans. In those days, ooh, that was hot! He wasn't extremely cute but he was tall and clean. During my shift, I learned a little bit about him, and he seemed nice enough to talk to. We got to know each other a little better and began to date. Eventually, we became engaged.

In time I learned that in addition to his full-time job, he worked part-time undercover in narcotics for the FBI. One night, as we talked over dinner, he told me that he used to own a café, and while at work one evening, his step-daughter stumbled in from off the street. She was so drugged up, it infuriated him. He found a new mission in life.

Life was starting to be fun except for the increasing level of pain in my right arm. I was much too busy with work, so I tried to ignore it and live with it. Plus, I started seeing more of Brian and Ken; we worked to rebuild our relationships. We never talked about me leaving home; we just picked up where we left off and tried to make up for lost time. We made it a point to do something together almost every weekend in the summer, often a day at the beach. Nights out together when I didn't work at the bar were a big deal, too. Go home after work and get ready for a night on the town, dancing the night away. Ken, the great singer that he was, often found himself on stage, singing with the band. Oh, I was so proud of him! He was tall, handsome, and sang like a pro.

My arm started to hurt more, but I continued to work my two jobs. My girlfriend Catherine and I took a cruise to Bermuda in early June 1975. I figured I would have my arm checked when we got back. Our trip was wonderful, and on the way home, we decided that next year, we would go to Hawaii. We dreamed big.

When I got back from my trip, I began going around to doctors. I received five different diagnoses, and my arm kept getting weaker and my use of it more limited and painful.

After James' and my first year together, we started to have just as much of a rollercoaster ride in our relationship as I had in my physical symptoms. He had ex-wife issues and child visitation problems, and more and more, his old-fashioned thinking that women belong barefoot and pregnant came through, exposing his insecurities.

Finally, though, it was October of the next year and off to Hawaii for two weeks Catherine and I went. On our way home, we spent two days and two nights in Las Vegas where we had a ball shopping, going out to shows, and enjoying fine dining. We said to each other, "Look at us!" Our hard work had paid off.

Once back home, I returned to my normal routine at the salon. One day my boss saw that I was in tears. I could barely lift my arm it hurt so badly. It certainly affected my work, and now we were both tired of having no solutions. By then, I had seen thirteen different doctors and heard thirteen different reasons for the problem. At that time, my boss was going to Boston's Leahey Clinic for her own health issues, so she called her doctor, explaining what I'd been going through and asked whether he could pull some strings to get me in with someone soon.

He did. Many tests and examinations later, I overheard the doctors talking outside my examination room, discussing something about me having a muscle disease. My muscle, well, it felt like I had no muscles.

Hell, no. As weak as I was, I got off that table in tears, thinking, *I have no disease number fourteen.*

But I was still in pain. I just knew I didn't have a disease and decided I was going home. When I opened the door, I ran right into them. I told them just what I thought. They calmed me down and sent me to another department for more tests—psychological.

Oh, great! Now they think I'm nuts.

Despite everything, I stayed long enough for them to discover the problem was my thyroid. The doctors explained that since the problem had gone undetected for so long—through no fault of my own—my muscles reacted like they were deteriorating even though they weren't. That explained why I was so weak and tired. The doctors said that when I hurt my arm, the muscle around it couldn't help or take over to allow me to heal. Therefore, I continued to get worse. *Well, at least now I have something to go on that might make sense.*

The doctors tried to regulate the thyroid for two years. I was either overactive (hyperthyroid, Graves' disease) or underactive (hypothyroidism). I gained weight, I lost weight. I lost hair, it grew back. My heart raced, then it didn't. It was a continual rollercoaster of emotions and symptoms.

I quit my night job and did the best I could at the salon. By the time my surgery date to remove part of my thyroid arrived, I was huge and unrecognizable. I looked like an overblown balloon that was going to pop any second. My long, shiny, brown hair was thin and short. My eyes protruded more each month. I just wanted it all to be over.

When it was time for my surgery and I really needed him, James wasn't available. He drove me to Boston and waited with me only long enough to see me rolled down for surgery, then drove back to Connecticut. I was in recovery all night and until noon the next day. I couldn't wait to get to my room. I didn't sleep a minute all night long. So many patients around me moaned and groaned, keeping me up. I felt caged, thinking, *Just let me out of here. I have things to do. I have no time for this s...*

James never managed to find time to get back to see me in Boston. I was so disappointed, especially right after my surgery, when I felt my worst, so far away from home, scared, and alone. He mumbled something about working on an undercover project, and he just couldn't get away.

The worst part was the first time I was able to get out of bed and look in a mirror. I was horrified. All I could do was cry. I looked like a monster—my hair was standing up and thinner, my eyes, even more pronounced. I was devastated by my neck. I didn't have one—just a big rectangle from chin to collarbone with six inches of staples across the middle of it. I dragged myself back to bed and cried myself to sleep.

Those five days in the hospital were long and lonely; being out of state, away from home, and all alone was scary. Catherine and Brian, who were now dating, came to visit. They were shocked at how I looked and tried very hard not to show it. They didn't visit very long; I sensed it made them nervous to see me. My appearance frightened me. How could I not expect them to react? I don't think they stayed longer than ten minutes, a short visit for driving from out of state. I had no other visitors throughout my stay. By this time, Ken lived at home again with our baby brother Sam and our mother as he underwent treatment for recently-diagnosed leukemia.

James at least managed to find time to pick me up when I was discharged. However, as we left the hospital, he told me I couldn't go home. He explained something big was going down that evening, and I wouldn't be safe. I wasn't pleased at all. After being in that hospital for five days, all I wanted was my own bed. He told me he'd asked my mother if I could stay with her for a few hours, which instantly infuriated me. By this time, my mother and I had some communication and a half-hearted relationship, in a sense, faking at playing mother and daughter with lots of unspoken words. But still, he knew that was the last place I wanted to be. What was he thinking.

It was her card night; all her friends showed up. Before long they were very loud; many of them smoked. I was miserable, lying in her recliner in the next room. About midnight, James came back for me. I was so exhausted, near tears, I didn't care about anything. I just wanted to sleep in my own bed, in my own home. To add to this confusion, James informed me that after I got some sleep, we had to leave town for a while. I couldn't believe I was hearing this.

I thought, *Are you kidding? I've just been to hell and back.* If only I knew.

Early the next morning, a girlfriend called me to tell me what she'd witnessed the evening before. On her way home, she drove past a local hotel where she saw flashing lights and the cops handcuffing James! I didn't believe her, but I soon learned that James had set up the bad guys and needed to pretend to be one of them. That was why the FBI said we needed to leave—for our own protection.

As we packed a few belongings, I screamed at him, "This is a nightmare! This can't be happening! I just got of the hospital! I just had major surgery! Look at me! No hair. No neck. Obese. Protruded eyes. I'm tired, weak, and fragile, for God's sake! I can't do this!"

The FBI set us up with an expense account in an out-of-town hotel. Once we were settled and I had accepted the situation a little more, all I wanted to do was to recuperate and get on with my normal daily life. As the weeks went by and I became stronger, the more aggravated and bored I became. I felt thwarted by the whole mess James got *us* into. After all, who recuperates from major surgery in a hotel?

Throughout the upheaval in our living arrangements courtesy of the FBI, following my discharge I waited patiently for my six-week checkup, anticipating good news and visualizing being back to myself, what I knew to be me—a young, healthy, slender woman with normal-sized eyes who wanted to get on with her life.

Only I heard the exact opposite of what I expected. Dr. Mark told me that I was healing great but, unfortunately, I was sicker than they expected. They had to take more of the thyroid gland than they thought they would, and I should plan on being heavy the rest of my life.

With tears welling up, I asked what was going to happen with my eyes. Would they return to normal? By this time I had to tape them shut at night. My eyeballs protruded so much that the eyelids couldn't cover the whole eye. It became quite uncomfortable, and during the night, my eyes produced so many tears that I would awaken with a wet pillow. Every night a sac-like of fluid built up in the corner of each eye that took all day to drain, only to reappear again the next morning.

Dr. Mark's comment: "The good Lord gave you big, beautiful brown eyes, which is making the situation worse." As he escorted me out of the examining room, he said, "Let's wait and see."

I left the office on that dreary, rainy afternoon upset, discouraged, and very angry. I hated everything about what I'd just heard as well as the mess James had us in. Trapped and vulnerable, like a caged animal just like I had been in the hospital—I decided, *I'm done. I'm going home.*

James and I had a big argument. I packed my bags and left. We had used my car this whole time because the bad guys would recognize James'. I jumped in it and left him there in the hotel.

I don't think I was home more than thirty minutes when there was a knock on my apartment door. I opened it to find three men who identified themselves as FBI. All they said was, "Miss, you can't stay here. It isn't safe for you." They insisted I leave immediately and followed me back to the hotel to make sure I did as I was told. I was frightened. I was mad, too. The reality of how serious the situation really was began to sink in.

Another long, boring month passed. James had just returned from a meeting. He started talking about relocating—again—and changing our names, never to return to the area. At first, we had fun playing with names, but after I slept on it, I announced, "I'm not going to do that." In the end, the FBI moved us to yet another town. I told James that I didn't want to know anything about what he was up to and I didn't want to live with these bizarre goings on—just stop it all, get out or I was done with that crazy life and him.

We found a new apartment and both worked third shift, James at his full-time job and I as a sales clerk while I became stronger. The whole time, I silently worried what he was getting into now.

Determined to create as normal a life for myself as I could, I concentrated on getting the weight off, no matter what it took, to prove Dr. Mark wrong. The more weight I lost, though, the more jealous James became. I lost close to 100 pounds. James became more unpredictable. I'd had enough of his jealousy and his questions, "Where were you? Who were you with? What time did you leave work?" day in and day out.

That's when I moved out of town—alone—and in with friends. I hated the daily commute, but the peace of mind was worth it. If I could have done it my way, I would have loved to get an apartment with Ken so we could support each other. But by this time, he worked on cruise ships teaching ballroom dancing between treatments. I always felt that he took that position so his family didn't have to watch him die.

I eventually went back into hairdressing, saved my money, and got an apartment close to my new job. James started to come back around, declaring his love and desire for us to get back together. I was leery and kept him at a distance, seeing him periodically. Easter of 1980, James and I visited friends and family and enjoyed the day. He went off to work that evening and I went home to bed.

In the morning, James brought me coffee from my favorite coffee shop. As I got ready for work, we talked and enjoyed some conversation. I was about to leave when he asked if he could lie down for a while, as he was very tired and didn't feel well. I didn't mind and took the phone off the hook so he could rest, then left for work.

My workday flew by. Around 3:30 p.m., I started to wonder why I hadn't heard from him. I called the house but kept getting busy signals.

I started to wonder why he hadn't put the phone back on the hook. I began to get anxious and was just about to ask my boss if I could leave early when she gave me another client. I rushed through the haircut, cleaned up, and asked to leave, telling her that I felt something was wrong. I told her I'd been trying to call my house for an hour and a half but kept getting a busy signal.

I ran to my car, drove home faster than I should have, and ran up the stairs to my apartment. As I unlocked the door, I called out to James. I turned into my bedroom to discover him lying on his back on my bed, his feet on the floor, his arms spread out. I panicked, sensing something was very wrong.

"James! James!" I called, trying to awaken him. I hopped on the bed beside him. I lifted his eyelids, still calling out his name. I shook his arm. It was dark purple all along the back of it, like he was bruised. *Was he beaten up? Why isn't he waking up?*

He's got to be unconscious. I panicked even more and with trembling hands, called 911. Then I called Brian and Ken, the latter who was home for his chemo treatments. "Come quickly."

The police and the paramedics arrived before my brothers. The paramedics pronounced James dead and took him out in a body bag. I was in shock. I couldn't believe what I'd just been through. As the police questioned me, my brothers arrived. They ran to me, asking the police to back off, telling them that I had been at work all day. The police said they would contact me if they had more questions.

During James's calling hours, the mortician approached me, asking if there was going to be an autopsy. I explained that James was estranged from his family, his boys were too young, and I was not his wife. He commented, "Well, there should be. I found blood in the nose and mouth, not typical for a heart attack victim."

James was buried, at age thirty-eight, wearing the black leather vest I had made for him. There was no autopsy.

Moving On

Just about a year had passed since James died. It was a beautiful March day when I ran into some friends of his, Jay and Bee. They asked how I was doing and invited me down some Friday night to the bar they owned called JB's café. They assured me I would be okay. They were always there on a Friday night.

A few weeks passed. As I drove home from shopping with Catherine, at the crossroads, I thought about whether I should go straight to visit Jay and Bee or turn right to go home. I decided I didn't have the courage to walk into their bar alone, so I drove home.

I was lonely. I had not lived in town long enough to make new friends. So I went to work and I went home. At the time, once a week, I would go over to my Nana's home, do her hair, drive her to OTB, and then we would have lunch together. That was my life.

Sunday, March 29, 1981, I went to the cemetery to tell James I wouldn't visit his grave any more. I never liked going, but I was doing what I thought I was expected to do.

Since it was such a gorgeous day, I decided to visit my brother Brian earlier than we had planned. Heading toward the town he lived in, I had to pass JB's café. I felt alone, empty, almost robotic, drudging through life. To make my life feel even emptier, Ken moved to California the week after we buried James. I missed my little brother so.

Coming upon the café, I recognized Jay's car. At the last second, I pulled into the parking lot. I immediately had second thoughts about my decision and sat in the car fifteen minutes thinking about the "what if's." *What if Jay isn't there? What if it isn't safe inside? What if I can't walk in there by myself?* What if? What if?

It felt so different to walk into a bar when I wasn't going to work. It took everything in me to go through that café door. Fortunately, Jay was sitting at the corner of the bar with a few men around him, drinking coffee and listening to a band practicing for that evening. He had a big smile, made room for me to sit right next to him to help me feel less out of place. Jay offered me a coffee, introduced me to his friends, and said Bee was on her way. A gentleman walked over from the band area to his spot at the bar.

Jay asked, "Do you know Tony?"

I answered "No" and couldn't help thinking how handsome he was. I was mesmerized by the most gorgeous pair of blue eyes. Everyone was very social and Tony was a great joke-teller.

I started to relax and enjoy the company. Two hours had passed when I looked at the clock.

"Oh, I have to get out of here. I'm late!" I was invited to bring my brother back that evening to enjoy the band.

Brian, Catherine, and I went back later that afternoon. We had the best time. It felt great to finally give myself permission to relax and feel alive again. The guys played pool and we girls played the jukebox and the bowling machine. When the band came on, Tony asked me to dance. I left by 9:00 p.m. to prepare for work the next day. We had so much fun that Sunday evening, we decided to return the next week and bring even more of our friends.

The following Sunday I was back at JB's with friends when Tony asked me if I'd like to take a ride with him. Once we were outside, he asked if I could drive; his car was in the garage. Bewildered as I was at that, I drove him to another bar, we had a drink and started to get to know each other. That evening he asked for my phone number.

At work the next day, I asked my boss if she knew Tony and should I get involved. Her perception was he came from a nice family, lived in town all his life, and his dad was a cop.

"Yeah, yeah. Date him!" she said, adding, "Oh! He's so handsome!"

I did start dating Tony, never thinking about taking inventory or recognizing the red flags. I enjoyed our first five years together, and meeting new people helped me build my clientele at work.

Casey Morley

I Was Hoodwinked

I turned thirty-three years old. I was tiring of the bar-hopping and wanted to settle down. I looked at the five previous years as the childhood I'd never had. I thought perhaps on a deeper level, I was a child at play, carefree for a change. In hindsight, I was mourning a life unlived.

I thought now, though, that it was time to take life more seriously, to think about getting married and making a home. Tony led me to believe he wanted that as well, but the more I pushed for it, the more arguments we had. His anger and jealousy grew every year we were together. I was tiring of him not being responsible and not holding up his end of our relationship.

We lived together on and off, usually because he had no other place to stay. The first time he asked to stay for the weekend only, explaining he had had an argument with his roommate and he was sure things would calm down by Monday.

I trusted and believed him but never really liked the idea. I felt bad for him. I didn't realize Tony manipulated me and used me; I was naïve to many goings-on in his life.

One Sunday, weeks later, Tony had not left and I thought that the argument with his roommate must have been over money. Tony still had no job, no money, and no car. I was getting angry and told him he needed to leave. Staying was supposed to be for one weekend to help him out.

He became furious with me, swearing, "Where the eff do you want me to go?"

I didn't care, really. I was tired of paying for him. I wanted my life back, my freedom. Tony had become a burden. This wasn't fun; it wasn't working. That's exactly what I told him. I left my apartment, expecting him to be gone when I got back.

I had a great day. I visited some friends and we went shopping, had some lunch, and just did girl stuff. I arrived home hours later, feeling much better, noticing no lights on in my apartment, and thinking, *Great, he's gone. I have my home back.*

As soon as I entered my apartment, I sensed an eerie silence. I slowly inched my way to the light switch to my bedroom. As I flipped the switch, Tony jumped off the bed and punched me in the stomach with such force, I couldn't catch my breath. I gasped in pain, thinking I might suffocate. He screamed and swore at me about how could I leave him stuck there all day with no car, no money, calling me an effing bitch.

When I was able to breathe again, I had no problem telling him just what I thought, asking him, "Where are all your drunken friends? Where's your father? You never have any problems any other time getting rides. Or, you could have walked!"

He yelled back at me, "You know I have no money."

I was quick to reply, "Get a job! But first, get out!" I reminded him again that his stay was supposed to be "only for ONE weekend. Remember?!"

Just as he said, "Eff you!" again, someone knocked on the door. I was grateful to see the police. A neighbor must have called. I told the cops the day's events and they escorted Tony out of my home.

A week prior to that, Tony had caused a problem with another neighbor over parking. Consequently, I received a letter informing me I had to make other living arrangements. I was devastated, angry, humiliated. It takes money to move—security deposits, moving truck—and the little I put away in savings each week wasn't enough. I was forced to put my things in storage and, gratefully, was able to stay with a friend and her family.

Humiliation

Tony moved in with his sister and her family who had moved back in the house they were raised in. Tony and I didn't speak for months and, yes, then, true to form, came more apologies and promises. It did seem that he meant it this time. He was staying home more, having meals with his family, and he got a job. Little by little, he wore me down, and we started dating again.

I don't remember how long I was able to stay at my friend's home, but her husband grew tired of not having his privacy and I was asked to move out. I ended up at Tony's sister's house, on the floor in her living room. Eventually, they made room for us in the front room right off the kitchen. I went out and purchased a sleep sofa, figuring I would not be there long and would soon be able to get my things out of storage.

This situation turned out to be horrible. I learned quickly why Tony was home more those days. They were doing things behind my back that they knew I wouldn't approve of. Oh, they tried to hide it from me. I may have been naïve, but I wasn't stupid. It sickened me.

I started to despise everyone. I was trapped once again. I was the only one working. Tony became more manipulating. Eventually, his sister and her family moved out. She hadn't paid their father any rent for months, and he started to put pressure on them. If I had to guess, my rent money never got to him, either.

Tony and I were alone at the house, and he did get another job. He started slowly telling me about his childhood. None of the stories were good; in fact, he told me he even hated being in that house because of so many bad childhood memories. At the time I didn't realize the depth of our connection or of our wounds. My empathy with him began to create a bond that, I believed, would get us through anything together. We would love and support each other through our healing.

But Tony's old habits returned. Once he got a little money in his pocket, he started hanging out at the bars again. Every move I made made him jealous or angry. I knew I couldn't stay there much longer—I was vulnerable to his every mood, without warning.

That Christmas my sister and I were invited to Tony's work Christmas party. Tony fixed her up with his cousin; the four of us had a wonderful night, dancing and enjoying the meal. On our way home, we all reminisced about the extra-funny happenings of the evening when just a half mile away from home, Tony turned nasty.

The three of us looked at each other, shocked, thinking, *Where'd this come from?*

Tony's cousin Jeff tried to reason with him, telling him to calm down, don't ruin a great night. There was no talking to him.

Once we were in the house, Tony exploded, telling us all to get the eff out; he didn't want us there. He was vulgar as he literally threw us out of the house. We girls were in high heels and dresses, slipping and sliding on the frozen ground.

I have no idea where my sister and Jeff ended up, but I went to the salon where I worked and slept on the tanning bed with hand towels for my blanket and pillow.

In the morning, once again all apologetic, Tony promised me the world. I despised the whole situation, but I knew I would have to go back—I couldn't live at the salon, and I had no other place to go.

At work I was promoted to a management position. I had more responsibilities, including ordering supplies, banking, petty cash account, and overseeing nine hairdressers.

I attended monthly franchise meetings, and, before long, the two big bosses who were partners took a liking to me and invited me to all the owners' gatherings. One afternoon, after a day out on the water, Jim, one the franchise owners, approached me and offered me fifty percent ownership. The deal was that ten percent of any money over $3,000 a week would go toward me earning my way to own half the business.

Wow! I thought. *Could this be real? Could I be getting such a break?*

I was excited and worked diligently to increase our numbers to accomplish these new goals. I saved all my money and started to look for my own place. I found a condo I could afford and started to move forward to buy it. The bank told me I didn't make quite enough. Discouraged about it all, I shared this with my bosses. The woman franchise owner, Frieda, offered to cosign for $6,000 that I would pay back upon selling the condo.

The price was steep, but I didn't care. It was my ticket out—out of the hell I was living. The day of my closing couldn't come fast enough. I told nobody about this; at times, I had to bite my tongue when Tony was an exceptional asshole, above and beyond his everyday run-of-the-mill asshole self.

Everything was perfect at the closing. I got my keys, drove to Tony's, grabbed my hidden suitcases, and left him a note on the table. All it said was, "I've moved out. I'm done."

What a feeling the moment I turned that key and heard the lock turn to open what was now my new front door. I just kept walking around, visualizing how my furniture would look once I could afford to get it out of storage, where it had been since leaving my last apartment.

I don't know how Tony found out where I moved so quickly, but that evening, just after dark, he pounded on my door. He kept trying to peek in the little windows at the top of the door. I was too frightened to move. I hid in the downstairs closet by the hot water heater, waiting for the banging to stop.

He kept yelling, "I know you're in there. Your car is here. Open the door! I know you're in there."

Tony finally left. I was so exhausted, I threw a blanket on the living room floor and fell asleep.

It was fun being in charge at work; all of us got along well and worked great together. And Tony got used to me being in my own place. I started to see him less. It seemed he could drink ten hours before he turned into an infuriated, indignant ass. Then it was eight hours, six hours, then four hours.

One Saturday after work, I stopped at the club to see him. I wasn't there a minute and I was in tears. I turned around, walked out, and knew suddenly that I needed to get back to church. That's exactly what I did—went to church. It had been so long since I was there. It felt wonderfully safe and peaceful. I used it as one way to break the cycle of the craziness. I didn't care anymore where he was. I just went to church and started to be more content, alone and quiet. I finally had some peace in my life.

About two years after the deal was made about ownership of the salon, a sheriff walked in one Saturday morning. He held this big orange sign explaining we all had to leave the premises for nonpayment of rent, leaving even our own personal property—our blow dryers and scissors, etc.—behind. I explained I knew nothing about it; the main office took care of our overhead expenses. I gave him whatever money was in the register to buy some time until Monday morning. It being Saturday, I knew I wouldn't get anyone at the office. He relented and we all continued to work, not knowing what the next week would bring.

Monday morning I learned there was no money—basically, the well was dry. I ended up arranging to pay the sheriff out of the register each week until the rent was caught up.

The sheriff experience made it clear that our employer and his company were on very shaky ground. The fear of what this meant for all of us was certainly in the air. I immediately held a staff meeting and had all the stylists express their concerns. They all agreed that whatever decision I made, they would follow, relieved I had their backs.

A Job Well Done

Six months later, I opened my own salon across town. It came out beautifully: 1,200 square feet, eight stations, three sinks. I had applied for a business loan, hired licensed electricians and plumbers, and negotiated furniture prices to fit my budget. I was proud of what I had accomplished all on my own. Plus, all nine stylists would still have jobs.

In the meantime, I expected the money that went toward my fifty percent ownership; after all, I had worked hard getting the totals up every week at the previous salon. I felt I was due that money. The owner's words will never leave me: "How can you own fifty percent of something that is no more?" Devastated and shocked, I could not believe what I heard.

I really wanted to call him a bastard for using me so, but I remained a lady, and as I started to walk away, I asked, "How do you sleep at night?" He didn't even have the guts to look at me. Another male crud.

One side of me was angry at this whole situation, the other side of me was proud. In hindsight, after about my first year of working toward fifty percent ownership, he never went over the line but certainly set things up at some meetings to be alone with me. To me, he was looking for a one-night stand or a fling. Had I been naïve enough, I'm sure he would not have hesitated. No matter how much I wanted to be successful in business, though, going down that road was never an option.

June 6, 1991. At noon, I received my certificate of occupancy. My salon was formally open. Wow! I was so proud of myself.

I thought, *Look at me! I did this!*

Although not everything went as I had hoped or planned. Just days before opening, two full-time hairdressers who were going to work for me told me they had changed their minds and were not coming. That meant a minimum $1,000 a week zapped out of the budget.

And then the second financial surprise. To this day, I have no idea how this never came up with all the people I worked with and all the things I learned. I never was taught about what I now call the "dreaded 941s." As my accountant's assistant taught me how to do payroll, she explained 941 taxes to me.

Panicked, I looked at her and said, "I have to add up what? And do what with it? Match it?"

Leaving my accountant's office, I worried how would I ever pay the bills; the 941s could cost hundreds more per month. I was more grateful than ever that I had a little money put away.

Only the good Lord knew how much I needed that money to survive. After the two financial upsets, the business was paying the bills, but there was nothing left for me. I worked all week for zero dollars. I lived on my tips and used my little cushion to pay my home expenses.

Aloof and Clueless

One year later, on Saturday, June 6, 1992, I conceived my son. It was the first anniversary of my salon. It had rained so much that by the time I closed up the salon for the day, the river across the street from my house had overflowed its banks and the police had blocked off the road. My plan was to go get some groceries, but on second thought, I didn't know whether the road would be reopened by the time I was finished. So I decided to stop at a friend's restaurant that was located in front of the blocks in the road. The place was crowded with everyone eating and drinking, appearing to have not a care in the world, as if the flooded road was no concern to them.

I don't know who called Tony to let him know of my dilemma, but it infuriated me. I had left him once again, broken off the relationship, and hadn't seen him in more than a month. I was still angry at him for not being there when I was planning to open my business. His only involvement was that he drove me to New Jersey one day so I could check out styles of and prices for custom salon furniture. This trip would give me negotiating tools at our local salon furniture companies. Even though I was grateful to Tony, I was disgusted with him for still not going anywhere in life.

So on this rainy night at the restaurant, Tony asked if we could go somewhere and talk.

"Let me buy you dinner."

I reluctantly agreed. He was sweet and gentle, soft-spoken—the Tony I fell in love with—when he declared how much he had missed me. After dinner he asked if he could come to my home to take a shower, explaining his hot water heater was broken. The road to my home had reopened, so I said okay. In hindsight, Tony once again had a secret agenda—sweet talk me, then use me. At the time, though...

I didn't see Tony after the weekend of conception. The next day we went to a pig roast and he started at 10:00 a.m. with the Jell-o shots.

I warned him, "Please don't do them. They have vodka in them."

He ignored my warning, telling me not to tell him what to do. I don't think I was there an hour before I looked for someone to give me a ride home. He could drink rum for hours and only get drunk, but vodka made him a totally vulgar, asinine idiot in a blink. I was so angry with myself for falling for the same old routine of sweet voice and empty promises.

Tony didn't know what to do when I told him I was pregnant. He didn't want another child—he never saw the two he already had. Their mother moved them out of state. He reminded me that I was thirty-nine years old.

"What are you thinking?" and mumbled he didn't want an "effing meatball," his term for a deformed child, a possibility, given my age.

Those words made me cringe. What kind of talk was that? I didn't care what he thought. I knew deep in my heart and soul that my baby would be perfectly healthy and normal. I just knew it. Nothing or no one was going to get in my way.

Tony wasn't around much my first four months of pregnancy. I told not a soul; I just continued my walking routine that I'd begun years ago, going to church, and taking really good care of myself. I made sure I didn't miss going to Al-Anon meetings, either.

My doctor was pleased. My blood pressure was the best it had been in twenty years, and my thyroid was normal. By the time I was in my fifth month, I had lost fifteen pounds. I ate well enough. I guess working full time, walking a lot, and the baby took it all. By the end of October, I had walked more than 300 miles.

For the first time in my life, I heard the words, "You need to gain some weight"! I asked the doctor if I could record him saying that. We both laughed, and he sent me on my way with a pat on the back. Oh, I loved every second of being pregnant! I always felt it would be the most important job I would ever have.

I didn't go anywhere during my pregnancy—just to work and church. On weekends I rented movies and often watched one of my favorites, *Pretty Woman* with Julia Roberts. I loved the feeling I got when she took her power back, letting her real self shine through and not settling for what she didn't want. The movie truly helped me stay strong.

I also had wonderful friends. When they could, we would share a meal. They supported me through my pregnancy more than ever. But they had lives of their own; my life still was very lonely. I kept busy having tag sales to save up for baby necessities.

Tony passed me one day on my walk. He stopped his car to ask how I was doing. It felt like I was talking to a stranger.

Wednesday, September 9, a big day. I was going to 9:00 a.m. Mass and right after Mass, having an amniocentesis, the test to determine whether my baby had any chromosomal abnormalities. The plan was that Tony would go with me to both. It ended up that he was a no-show for church and a no-show for the test. I was frantic, trying to find a ride. At the last second, his sister rushed to town to drive me and be there for me. Of course, Tony had an excuse and blamed me for telling him the wrong time.

On September 21, the doctor called, saying, "Baby is just fine. Keep up the good work." Two days later, I told my mother and Tony's dad.

My mother kept repeating, "No, you're not. No, you're not," not believing me, while staring at my belly. She even asked me to lift my shirt.

When I did, she still said, "No, you're not. No one looks like that being five months pregnant."

I left her home saying, "Well, February 26, 1993, is my due date. You'll see."

When I told Tony's dad that he was going to be a grandfather again, his comment was, "Who?"

To this day, I'll never forget the expression on his face when I said, "Me." He called me Murphy for a long time after that, referring to the television character Murphy Brown who had a baby but wasn't married in the storyline.

Tony was pleased to hear everything was fine with the baby and started to come around a little more, trying to make up for lost time. He tried to be more attentive and cooked some meals. He was in my life one week and out the next.

November 12, 1992. My phone rang. I was already in bed.

A male voice asked, "How are you doing?"

My silence while I tried to determine who it was went too long.

He finally said, "It's your father."

All I could say with a question to my tone was, "Dad?"

It was the first time in my life my father ever called me. Not much contact since I was fifteen when he pulled up in his truck to visit with us kids. He never made any attempt to be a father.

I thought, *Gee, maybe we'll move mountains after all.*

That Christmas the salon was very busy. I was exhausted by Christmas Eve. We had plans to go to Tony's dad's for dinner.

By 8:00 p.m. I just had to say, "Tony, please take me home."

Then it was 9:00 p.m. I asked him again to please take me home. Aggravated with me for disrupting his drinking for free, he drove me home, griping all the way about how he didn't know why I was so tired. I couldn't believe my ears. Why was I so tired? Angrily, I started listing what I did every day and besides that, remember? I'm seven months pregnant.

What a selfish asshole, I thought to myself.

He dropped me off and went to Jay and Bee's house for the annual Christmas party they had for their friends and family. Tony showed up the next morning as I was coming out of church. By now his "I'm sorry" just disgusted me.

January 24, 1993. Catherine gave me the most beautiful baby shower. I received many beautiful baby items, and all my friends were there to support me. We brought home a small truckload of sweet things to welcome my baby. It was a wonderful, long, exhausting, day.

Another dear friend, Michelle, was my coach for Lamaze classes. Tony said he couldn't go because he was in a dart tournament at JB's café. That was probably best, as he would have made me nervous or aggravated me, causing my blood pressure to go up, something we couldn't afford at that point. My girlfriend and I chuckle to this day when we think about the day we were in class and I told her I worried about getting to the hospital on time and forgetting my lipstick. You know, like in the movies. She already had two babies, so she had the scoop on what to expect.

February 26 came and went. No baby. I was going to the doctor's weekly by then, and each visit I was told, "Big baby." The guess one week was nine to ten pounds. Seven days later, they estimated twelve pounds. I was in tears and scared.

I cried to my girlfriend, "I'm having a toddler!" next asking, "What will we clothe the baby in?

March 9, 1993. I woke up in labor, back labor. Oh, getting in the shower was tough. I called Tony to let him know what I was feeling. Tony didn't know what to do. He kept coming and going. He would be in the house one minute, then gone the next. Michelle showed up at noon. We monitored my contractions, and Michelle drove me to the hospital at 5:00 p.m. per my doctor's orders. Tony followed right behind us.

Nicholas James was born 6:42 a.m. the next morning. Eight pounds, four ounces, and twenty-one and a half inches long—actually, a small baby for being two weeks late. The doctor had a great big smile as he shared that I had a perfect baby, healthy and strong. Just as I predicted.

Baby and Me

As I anxiously waited for the nurse to bring my baby to me, I contemplated all that had happened in the past thirty-six hours. Surely, it was nothing I had envisioned or was prepared for. Even after all those Lamaze classes Michelle and I attended while Tony played in his dart tournament.

After I was admitted and examined, we were told I had dilated 5 centimeters.

Great! I thought, *only 5 more to go. That should be fairly easy, and my baby will be here soon.*

Five hours later, 10:00 p.m., nothing had changed. I was still only 5 centimeters dilated and now eighteen hours in labor.

Michelle decided she would take the night shift and sent Tony home. I was wheeled into a small birthing room and hooked up to a machine to monitor the baby through the night. Michelle was given a thin mattress on the floor so she could get some rest. Certainly, it was not your ideal sleeping arrangement.

I was given something to relax me and to help me get some sleep, so I was only half aware of the nurse slipping in and out of the room every hour.

Suddenly, the birthing room door flew open, startling me awake as the nurses tripped over Michelle's mattress. The baby's heart rate had dropped to 80. Through the grace of God, it quickly returned to normal and things calmed down until the 5:30 a.m. decision to do a caesarean section.

I was frightened and discouraged, thinking, *Almost twenty-six hours in labor, still only dilated 5 centimeters, and now they're going to cut me.*

Michelle called Tony immediately to inform him of the doctor's decision. Once he arrived, I overheard their conversation outside of the birthing room. Michelle pleaded with him to go in the delivery room with me, assuring him he wouldn't want to miss the birth of his child, but to no avail. Tony pleaded with her not to make him go in and chose to sit out in the hallway as I was prepared for surgery. Michelle sat beside me, holding my hand, as she watched Nicholas come into the world.

They had a sheet draped over me from the waist up. All I could see was Michelle, who suddenly exclaimed, "His feet!"

The sheet draped across my cheeks annoyed me and frustrated me. I couldn't even watch the doctor's expressions.

I looked to Michelle, worried, thinking, *Oh, my God! Are they there?*

I was able to squeak out, "What?"

She turned to me with a great big smile and proudly proclaimed, "They're big!"

We both laughed. I was now relieved that he had them.

As I nursed my baby that next morning, I decided now that I had another life to take care of, I would try to put Tony's despicable behavior during my pregnancy behind me. Once he heard I was pregnant, he started to drink even more. I had kept a journal. The first five months, all I wrote about, it seemed, was how long Tony spent at the bars or how often he was in one. My journal pages were filled with "called drunk," "called swearing," "filthy-mouthed," "blamed me" for whatever's wrong in his life. The list of lies grew as well. Tony just about lived at JB's café or the club, often eight to ten hours a day, drinking more days than not. His engrossment in this toxic lifestyle clearly was escalating.

My stay at the hospital wasn't the most pleasant. Five long days, and my body didn't seem to want to resume its normal functioning. Because of all that, I was only allowed to have ice chips, and I became hungrier by the day.

On the morning of day five, I called Tony to let him know we were probably going to be discharged that day.

All he said was, "Can't you stay another night? I'm plowing snow."

When my doctor came to see me that morning, I explained I didn't have a ride until the next day.

He replied, "What do you think this is, a hotel?"

In tears and now realizing I was also anxious about going home alone with my new baby, I started calling friends I thought might be able to come for us the quickest.

Kim, an employee of mine, with joy and excitement in her voice, said, "I'll be right there."

Two hours passed before Kim was able to get to the hospital. Nicholas came into the world during the Blizzard of 1993. The snow was piled high everywhere, and many streets were still not plowed, all the more reason not to have asked Michelle to make the drive.

Kim had the car all nice and warm and was able to secure the baby carrier by herself. She was honored to be the one to pick us up and tried very hard not to show her disgust with Tony's priorities.

We arrived home safely, and Kim stayed long enough to take some pictures and help us settle in. I was exhausted but happy to be in my own home and didn't care Tony hadn't been around much in the last three days. We didn't need his crabby disposition around us anyway.

Our first week home was difficult. Nicholas cried most of the night and, like a lot of babies, had his nights and days confused. I didn't get the sleep I needed and still was not achieving normal bodily functions.

On the fourth morning after this kind of night, Tony came over in an attempt to help. Soon he discovered it seemed nothing helped the baby settle down. After just an hour, he had had enough. He came looking for me, yelling that he didn't know what was wrong. He found me in my bedroom on the phone in tears. I had just learned that Michelle was out of town on a business trip.

Tony looked at me and screamed, "What the eff are you crying about?"

I was close to hysterical at that point, no food, no sleep, a crying baby all these days later.

I screamed back at him, "Get out of my house. Leave us alone!" Then I told Michelle how difficult the days of adjusting with no help had been. Expressed that I had no patience for a clueless, inconsiderate, hung over, irritable anyone being around us.

Baby Onsite

Slowly but surely, we started to adjust to our new lives, Nicholas and I. Within three weeks, we were out visiting loved ones. Three more weeks later, I received the okay to go back to work.

Our days were quite difficult and exhausting. Trying to run a business with a new baby onsite was hard on everyone. It was hard on the employees, clients, baby, and me. In between all the craziness, we did manage to enjoy watching my son in each stage of development. Each month he grew more alert and adorable. Most of the clients understood, and some even tried to help. On occasion, though, there were some unbearable moments.

The first schedule I drew up was to work three hours, go home to nurse Nicholas, have my lunch, and return to work for three or four more hours. One morning it was near time for us to leave for lunch. I was just finishing up a client's new hairstyle when Nicholas started to whimper. His whimpering increased to a cry rather quickly as I tried to calm him and finish my work.

The tension rose. I was getting upset as well. All my employees were busy; no one to settle Nicholas down. Then my client claimed she loved her new hairdo, but could I go just a little shorter?

I was overwhelmed; I wanted and needed to tend to my baby. My heart was racing. My baby was crying harder when she shouted, "Can't you give it a cracker?" I rushed through the new, shorter hair cut.

In tears, I raced home to care for Nick, praying and crying all the way, *Dear God, please show me the way. This is impossible. How can I keep everyone happy? I need to work. I need to care for my son. How do I do it all by myself?*

I still wasn't able to take a paycheck. Starting up a business was expensive. So many other bills needed to be paid first. Tony had lost yet another job and was only contributing ten dollars a week—when he could. One week his contribution was two cans of formula, just what this nursing mother didn't need.

I felt trapped, cornered, not having enough money for daycare. Yet where else could I go with a three-month-old baby and do my job?

Every night I arrived home exhausted, frightened, lonely, and hungry, once again eating cereal for dinner and choking back my tears. Because I was nursing Nicholas, I worried whether my milk was adequate for him because of all the stress I was under. I was anxious about how I would ever get through this. At the same time, I was delighted. I was blessed with such a beautiful, healthy baby. Through my tears, my mantra became, *God, please show me the way.*

When Nicholas was four months old, Dr. Chris, his pediatrician, said I was doing a wonderful job and that Nicholas was the "tallest kid in the class," meaning out of 100 babies, at twenty-seven inches and eighteen pounds, six ounces, Nicholas's numbers put him at the top of the pediatric charts. I needed to hear I was doing a great job. Life was a whirlwind of emotions and hard times.

Our days started to smooth out a little once I switched to different hours. I now was able to work 11:30 a.m. to 7:00 p.m. until Nicholas was eight months and his teeth started to come in. Unpredictable bursts of irritability from a very unhappy baby made our days—mine, Nicholas's, and my clients'—very long and tense.

Tony came to the salon once in a while to take the baby home at 5:00 p.m., usually only when he wanted something. I would find telltale signs that he ate my food, used my washer and dryer and, sometimes, even took a shower. It infuriated me, but, again, I was trapped. I still didn't have enough money for daycare, and it was better for the baby to be home and easier for me to run my business.

We made it through year one. For Nicholas's first birthday, after getting him dressed for his first party, I put him down to hold onto the sofa, and he decided to just walk away. The guests who had come to celebrate all screeched, "He's walking!" It was a great moment.

Dr. Chris continued to repeat how Nick was way ahead. His molars were early, and he was the size of a two-year-old.

Could My Hell Get Any Worse?

Two months later, one by one, my employees gave their notice. And right after that, Tony, Nicholas, and I were in a car accident. As I waited to pull into my driveway after grocery shopping, my little red Mustang was rear-ended. My foot was on the brake and my right hand was on the steering wheel.

The impact from the collision sent a tremendous jolt through my whole right side. Pain shot down my right leg, and when I tried to get out of the car to go to Nick, my right hip gave out and I fell to the ground. Tony was moaning and the baby was crying. A neighbor came to help while we waited for the ambulance and the police.

It seemed like my world was caving in. No employees. No car. No money. No child support. I was in such pain; my back, neck, and hip hurt constantly because of whiplash from the accident. Nicholas started not sleeping through the night, making our days even harder. Again, I thought about what to do next, wondering, *Who would hire me, lugging a baby along?* It seemed Nicholas and I both cried until we were exhausted.

My only choice was to make a new budget for the business. I met with my landlord to ask for a reduction in rent while I attempted to rebuild. My landlord agreed to help me, for which I'm eternally grateful. I worked as hard as I could but still couldn't make ends meet. One month I had to decide which electric bill I would pay, the one for the salon or for my home. I chose to pay the business bill, and my home electricity was shut off for the $176 due.

Having no other choice, I asked Tony to come over to watch the baby so I could go to social services for some help with my bill and get to work. In prayer that morning, I remembered that my neighbor had passed away, but the electricity in that condo was still on. Out of desperation, I decided to plug my refrigerator into that outside electrical socket, believing the thought was divinely guided. It was the only way I could keep Nicholas's things cold.

Upon returning from work that evening, I was livid. Tony had extension cords connecting everything you could find throughout the house. The television was going, the lights were on, the toaster was plugged in, and the coffee maker was still warm.

Fierce rage raced through my body as well as an awareness of *Oh! my gosh! What would he teach my child?* as Tony sat on his ass relaxing while he mooched off people.

Infuriated, I once again shook my head in disbelief at his actions. I couldn't help but to ask, "What were you thinking? This is way past keeping the baby's milk cold!"

Instantly he raised his voice. "What the eff did you want me to do all day?"

"How about find a job!"

Desperate for more reliable help, I started to look for teenage assistants, figuring maybe they wouldn't be too expensive. I decided to try the niece of a friend. Nicholas couldn't pronounce her name, so he called her Aba.

I made another new schedule, for Mondays at least. I would bring Nicholas to a friend's house at noon, and at 4:00 p.m., she would bring Nick to Aba. I then would pick him up after work between 7:30 and 8:30 p.m. This new help gave me a little reprieve, and life went a little smoother—at least for one day a week—and I could concentrate on building up the business.

Nicholas was seventeen months old when I was done, so done, with Tony. I left him for good; his DUI was the absolute last straw. He hit a bus carrying senior citizens on their way to an event.

He rang my doorbell the next morning at 5:00 a.m. looking for a ride to the garage where the police had towed his car so he could get his wallet. I was revolted by the whole situation, but I took the opportunity to talk to him on the way to the garage. I made it clear to him that I was sorry his Mom passed away only the week before but that I would no longer put up with his toxic lifestyle or excuses.

Tony spent the next six to eight months making fervent attempts to get back into my good graces from every ardent angle he could come up with. One day he even proclaimed if I gave him back the engagement ring, I would never hear from him again. I instantly went to my bedroom where I'd tucked the diamond away to return it to him. Tony's promise lasted exactly one hour.

Nicholas turned two. Again, Dr. Chris said he was the tallest kid in the class at thirty-seven and a half inches and thirty-five and a half pounds. The doc also added, "Keep up the good work, Mom."

His words once again were comforting. I needed that pat on the back, especially with the constant struggle with what was right or best for my son. One month after Nick's birthday was Tony's. It was a Saturday. Nicholas was at work with me from 8:00 a.m. to 3:30 p.m., and Tony kept calling the salon, asking for a "family day."

Here we go again, I thought. *Another battle, another round or ten of him swearing and yelling.*

At the end of the day, all he really wanted was to squeeze a so-called family day in between his drinking sessions. With each call, he was more intoxicated than the last. When the calls stopped around 3:00, I figured he must have found something better to do, or he passed out. Either way, hopefully, we would not be bothered anymore for the rest of the day. I was right.

The next day, of course, he was all apologetic, asking to see his son for his birthday. I agreed to allow him to visit in the backyard at four in the afternoon and hung up the phone. By noon, Tony was on the phone again, feeling good and now with an attitude, griping about how unfair I was to him.

He said, "I'm sure going to dinner is a 'no.' All you ever do is say no."

Shaking my head, wondering where that came from, I responded, "You're feeling good already."

Before he hung up he mumbled, "I'm tired. I need a nap. But all you ever say is no." He didn't make it over to see his son that day, either.

Early the next morning, he was back on the phone with a worse attitude, now very defensive, with his typical "it's your fault, not mine" attitude, blaming me for his misery. I had no comment, just hung up the phone. As usual, that prompted another call. I let the answering machine take it.

He assumed I already had plans for Nick and called me a "mean, rotten, effing bitch." Now, that is some very sound, grounded thinking.

What a nut, I thought, and off to church Nick and I went.

Coming out of church, I softened and made several attempts to contact Tony. I called his home phone at least a dozen times and even went and knocked on his back door. No response. Around 2:30 that afternoon, he left a message on my answering machine. He needed to go home for a nap. Could he come over to see Nick for dinner? Again, his drinking was his priority, and he expected me to jump through hoops for him.

That evening I waited until 6:20. No Tony. I fed Nick. We went to the park and later watched a movie. The sad part was that Nicholas had waited now for four days to sing happy birthday to his father, and Tony couldn't seem to stay sober long enough to fit his son in for ten minutes.

To end our night, a typical abusive message from Tony blamed me for all that was wrong in his life and accused me of keeping his son from him. And, of course, more name calling—Tony's psychopathic insanity was constant in our lives.

He just never stopped. He woke me up in the middle of the night. He just had to tell me I was a despicable creep for keeping his son away from him on his birthday. This went on for days. His hostility grew and grew, and he repeated that I was keeping his son from him. He just wanted to see "his boy."

I was just as consistent in saying, "No, not when you are drinking or DRUNK!!!!!"

Not once did he take ownership of his own behavior—the cause of this nightmare. Not once.

A Confused Easter Bunny

I was exhausted from trying to keep all Tony's alcoholic craziness from Nicholas. How long could I go on pretending? How long could I keep this away from Nicholas and maintain a happy, safe home without cracking?

When Tony couldn't handle me not backing down about his drinking and being sober to be around Nicholas, he would start in with, "I'm taking you to court." This time, that threat went on for weeks.

By now, I never knew what Tony's behavior would be, but I did know it would always be bizarre. He was not of sound mind most of the time. If he held a job longer than a month, he developed a pompous attitude, thinking he had more power.

I was preparing Easter dinner when there was a knock on my front door. I thought it was my neighbor, for we had spoken at church that morning. We were going to share a recipe.

When I opened the door, Tony pushed right by me, barely able to walk, and fell into the rocking chair.

He immediately started in on me, "Are you having sex?" and swearing at me, "You're an ass. You're really making me hate you."

I asked him to leave, but all he did was growl at me like an animal and didn't move.

He kept threatening that he was going to take me to court, that I was keeping him from his son, that I would have to pay for his lawyer. "You think you're such a smart ass. I'll show you." He turned to Nicholas and said, "Nicholas, your mother is a jerk."

Nick responded, "You jerk, Dada. You jerk."

Then Tony yelled at the baby, "Don't you talk to me that way!"

In his next breath, he asked for the Easter gifts he had just given to his son. He put them back in the bag he brought them in, handing back only one of them.

When Nick asked his father to open it, Tony said to his two-year-old son, "Go ask your jerk ass mother." As he walked out the back door, still carrying the baby's gifts, he yelled back to Nicholas, "Mama is jealous because you love me more."

I couldn't lock the doors fast enough. Having to deal with such crazy behavior was tough on me, but my main concern was the damage being done to my son. I barely felt safe and sane; I worried so for the confusion Nick was going through, constantly concerned about how much we would have to undo. The subconscious mind is already programmed by the age of six.

Two hours later Tony called. "Presumably you're not going to let me see my son. You should know I gave a lawyer a $250 retainer." CLICK!

I always did my best not to appear fearful about his words, but these frightened me to the point of being sick to my stomach. It took me all evening to calm the baby down and to get him to stop repeating his father's words. "Mama jerk. Dada jerk."

A Mother's Nightmare

April 24, 1995, Monday, would be a little different. Nicholas went to daycare a little earlier than usual. One of my new employees and I had a hair show to attend. I was anxious about not working that day, because every penny counted, but it was just as important to build a new team and stay up on what was new in the industry.

Ten minutes after we arrived back at work from the show, I received a phone call from Aba, Nicholas's daycare provider. They were on their way to the hospital. Nicholas had been bitten by one of their dogs. I had one of my staff finish the haircut I was working on and raced to the hospital. I prayed all the way there, *Please, Lord, let my baby be okay!*

When I arrived at the hospital, I found Nicholas crying, terrified, his little grey sweats covered in blood. The right side of his nose was gone—just gone, a vacant space. The dog bit it off.

As soon as he saw me, he began crying, "Mama! Mama!"

I picked him up to comfort him, and I thought I was going to be sick, or, worse yet, possibly pass out. My knees weakened, fear took over.

The emergency room personnel informed me that they couldn't do much to help. We needed to wait for a plastic surgeon. I paced the hospital floor with Nicholas on my hip for four hours, comforting him, waiting for the doctor.

My little guy kept pointing toward the door, repeating, "Mama! Nicky home. Mama! Nicky home!"

As I prayed and paced the floor, I kept my eyes fixed on the doorway to catch the surgeon's first reaction. Somewhere in my denial of this mother's nightmare, I pretended.

My baby has a half a nose missing. Maybe it's not that bad.

It was too much to bear, though in my logical mind, I was very much aware this was horrible. I kept trying to push the thoughts of how would life be for my little guy with such a deformed face out of my mind, because I knew Nicholas would pick up on my distress if I continued with that thought process.

I was right. The surgeon's first reaction was an expression I will never forget. Dr. Daniels decided to do surgery right there in the emergency room to not waste any more time. He apologized for taking so long to get to the hospital from his out-of-town office.

My little boy was immediately put in a baby straightjacket and given needle after needle in his little face to prepare him for surgery. During the procedure my son screamed, so frightened that his little hands broke out of the jacket.

Dr. Daniels assured me that Nicholas didn't feel anything, which I could not conceive, as the baby had to have felt at least the first few of the twelve needles into his face. Dr. Daniels went to work and pulled flesh from under Nicholas's cheek to form a new nose.

Nicholas continued to scream, so the doctor asked me to hold the baby's head still.

Nick wasn't settling down, so I began to say aloud, "Sssh, Baby. Pray with Mama. Sssh, Baby. Pray with Mama."

I started to talk about another little boy he knew who had heart problems.

I prayed, "Baby Jesus, pray for Anthony. Nicholas, pray with Mama." I kept my voice low and steady. Nicholas started to calm down, and Dr. Daniels glanced up, gave me an approving nod and a look of "keep up the good work."

Somewhere in the middle of all this, Aba's mother decided to go find Tony. They arrived at the hospital after the surgery had started, and Tony was not allowed into the procedure room. He made matters worse by being his drunken self, yelling up and down the hallway. I thanked God he wasn't allowed in that room, angered why that woman went to find him or even told him what had happened after seeing his condition.

When Dr. Daniels finished putting twenty stitches in Nick's face, he came over to me and said, "I just want you to know, you're a wonderful mother. What I just witnessed was amazing. Your baby did well. He'll be fine."

As he patted me on the back, the tears just streamed down my face; I was unable to control them another second. His words and comforting look helped me feel Nicholas and I weren't alone in this nightmare and the doctor would help us get through it.

I carried my baby out of the hospital, grateful the surgery was over and just as grateful the doctor we waited for hours for was the man and surgeon he was. I tried not to think past the next hour. At that point, it was more than I could bear.

To make this nightmare worse, I was now stuck with Tony because his car was still at the bar. We barely made it to the pharmacy where we needed to pick up medical supplies and Nicholas's prescription when Tony started his ranting and raving.

"How could this happen to a baby! Who was supposed to be watching him? Where the eff was everybody?"

I struggled to drive. My whole body trembled. It took all of me to stay composed. I was so upset over what my beautiful baby had just endured, and Tony's behavior only escalated the fear of what was ahead for us. Once we were home, I changed Nicholas and got him ready for bed.

I knelt beside Nick's crib to hold his little hand while he fell asleep. My body started to rock back and forth as the tears again started streaming down my cheeks.

I prayed, *Dear God, please heal my baby.* Over and over again. *Please heal my baby.* Those were the only words that would come out of my mouth.

In the meantime, Tony was still lying on the living room sofa, STILL yelling, "There is no effing God. How could this happen to a baby?"

As I got up to close the nursery door, I wondered if it was possible for us to grow any more apart or be more opposite than we were. I fell asleep on the floor next to Nicholas's crib.

Five days after the dog was put down for biting Nicholas, my friend stopped in at my salon. I asked, "How is everyone doing?"

With a disgusted shrug of her shoulders, she responded, "Well, they lost their dog."

She had such an attitude in her voice.

I quickly replied, "Nicholas lost HIS NOSE!!!!"

With a that's-not-such-a-big-deal attitude and shrug, she said, "Oh, it will give him character."

Her words stopped me in my tracks. I couldn't believe what I heard or her nonchalant view about my baby's nose. She valued a dog more than a baby's nose. Instantly I knew that friendship was over. I didn't need or want people like that around us. It will probably take me a lifetime to forgive her words.

Two weeks passed. We did our best to survive the horror of what seemed to be a very bad dream. Tony called, wanting to take us out for pizza to take our minds off our troubles for a while. In the middle of dinner, Tony called the baby "zipper nose"—twice. He had a smile on his face as if it were a term of endearment.

Not believing my ears, I asked, "What are you doing? Hasn't he already been through enough?"

Tony looked at me as if I were crazy, then called the baby "Rudolph."

That was it; I couldn't sit there another second. I packed up Nick's things and started toward my car.

As Tony rushed to catch up, I asked him, "How can you be so cruel?"

As Tony strapped Nick into his car seat, Tony said to the baby, "Mama doesn't love you anymore."

Was it just me? Those were not words a parent would or should ever say to a child! I was so upset I was trembling. I wanted to run Tony over with the car. I pleaded with him to stop messing with the baby's head. Why would he put such untruths in Nicholas's mind?

Tony yelled back, "I know what I am doing. Just shut up!"

The more I asked him to stop yelling and swearing, the worse he got, repeating, "Eff you, eff you!" Then he called me "an asshole," "a bitch," "a rotten zero," "a nothing"—almost all the way to my home.

Then, at the last second, he asked to be dropped off at JB's café. No surprise. His bar life kept him from being supportive during surgery, and now he needed more booze after upsetting us. So much for taking our minds off our troubles.

I drove home thinking, *Good riddance, you blazing maniac.*

I was exhausted, once again trying to juggle it all, trying to keep peace and protect my child. I was furious as I reflected on the events of the past week.

As usual with Tony, it was never, ever enough. I allowed him to come over and have breakfast with his son. I let him borrow my car to go to the hardware store. I let him take Nicholas to the park, and this was the thanks I got.

You bastard! I thought. I clenched my teeth not to scream it out loud. I silently repeated continuously, *You bastard!* as my hands gripped the steering wheel until my knuckles were white.

I couldn't help but to think he was losing his mind. Plus, early in the week when he had breakfast at our house with Nick, he kept saying to me, "Let's have sex. Let's have sex."

He just didn't stop with "Let's have sex." He moved on to, "Nicky! Tell Mama 'Get naked.' Tell Mama, 'Get naked!'"

"Oh! my God, stop!" I pleaded. "He's only two years old."

This whole scene was beyond anything I could tolerate. Tony would not stop or leave, so I picked up Nicholas and we left. When we returned home, the answering machine was flashing. "I don't care what or when. You will be giving up something, even if I have to rape you."

Tired of feeling trapped and desperate, I put a call in to Dr. Chris to discuss Tony's abusive behavior toward Nicholas, totally aware I was adding another professional to my list of avenues for help, another piece of documentation for the courts. Dr. Chris referred us to a clinic to get Nicholas into therapy for the trauma he had just been through because of the dog bite.

I did what Dr. Chris suggested, hoping it would help, but, my gosh, Nicholas was only a baby. I was so annoyed that once again, Tony's abusive adult behavior was just shoved under the rug. Tony had no consequences again. Well, if anything, a record of his behavior would be in the doctor's chart, I hoped.

I only had to put up with a few calls from Tony the next week. I told him that, at Dr. Chris's recommendation, he could no longer see Nicholas near me or my home. He would have to find another way. I hoped that this way, Nick would be subjected less to his father's anger over me leaving him and to his escalating drinking habit.

Tony didn't deal well with this change, saying often during his phone calls and messages that he'd disregard the therapist's advice about keeping Nick's schedule as consistent as possible.

"I'll do what I damn well please. My son is going to have a fun life, not like mine." Tony declared it was I who needed the therapist.

Damn straight, I thought to myself. *Nick and I shouldn't have to put up with such abusive behavior.*

I stood my ground, insisting that Tony needed to do what was best for Nick; if he didn't, I would limit his time to only one visit a week, somewhere safe and supervised. Then I hung up the phone.

About an hour passed, and Tony was back, slurring and yelling, "I want to see my boy. I want to see my boy!" His dragging and slurring increased the more he tried to speak. The last words I heard were, "You're a rotten, miserable person." CLICK!!!

I hung up without saying one word to him.

Unfortunately, the calls did not stop. Tony called back every fifteen minutes, leaving the same message, for four more hours. By the time the calls stopped, my nerves were shot; I was a wreck because of his continuous woodpeckering.

Nicholas had been in therapy three months and we were getting by, things were settling down, when Tony called with his new brainstorm. "Let me have my boy Friday through Sunday."

He didn't care for my quick "NO!" I reminded him of his choices and sarcastic manner in front of the baby. He mumbled that he wouldn't tolerate not seeing his son, of course letting me know he thought I was the "abusive parent."

My Deterioration Becomes Evident

I was growing weaker and weaker physically, emotionally, and psychologically. I was extremely tired. Tony's calls and threats frightened me. I was exhausted, dragging through every day, nervous, and constantly sick to my stomach. I had a headache that just wouldn't go away.

I was then diagnosed with fibromyalgia, not surprising considering the emotional and physical stress I lived, putting me at high risk for the disease. Everything in my body hurt. At times, the pain just flowed through me like waves in the ocean.

It became harder and harder to do my job, to smile, to pretend that everything was fine. I feared sharing the hell I was living, and I was so ashamed, thinking, *How did I get into such a mess? How could I not have seen the writing on the wall? Who could have known it would turn out this horribly?*

I never imagined that Tony would get continually worse. His drinking and crazy thinking were out of control. His new angle was, "We know how terrible it was as children without a father around. Why are you doing that to Nicholas? God is going to punish you."

I couldn't sleep at night. I worried constantly and lived in fear. *What would happen next?* I did my best to remain calm and respectful to Tony, thinking two wrongs don't make a right. I didn't want Nicholas to be subjected to two out-of-control parents.

I needed help. I needed rest. I needed money. It was a vicious cycle. When I treated Tony respectfully, he took it as hope we could be "a family." He had no idea I'd grown disgusted and embarrassed by what he had become. I didn't want to see him or be seen with him. His escalating physical deterioration became more evident each time I had to deal with him. It was difficult to watch and even more difficult to be around.

Trying to stay sane and protect my son became a constant battle as Tony continued to pick and choose when it was convenient for him to show up in Nick's life and ignored all my set limitations and boundaries. Constantly trying to discern whether I was doing the right thing, making the right choices, plus anticipating Tony's erratic behavior was a full-time job.

I met a woman at one of my networking groups. She listened to my dilemma about getting some help to care for Nick while I worked. She made one phone call and, miraculously, Nicholas was accepted through Catholic Family Services and was in a happy, safe environment. They charged me on a sliding scale. I could only afford a few days, but that help allowed me to keep Nick safe and concentrate at work.

While I was at work one day, Tony called, as sweet as could be, pleading, "Please let me borrow twenty dollars." He claimed that he hadn't eaten in days. I thought, *You should be helping me.* In minutes he was at my salon. As he left with his twenty dollars, he commented, "You're doing an injustice to Nicholas."

Ten minutes later on the phone, "It's really too bad you're jealous of Nicholas's and my relationship. Your behavior must be some form of child abuse. It makes me wonder if you are any good for him at all." The call ended with the observation that he was a much better influence on his son.

I said to myself, *When will I ever learn? You sick bastard.* The booze had really gotten to him. He certainly didn't hear himself or realize how irrational his thinking had become.

God Spared Them Both

A half-hour later, I received a phone call informing me my youngest brother Sammy was found dead that morning. It was December 15, 1995.

As I raced to his home, I feared what I would walk into. What would I see or be told? He was only thirty-five years old. What could have happened?

I prayed, *Please don't let this be true.*

In between my prayers and trying to control the speed of the car, I was grateful that Nicholas was not with me at work. What would I have done with him? I certainly could not have had him with me then, not knowing what I would find when I reached my brother.

The drive took forever, even though it was just to my mother's house. It was true. My baby brother Sammy was gone. Being in the room he died in was horrific; it felt dark and shady, just like two of the three people who were in the house. They were strangers to me, and the man who was once our mother's boyfriend just hid in his room. The snake. He couldn't even come out to talk to me about what he knew. Obviously, with Mother in a nursing home, things were not the same. She would not have tolerated the goings on in that house.

The reality of Sammy's death devastated me. When he was a baby, I would come home from school to find my mother sitting with her feet up, watching her soap operas. I was the one who had bathed Sam, changed his diapers, played with him. I had lost my baby brother, but, somehow, it felt like I had lost my own child.

The blessing in my brother's death was that he was finally out of pain. For the preceding ten years, he had had one back surgery after another to repair an on-the-job injury. He seemed to become more disabled after each. The strength of his pain pills continued to increase, as did the amount of his pot smoking. Then he added some vodka to the menu. He also struggled with not feeling useful.

Being that he was so disabled, his days were long and lonely, especially once our mother was in a nursing home. Sammy believed she was coming home soon, but I knew better. Mom at that point was not even aware of everyday goings-on. Some days she didn't even recognize her own children. She was sent there for rehab but seemed to only deteriorate once she hurt herself at a physical therapy session. She was spared on one level. She could not have gotten through burying her baby, and Sammy could not have handled burying his mother. I thanked God for sparing them both.

Spots Don't Change

Tony knew Sam's death was tough on me and did try to be more cooperative for a while. But within weeks, right after Christmas, he was back to his old behavior, berating me, yelling and swearing about everyone and everything.

It was Valentine's Day 1996. Nicholas had been in therapy for the trauma from the dog bite for ten months. His therapist felt it was time to bring Tony in on a session, since Nick brought him up often.

Tony didn't like any part of that hour. I watched him desperately try to control his anger. We had barely closed the door after the session when he snarled at me, "Well, enjoy the tax deduction for Nicholas because it's your last year."

As I thought, *Where'd that come from?* he continued, "That was bullshit in there."

Nick repeated "Bullshit," and, of course, Tony yelled at him for swearing, then told him to "SHUT UP!"

Oh, I wished the therapist was within hearing distance.

I was very pleased at how the office visit had gone. I could tell the therapist recognized Tony's nature by his comments and agitated state by her words on Nicholas's behalf before we left. Another little piece to the support I was trying to build, another professional on my side.

I felt consoled when I thought about the therapist speaking on Nicholas's behalf if I ever needed her for court. I never knew when or if Tony would follow through with his threats about going to a lawyer for more time with Nick. Slowly but surely, Tony revealed his true self, and just as slowly but surely, I was building my case without any "he said, she said" in the story.

Tony sped away from the therapist's office, tires screeching, for many to witness. I shook my head and laughed. Just an hour prior to this visit, he had declared his love for me, asking me to let him take me away from "all this."

Finding a Middle Ground

As I continued to enforce limited visitations and boundaries, the more crude, sarcastic, and cocky Tony behaved, constantly playing head games, putting Nicholas in the middle, showing up at our home without any notice, disrupting whatever serenity I had achieved. We had argument after argument about his disrupting Nick's schedule. He never tried to imagine what it was like to bring a toddler to work and how important it was for Nicholas and me to stay on task.

One afternoon, without warning, Tony stopped by the house. He wanted to wake Nicholas up from his nap just to say goodbye; he argued with me about it loud enough to wake the baby up.

Now Nicholas was crying, and as Tony headed for the front door, he yelled up the stairs, "Nicholas. Nicholas. Mommy wants me to go. She's throwing me out again. I can't stay and play with you. Mom's keeping us apart."

As he walked to his car, he continued yelling up to Nick's bedroom, "Your mommy is making me leave again, Bud. She's the mean one, not me."

Tony's patterns did not change. Hours later, he called to borrow money so he could get to work. He always thought that excuse would soften me since if he worked, I might get a little financial help from him. I knew there was little chance of that. It was quite clear the bars got all his money. I was sure that as he spent the last of his money at the bar, he didn't think he needed money to get to work. He just thought about the next drink.

Confusing me, he rambled on about how I always got my way. Whatever I wanted, I got. And now, he was being set up by "some chick" [Nick's therapist] for the trauma from the dog bite.

"And now this bitch is going to tell [Nicholas] I don't want him around."

It seemed that subconsciously he was aware of the harm he was doing to Nicholas, but I still couldn't get him to admit that he was hurting and confusing his son. His drinking had taken over his life, and Nick and I were paying the price.

Right after Nicholas turned three, his therapist said we were done, saying that Nick did wonderfully.

She said, "He worked harder than most adults."

I was just amazed by and admired how she worked with such a little guy who barely had a vocabulary. It took me the whole year of asking in my daily prayer for help with forgiving all who were involved in not protecting my baby the day of the dog bite.

On September 23, 1996, the nursing home called. My mother had passed away that morning at the age of sixty-four. I sighed a breath of relief for her; it was no way to live. She didn't even notice Sammy didn't come to visit anymore.

Sadly, the day we buried her, my tears were not over her passing. My tears were for the years and years of never understanding why I was never good enough for her, why she did what she did, why she never protected me as a child. Why didn't I matter to her? My tears also reflected relief that her hell was finally over.

I showed up at her service because I thought that was what I was supposed to do but spent most of the time worried about work. I couldn't afford to miss any. I still needed every penny to make ends meet. An employee commented on how strong I was returning to work that afternoon. Oh! Not strong. I needed to be able to feed my baby more than I needed to grieve. It was as simple as that.

Nicholas, Not Nichole

Life settled down a bit, but finding daycare help for Saturdays was still a dilemma. It was difficult for anyone to commit to every week—their lives were all too busy. My Saturday schedule included anywhere from ten to fifteen clients over eight to ten hours, and having a toddler at work that many hours made for a long, rough day on everyone.

Tony diligently tried to convince me he would be responsible and promised to show up on time if I allowed him to watch Nicholas on Saturday. His harping got to me, but, really, I had no choice.

Reluctantly, I agreed to try it for a while, knowing only too well how difficult it was on Nicholas to be at the salon that long, and it wasn't so easy keeping him busy anymore. He wanted to be outside playing with other children, and I felt strongly that he should be allowed to be a child.

I called home one Saturday to check on how things were going. Tony answered the phone all annoyed; he spewed that Nick was afraid of a worm.

Then he started ranking on Nicholas, "Nichole, Nichole, do you want me to buy you a Barbie doll?"

I pleaded with him to stop.

Nicholas got on the phone all upset, asking, "Mama, I'm a boy, right?"

His father continued to rant and rave in the background.

"Nichole, Nichole. It is really clear to me that your mother and godmother have too much influence."

I was so upset. My child was being emotionally abused, and I was trapped at work. I couldn't even leave for minutes; I had a perm to rinse in two minutes. I had to choose between rescuing my son and destroying my client's hair through overprocessing. A lawsuit I did not need.

The battle continued 24/7. The more I tried to find a normal balance and keep the boundaries clear with Tony, the more he put Nick in the middle. Tony would argue with me to see his son more, then on Saturdays complain I took advantage of him.

Every Saturday when I arrived home, we had the same disagreement. No matter if I worked six hours, eight hours, or longer, he always had a problem. He felt I should only work the hours that were convenient for him. To get him to stop arguing with me and leave, I would attempt to get to the phone to call the police. A few times when he didn't block me from it, I actually started to call them. More than once, Tony pulled the phone out of the wall.

He often told Nick that I was rotten and mean and that "Now Daddy is going to be all alone." He kept repeating, "You have a rotten, mean mother. Let her effing boyfriend watch you."

Always feeling at the edge of my breaking point, I consulted two attorneys who both warned me that if I took Tony to court, he would get more time with Nicholas and could be granted sleepover visits or every-other-weekend custody. I could not or would not *ever* chance that.

Desperation to find a way to protect my child never left me. Every day I prayed for answers or a miracle and hoped I would find someone to guarantee our safety and a good outcome. I lived in constant fear, never knowing what Tony might do next and/or get away with, being a cop's son, or how crazy he would make me look.

I started to talk weekly with a nun from my church. She would calm me for the moment but kept encouraging me to trust the authorities. She witnessed me stuck, frozen with fear. The vicious cycle of trying to discern what was right, what was wrong. Some people would tell me, "Nicholas needs his father"; others would say, "He doesn't need his father" or ask, "Is his father sober or is he drunk?" The concerns were endless, yet I couldn't chance the authorities giving Tony more time with Nicholas and never, ever an overnight visit. I would be dead and buried before I would do anything to let that happen.

That October my grandfather, my mother's dad, passed away. It hadn't even been a month since Mom passed away, making it three deaths in ten months. Sammy, my mother, and, now, my grandfather. I didn't have the time or even the energy to mourn him.

I always worked late on Mondays, often until 7:30 or 8:00 p.m. Suddenly, my part-time employee who babysat for Nicholas on Monday nights decided to change careers and was no longer able to help.

Oh! What next, I thought.

When Tony learned about it, he worked on me long enough to break me. I said I would let him try to add Monday night 4:00 to 7:00 p.m. to his visitation. It would be a trial run; I really didn't have much choice. Leaving work to pick up Nick at daycare and bringing him back with me would only delay his schedule for dinner and bedtime even longer.

I made what I expected of Tony and the responsibilities he needed to abide by very clear. There would be no drinking. No bars with Nicholas. Show up on time and prepare a decent, healthy meal. More important, certainly no yelling or swearing. I got lots of thank yous and "I will, I will."

Weeks passed. Tony couldn't seem to honor his commitments for one reason or another. He asked me to leave my door unlocked all day so he could let himself in to feed Nick because he had no money or food.

I reminded him, "It's been six weeks and you have yet to accomplish one night without my help."

His pathetic answer: "Give me a break! I'm doing the best I can. I have no money."

I wanted to respond, "Stay out of the bars" but knew only too well those words would fall on deaf ears or cause a bout of nastiness. The only thing that stayed consistent was the inconsistency of Tony's words and actions.

Always Something Better

The ebb and flow of Tony's unpredictable, antagonistic behavior caused a constant upheaval in Nick's and my lives. Even when I thought there would be peace among us for the moment and we might get through an hour or two, often, I was wrong.

Halloween was just a few days away. Nicholas was excited about picking out a Halloween costume, trying to choose between Batman or Spiderman. Tony had been tormenting me nonstop to partake in our festivities. Halloween night arrived. Tony showed up only long enough to tell us he had been invited to a party and I would have to bring Nicholas to Papa's house myself.

The pattern of Tony arranging to see his son unless something better showed up never altered; neither did his lack of awareness of the example his lifestyle or his swearing set for his son. He couldn't get through thirty minutes before we would have a problem with his language. It was as if he were among a bunch of adult low-lifes.

I could never anticipate which side of Tony would show up—but what I could count on without fail was that his deep-down real priorities would always shine through. It was not the first time that spending time with Nicholas took a back seat to the alcohol.

Christmas week, he came over "just to put the tree in the stand for my son." In minutes, we were listening to "effing tree."

I started to sound like a broken record. "Stop with the language."

It didn't matter. His response, "Shut up! Just shut up!" Clearly crabby, irritable. Most likely a hangover.

I remained calm when I asked him to stop ruining every event with his filthy mouth, asking, "What kind of memory will this be for Nicholas?"

In the meantime, Nicholas started saying, "You shut up, Dada."

Tony hit him with his baseball cap.

"Please," I pleaded. "Just go. Please just go. We don't need a tree."

Instead of Tony enjoying creating a happy holiday memory with his son, he became a jealous, ranting idiot, putting Nick in the middle again by talking to him in a totally inappropriate way and ruining the moment.

"Yeah, Nick. Mama must be up to something. She must be going on a date. If I catch him, I'll rip his nose off."

Tony's sick, troubled mind then produced, "Nicholas, you better come home with Daddy. Mommy's going out whoring around."

By this time, I was trembling so hard, I could hardly scoop Nick up in my arms and rush out the front door. My rattled thoughts were that if we left, Tony would. I was so upset, I could hardly open my car door. My hands shook so, I couldn't hook the seatbelt over Nick's car seat, giving Tony time to catch up to us.

I told him if he continued with this type of behavior, I would take him to court for child abuse. Just before I closed my car door, he yelled back, "If you do that, you will be DEAD!"

At the same time, he blocked my car with his to prevent me from driving away. I quickly locked the car doors, fighting back tears so I wouldn't upset Nicholas any more than he already was.

I prayed, *Lord, please. Help me to know what to do to keep us safe.* As the tears streamed silently down my cheeks, I asked the Lord to forgive me for wishing Tony dead.

I kept the phone off the hook for days after that evening so I wouldn't have to listen to Tony's mouth and his crazy accusations. Nicholas and I lived like prisoners behind tightly closed blinds and bolted doors. Any little noise startled me. I was constantly afraid of what Tony was up to.

He came over often, banging on the front door, banging on the back door, yelling, "Put the effing phone back on the hook! Open this effing door! Let me see my boy!"

At this point, his father's daily outbursts had gotten to Nicholas and he started crying. I opened an upstairs bedroom window and called down to Tony, telling him that if he didn't leave immediately, I would call the police.

He switched to his sweet voice. "Oh, stop," he said. "Yes, I was out of line [when I came to help with the tree]. I apologize. Don't hold a grudge."

I just closed the window and went to comfort my son—again.

As the weeks passed, I was able to keep Tony away from our home, only allowing him to pick up Nick at my work. But I wouldn't let him inside the salon. It was located in a strip mall with four designated parking spaces right in front of my storefront. Tony would pull up to the front windows. I could kiss Nicholas good-bye and watch him get right into his father's car.

One evening, as I put my son to bed after a short visit with his father, he said, "Mama, Daddy says you're a liar and we're going to go to Florida next Monday."

It took me more than an hour to ease his mind enough for him to settle down and fall asleep.

The next morning, after I took the trash out, there was Tony, standing in my kitchen. I had no idea where he came from, where he'd hidden. I was angry, so angry I wasn't even frightened. I wanted to hit him or hurt him in some way for startling me like that.

I pushed him out of my way and poked him in his chest, asking, "What the hell do you think you're doing, telling a little boy you're taking him away? Get the hell out of my house."

He said not a word and started to walk toward my front door. I thought he was leaving when, in fact, he ran upstairs to Nick's room and woke him up. I hurried after him to stop him.

When I reached the top of the stairs, I overheard, "Good morning, Buddy. I can't stay. Your Mommy is making me leave; she won't let me see you. You're my best bud, right?"

I really don't know how I ever controlled myself. I wanted to push him out the second-floor window. I still believe today that I only controlled myself for Nicholas's sake.

As calmly as I could under the circumstances, I tried to reason with Tony. "You say you had a horrible childhood. Why, then, are you doing the same to your son?"

Ignoring me, Tony continued, "See, Nicholas, it's all Mommy's fault, Buddy. She's making me leave. It's not Daddy who is bad."

Tony had upset Nick so much, the boy was crying, "I hate you!"

As I went for the phone to call the police, Tony left.

I rocked Nick until he calmed down, explaining that I was not keeping anyone away, but that everyone has to behave properly with inside voices and good manners. Despite how upset I was, I had to show Nicholas a calm exterior to reassure him that his home with me was, indeed, a safe haven. That despite his father's actions, he could count on me to do my best to keep him safe.

Within the next half-hour, Tony attempted to leave a phone message, letting his son know he was all right, for Nicholas not to worry about him, and that he couldn't help himself. I picked up the phone in the middle of his message, said, "Please, Tony. You're forty-seven and he's four," and hung up the phone.

That afternoon I called the Department of Children and Families (DCF) for documentation reasons.

Losing the Battle

I felt like I was going to have a nervous breakdown and was fearful of what would happen to my baby. I hurt all over, crawled out of bed every day, dragged through my responsibilities, sick and tired of faking it. This never-ending cycle caused havoc with me on every level—physically, psychologically, mentally, emotionally.

A few months of peace followed. Then, Tony started to come around again, begging to see his son, pointing out that he had been working hard and not going to the bars.

"Please let me see my son." So it seems that when he was sober, he did get it.

However, it didn't take him long to exploit the situation and revert to his nasty self. A very loud voice. A few "shut ups." A few "effing this or that."

When I reminded Tony of the rules, he interrupted me with, "It's no big effing deal." Once again I asked him to leave.

He got two inches from my face and screamed, "I hate you, you fat, effing bitch!" I was able to push him out the back door and quickly locked it.

Oh, I thought. *Why can't I find someone to help us? Who would believe this craziness, anyway?*

It was almost Christmas again. In 1998, Nicholas was five and excited for Santa to come. Life had been a little easier. We were accepted at a daycare closer to home, and it also went by a sliding-fee scale. The whole staff was so wonderful to us, and the center was safe and clean.

Tony was now only responsible for four hours a week on Saturdays. He was a continuous no-show, hours late, or often brought Nick back to me early, without giving him lunch. Before long, I heard that he had started bringing Nick to the bars in those few hours of visitation.

Nicholas started to cry about going with his father. One Saturday when I tried to explain this to Tony, it only aggravated him to the point he threatened to sell Nick's dog (which really wasn't Nick's dog; it was a mutt Tony picked up at some bar).

Nick was fearless for the moment, replying, "I don't care. Mommy will get me another one!"

Standing up to his father like that was unbelievably brave for such a little guy. I was so proud of him. I felt a spark of hope that he truly understood he was safe with me, no matter what was going on around us.

Infuriated, Tony responded, "You know what, Nicholas? Why don't you find yourself a new dad."

This all happened in only five minutes in Tony's presence, but it upset Nick for the whole day.

This situation was so destructive, all I could do was pray. At times, I prayed so passionately, I would forget what I was doing, where I was going, as if I left the world for a while.

More Professionals

Fear ate me up. I lived in terror. Which is worse? Go to court. Don't go to court. Trust the system. Don't trust the system. Am I crazy? Not crazy? Not enough money. And again, not enough money. No child support and still no child support.

Tony seemed to finagle ways to continue to put Nick in the middle, disregarding his limitations and our boundaries, poisoning my child's mind.

Out of the clear, Nick would make comments like, "Papa is mean to Daddy," and, "Daddy says you're a liar."

It was clear to me that I was losing the battle. As hard as I tried, I realized that I was failing. Nick's behavior was changing; he began showing symptoms like bathroom issues, outbursts, sticking his tongue out at me. One day as I put him in his room to calm him down, he yelled out that he wished he would die right then and go to hell.

As I wrote this down in the journal that was filling up with innumerable abusive situations that I kept in preparation for court some day, Nick came to my bedroom door and said, "All I am is a piece of junk, right, Mama?"

I took him in my arms, and he cried and cried as I rocked him and hugged him, explaining that God doesn't make junk.

Still teary eyed, he looked up at me, "I'll never get a trophy at karate. I don't do good."

It broke my heart to see my little boy so broken. Tears were now streaming down my cheeks. We seemed to rock each other until we were exhausted and fell asleep.

The next morning I contacted the school counselor. She suggested I call our local safe haven and DCF. Shortly after, the school social worker called to let me know when she could see Nicholas at school and suggested I call the local police with my questions. She told me that she was impressed that I had called her office for help with Nicholas—usually the school has to call the parents. She commented how wise it was of me and what a good mother I was. I needed to hear that. Her words were comforting, and I knew I had taken another step toward building a case against Tony and a support team.

That afternoon, I called our local police department. I explained some of the problems I'd been having concerning Tony's behavior around Nicholas.

The officer told me, "He has every right to see his son. Why are you trying to cause a problem?"

I was so frustrated but certainly not surprised. The police seemed to exempt Tony from any consequences, no matter what happened. They just looked the other way. I was also frustrated because none of the suggestions anyone made helped at all.

Three days later, we had a snowstorm and afternoon kindergarten was canceled. Tony was able to pick Nicholas up for me and bring him to my work. The client I was working on was a psychotherapist. In the three minutes it took Tony to drop Nicholas off, she witnessed Tony's behavior and urged me to get help for Nicholas and me, commenting on Tony's self-centeredness.

I was grateful for her unexpected input. Getting that affirmation helped me feel that I wasn't crazy, at least for the moment, especially because I always questioned what was right and what was wrong.

Another client picked up on how overwhelmed and stressed out I was and one afternoon suggested that we pray together. I looked forward to Carol's appointments after that first prayer session; they comforted me so, believing with all my heart Matthew 18:19-20: "Again I say to you if two of you agree on earth about anything, then ask it and it will be done for them by my Father in heaven. For where two or three are gathered in my name, there am I in the midst of them."

Unacceptable Behavior

Tony's excessive drinking and his deranged thinking had taken a toll on the three of us. My life had turned into a battlefield, worrying about every move I made, wondering where I would find this monster lurking next.

Tony's impact became more and more evident through Nicholas's unsettled behavior and outbursts. One minute he hated me. I was a mean mother, or I hated him because his dad told him so. Or he thought he should go to the bars with his dad; that was more fun than listening to me.

I needed help. But where could I get it? How could I chance what the attorneys said "could" happen? I decided to just continue on my silent path of building witnesses and keeping my journal up-to-date.

A new neighbor and I became friendly and started to hang out together. She was a single mom as well with a son a little younger than Nicholas. We were company for each other, and she would help me out last minute when Tony was a no-show.

By this time, Nick started to open up to the school social worker, giving him the ability to open up to our new neighbor as well. Our new friend also started to take notice of Tony's irresponsibility and his many no-shows, and witnessed him leaving JB's café with Nick in the car. *Another witness*, I thought.

When I asked Tony about coming out of the bar at 11:00 a.m. with Nicholas as my neighbor reported to me, all he had to say was, "I had to go to the bathroom." He lived five houses from the bar.

The next week, Tony couldn't come on Saturday to take care of his son. He had fallen down his cellar stairs. He claimed he was too sore to move. This went on for weeks.

Rumors came to me about drugs. Not trusting what was going on at Tony's house, I reluctantly had to let him watch Nick in my home. After working a ten-hour day, I would come home to a house that was a total mess. The trails of their day's activities were evident everywhere.

Tony would also be aggravated at how long I'd had to work, saying he had "things to do." I wanted to tell him that if I received some child support, maybe I wouldn't have to work so long, but I knew that would have just been another battle. After he left, Nick sadly whimpered, "Mama, Saturdays are boring. All Dad does is sleep on the sofa and make me get him stuff."

In the past, on Mondays and Thursdays, I worked late. Because of the extra problems with leaving the salon to pick Nick up and go back to work, I stopped working on Thursday evenings. Tony was then only responsible for picking Nick up from after-school care and bringing him to me on Mondays. He didn't even have to feed Nicholas. I had food packed for his dinner.

Tony continued to regress as a responsible parent from May to October. He never showed up on time, if at all. Often he was in no condition to care for a child. The staff at my after-school daycare was concerned. Tony had been drinking more often than not when he came to pick Nicholas up, and the staff watched closely. I was thankful for the great job they did protecting Nick. A daycare staff member even commented about how he only picked Nick up once a week. What was up with that? Why was it so difficult for him to not drink one day a week?

One Monday Tony called me at 2:00 p.m., sounding pretty drunk and telling me, "If you don't hear from me by 5:00 p.m., you'll have to pick Nick up."

He knew very well how difficult it was to leave when I worked by appointment. (Which I needed to do to make ends meet. His now-court-ordered seventy-six dollars a week child support hardly ever showed up. He was thousands of dollars behind.) I explained I couldn't leave at five to pick Nicholas up; I was booked solid with three colors and cuts that evening.

His response, "That's your problem."

I called Papa's house to see if someone there could help me out by picking up Nicholas.

Their response was, "Oh! Let's give Tony some time."

They waited and waited. The clock was ticking, and I got more anxious by the minute.

I called them every five minutes, and they kept telling me, "Tony'll get there in time."

"No. You're not listening to me. He called DRUNK! He is not capable. Please, please," I pleaded, "just go get Nicholas. In twenty more minutes, I'll be charged a twenty-five dollars late fee, and I cannot afford that. Please," I begged. "Go get Nicholas. Tony is obviously in no condition to do it."

Now quite aggravated with the back-and-forth phone calls and my persistent pleading, Papa went to pick up Nicholas. At 5:50 p.m., only fifty minutes after they picked him up, Papa's girlfriend Jean brought Nick to my work, telling me, "We fed him a sandwich. We can't have this. We were just about to sit down to dinner. You'd better find another way."

I thought, *How can you be so cruel?*

I was so angry with Papa! That he couldn't keep his own grandson for a few hours or feed him what they were about to eat disgusted me.

Never mind being such a coward that he sent the girlfriend to bring Nick to me.

Before Jean departed, she told me the daycare staff told her Tony was no longer allowed at daycare and could no longer pick up his son. Even though it was another dilemma, I was pleased that I had another witness, such as she was, to what we were subjected to.

A friend was married to a police officer. I went to their home to discuss how Tony chose to bring his son to the bars when he had visitation. Unfortunately, her husband told me that no law prevents that. If a parent wants to bring his or her child, no matter what age, to a bar, it's the parent's business.

I sought advice from another lawyer I was referred to with this new information about the bars and now the daycare restriction. Again, I was told that if I pursued this in court, Tony could still get more visitation time because four hours a week was nothing. I was so, so frustrated with all of this. Why? Why is this so when he can't even handle the four hours he had?

Nicholas started to tell me some of the things his father had said to him.

"Daddy called you a bastard. He called you an effing asshole. And he told everyone in the bar you gave him the finger."

Once again, I explained how sorry I was he had to hear such language and such lies about his mom.

"Sweetie, Mommy never did that. It would be unacceptable behavior, especially at work. If people go around acting like that, no one would want to be around them or be their friends."

It always took me days to undo the damage his father caused in just those four short hours. Some days, Nick would even emulate an alcoholic. I started to have him draw his feelings. One afternoon he drew four little boy bodies and asked me how to spell angry, sad, happy, and delightful.

I fell asleep that evening wondering where I could find a positive male influence for my son and became excited when I thought about the Big Brother Big Sister program. But when I investigated, I discovered that they would have to inform Tony that I wanted to enroll Nicholas. I just forgot that idea, knowing only too well that Tony would make it impossible for everyone involved.

Isn't Anybody Listening?

That Thanksgiving, I decided Nicholas and I would go away for the holiday. I wasn't going to allow Tony to repeat the previous Thanksgiving Day horror. He upset our whole day with just one hour of his presence. Only moments after he arrived, he became angry that I wouldn't have a drink with him. I explained that I had a lot to do to finish preparing a beautiful meal. He started swearing. His voice and the tension in my home rose quickly. I insisted he leave immediately. As he walked out the front door carrying his box of liquor, he continued with the foul words.

He looked over at Nicholas sitting on the sofa and said, "Nick, it's your mother. Thank your mother for ruining the effing holiday."

Nicholas ate his Thanksgiving Day dinner confused, choking down some food with tears in his eyes.

Right after the holiday, I called Dr. Chris. I shared that I didn't know where to turn next for help. I reviewed my steps, telling him that I had spoken to the police and even they wouldn't help. I had met with four attorneys. They couldn't guarantee anything safe for Nick.

I told him about my steps to get help from Nicholas's school, explained the hell we lived in, and asked the doctor where or how I could get some help to get this man to stop his abusive behavior. After my forty-five-minute consultation with Dr. Chris, he advised me to not stop visitation but to put Nicholas in therapy. Again.

That was it? It just got crazier and crazier. That didn't address the issue of Tony. He was still in our lives. Still disruptive. Still abusive. What could we do? What could anyone do? Couldn't *anyone* help me? My child?

That advice put me right over the edge. It was just one more thing to take care of, by myself, when I was already sick and exhausted, barely making it through my day. How much more could I take? But, of course, I'd take it. I had to, for Nicholas's sake.

After that consultation, I contacted DCF and explained our situation, explaining that I could not stand by and let my child have to live this way. The DCF worker agreed that Tony's behavior constituted a case of risk of injury to a minor. Her suggestion was to get a lawyer and go for full custody, adding that Tony could get more visitation time with Nick.

So in the end, I was back to square one. I would never chance getting a judge who might not take the time to listen and who would treat us like we were just another number. I felt this way even more so after I learned of the drug bust that had gone down at Tony's house a short time before. I couldn't even imagine the type of people in and out of that house. Oh! The thought of what my son would be exposed to with a possible overnight stay frightened me. Again, I would *never, ever* chance doing anything that could give Tony more exposure to Nick, or Nick more exposure to Tony's toxic lifestyle. The way the system was stacked against us, I'd die before I let that happen.

Tony continued with his "do as I say, not as I do," expecting his son not to emulate him and when he did, punishing him to the extreme.

And, Tony's responsibility record didn't improve. In the preceding eleven months—forty-eight weeks—my journal records show that Tony had thirty-two no-shows or was incapable of showing up for one reason or another: too tired, too drunk, too busy, something better to do, or the car wouldn't start—for the fourth time.

So, no, no repeat of past Thanksgivings. We went to the beach instead.

Christmas 1999 was a Sunday. Tony went ballistic when I wouldn't agree to let him have Nicholas for the whole day. I really didn't care. I knew only too well from past experience how Tony liked to spend his holidays hopping from place to place having a drink or two, maybe more, at every stop he made. At 2:30 a.m. the day before Christmas Eve, the phone rang, startling me awake.

When I said hello, I heard Tony say in a deep, threatening voice, "You never know what kind of bad things could happen to you."

I wanted to call the police right then, but I didn't want to chance that their arrival would wake Nicholas up. How frightening to be awakened with the police in your home in the middle of the night.

That morning, December 23, once at work, I called the police to document the time of the call and his threat. An officer arrived shortly after I called, and as I was explaining what occurred the preceding night and what had been going on in our lives, the business phone rang. It was Tony. As soon as he started speaking, I could hear he was still in a foul mood, so I handed the phone to the officer.

The officer listened for only seconds when he identified himself to Tony. He didn't have any luck getting Tony to cooperate; he made plans to meet Tony later in the day to talk.

As the police officer left, he assured me he would make my new stipulations clear to Tony, putting an end to his coming to my home whenever he felt like it. Tony would only pick up Nicholas at my work on Saturdays and keep him from 10:00 a.m. to 2:00 p.m.

I smirked a little as the officer walked out, thinking about how Tony's timing to call and harass me worked out perfectly this time, alleviating the problem of my word against his. The officer heard him, "live."

The next day, Saturday, was Christmas Eve. Before 8:30 a.m., Tony was on the phone trying to explain to me how he hadn't slept in two days and wasn't capable of taking care of his son.

It took all my strength to say nothing, knowing this would make my case against him even better, but my anger built quickly, the same old thoughts racing through my mind: *He isn't working, still no child support. Plus, it's Christmas week, and I'm extremely busy trying to accommodate all my clients' needs.* I thought, *You selfish bastard.*

I just hung up without saying a word, grateful that I'd brought plenty of things for Nick to do; I had a nice little area set up for him to play in or to watch a movie without disturbing anyone. Of course, I had plenty of goodies and drinks to keep any child happy. He was such a good boy, but no matter how well I tried to prepare with toys and snacks, it was always a very long day for a six-year-old to just stay in one corner of the salon.

The following weekend Tony showed up twenty-five minutes late and brought his son back to me two hours early. That was missing his boy, wasn't it? Again, he had no food or any money to feed Nicholas. How much did he really want that visitation with his son, or was winning the battle the real agenda for him?

The New Year arrived. I went out back to drag my Christmas tree over to the woods behind my home. When I got back to the house, I found Tony standing in my kitchen—again—this time reading my journal and, of course, not liking one word he read about his behavior.

He started in on me with his usual filthy mouth, trying to assure me, "I don't do anything wrong by taking him to bars. There is nothing wrong with that. I'll take you to court."

He stormed out the back door. Two drinks and a half-hour later, his typical call came in. He left a message saying he was going to a lawyer at 3:00 p.m.

"This is war, and I am going to win."

Fearful that this time, he might go through with it, I called the abuse line and shared my story, cognizant that I was adding to the trail of help and, more important, that someone would listen to me, help me calm down. Four conversations later over a period of days, she suggested I file for sole custody and set visitations.

She ended her conversation, "Yes, Tony most likely will get more than four hours and possibly weekends."

This was so crazy! How many people in authority had now told me to go to court BUT Tony will get more visitation? How could I protect my child from this insane situation and the broken system?

My next step was to call our local safe haven. The people there suggested that I contact my local police department (!) and speak to someone in domestic violence. I explained that dilemma to her, and in the end, it turned out to be just another dead end. Tony's dad was now a captain in the department.

Tony continued disrupting our schedules, kept asking for overnights; I swear he was losing it or had already lost it. He had no phone, the refrigerator was broken—he had no food—and he certainly didn't care about bedtime or homework or a schedule of any kind.

I didn't know which was worse. I now had some peace at home, but Tony's behavior in front of my clients was embarrassing. He didn't care who was there or who was listening and continued to show up late and come back early. Nicholas was almost always upset and started having bathroom issues again. The little guy was in turmoil.

One of Tony's normal departure procedures was to give the finger for all to witness—clients, neighbors—and his child. Some clients were frightened of him, some were disgusted. And, add to that, I had to console Nicholas. It was a wonder I still had a business.

Nicholas, again in tears, said to me, "Mama, all Daddy did was yell and swear at me. Mama, Daddy called you an effing bitch again."

All I could do was hug my little boy and tell him again I was sorry he had to listen to such naughty, unacceptable words. How did I explain to him there was no one to help us? I felt half out of my mind. Fighting back my own tears, I got back to work and pretended I had it all together.

I set up an appointment for Tony with Dr. Chris, hoping the doctor could get through to him. But Tony was "too sick" to go. The abuse line suggested that family services get involved and, perhaps, do a substance-abuse evaluation. The Department of Children and Families agreed with Dr. Chris, and so I put Nicholas in therapy again.

Nothing else changed. All my words fell on deaf ears, and Tony continued to bring Nick to the bars. I continued to call the police, and the police continued to tell me that there was nothing they could do if a father chose to raise a child like that; there was no law against it.

Evil, Cruel, or Both? You Decide

Just when I thought things couldn't get any worse, they always did. Special Persons Day was coming up at school. I called Papa to invite him to the gathering. I had to beg him to accept the invitation, but he finally agreed. Three days before the event, Jean left a message on the machine. Papa wasn't able to attend after all.

This disturbed me. Nicholas was all excited to be able to show off his Papa because he was not only a police officer, but the CAPTAIN, in Nicholas's view, the boss of everybody. Papa just couldn't find time in his schedule to show up for an hour to make *his* grandson happy and proud.

I listened to the rest of Jean's message. She accused me and Tony of forcing Nicholas on Papa.

Totally not understanding what the hell she was talking about, I had to call her and ask, "What do you mean, 'forcing Nicholas onto Papa'? He hardly sees his grandson. Maybe one hour a month and Papa never comes to take him anywhere."

All she could come up with was, "Hug Papa. Kiss Papa," referring to when it was time for us to leave their home, I would say, "Nicky, come on. We need to go. Give Papa kisses" or "Give Papa hugs."

In disgust, I asked her, "Isn't that what families do when they are departing from loved ones? To me, Jean, that's teaching love and respect."

Jean jumped back with, "What are you forcing your son on him for, his money?"

I was livid, thinking, *What kind of distorted, dysfunctional thinking is that? You're toxic! (Evil, cruel, or both? You decide.)*

I listened in disbelief as she continued knocking me about how I'd raised Nicholas. Telling me that I was keeping him a baby and criticizing me for putting him in therapy.

She ended, "You wanted a [Papa's last name] baby, now deal with it. The sooner you realize it's in their genes, the better off you'll be," insinuating that all the men in Papa's family were no good, abusive, women-beating drinkers because it's in their genes. She was blind to the part she played in the whole cycle and the goings-on in their home.

I was enraged as I hung up the phone, declaring out loud to myself, "What was I thinking?"

I struggled to show Nick some sense of family when, clearly, she would have none of it. I had no idea she was so jealous. I guess she only wanted Tony's dad to spend time with her grandchildren, which he did plenty. Or was she in it for Papa's money?

The school social worker called to check in. She said that Nicholas was still a little uncomfortable but stayed consistent with "I hate my dad. He's mean and all he does is yell and swear at me."

Special Persons Day arrived. I dreaded going in to wake up my son because I had to tell him Papa couldn't make it after all. As Nicholas lay in bed, his eyes teared up, his little lip quivered, and he responded, "That's okay, Mama. Maybe I could ask some other Papa to help me." It was heartbreaking to see my little boy so sad and disappointed.

After getting Nicholas off to school, I called Jean to let her know how upset Nick was and couldn't help adding that there was more to grandparenting than sending savings bonds twice a year.

Of course, when I arrived home that evening, there was a return message from Jean. They "didn't need to hear all this shit about how his eyes teared up and his lip quivered. Really, dear, you belong in Hollywood." *(Evil, cruel, or both?)*

All that mattered, though, was that Michelle filled in for Papa and Nicholas didn't seem so sad.

The Bastards

As Tony's preposterous behavior continued, Nicholas became more affected. His anger grew; he began using unacceptable words, and signs of physical distress increased in frequency. I was able to find a new therapist only one town away, and we went once a week at first.

My friend Angela and her husband Jeff had been picking Nicholas up after school on Mondays for the past three months since Tony was no longer allowed to. Their business was very close to Nick's after-school care, and the arrangement was working out nicely. Nicholas was safe. Angela and Jeff were responsible, loving people who fed him a healthy meal and always included some playtime.

It was such a blessing to finally be able to allow someone to help without paying a price. It was very difficult for me to trust anyone. Nicholas enjoyed his time with Angela and Jeff and soon settled down enough to share some stories about his father's behavior, saying that his father was mean and that he never wanted to see him again.

Because Nicholas was six, Tony signed him up, without my knowledge, to play flag football. Tony thought it would be great.

It didn't go very well. Every week, Nick came home upset. I heard from the coach that Tony seemed to think he was the coach and stood on the sidelines, yelling and trying to take over, always bringing Nick to tears.

Nicholas's coach quickly became aware of Tony's absurd antics and kept Nick close to her side for protection. When she called to express her concern, she said it was terrible for her to watch.

She mentioned the other coach's comment about Tony: "He certainly doesn't have all his faculties." She said she would write a letter expressing her observations if I needed her to.

No matter how hard I tried to alleviate a problem, something went wrong. Nicholas's issues were escalating, and, at times, he emulated his father's behavior. Leona, Nicholas's therapist, suggested we try this or try that and that I should speak to Tony about his mouth. I almost laughed out loud! As if I haven't thought of that on my own!

It was quite a fiasco, but I did share Leona's words with Tony.

He was quite clear about his view: "I didn't effing teach him anything. He effing learns it from effing school" and hung up on me.

When Leona asked Nick about his behavior, he replied, "My dad does it."

In therapy Nick had less and less to say. Leona feared he was shutting down and now wanted to bring Tony in for a session.

When I attempted to tell Tony her suggestion and how Nicholas's symptoms were worse each week, all he had to say was, "Oh, no. This is not on me. You created this monster!"

Tony arrived minutes later to take Nick to football practice.

All I asked was, "Please, just don't yell at him."

An hour and half passed. Tony pulled up in front of my home. I quickly rushed outside to prevent Tony from entering my home. I couldn't help but notice his angry body language.

I opened the car door for Nick to get out. He hung his head in discouragement, fighting back tears. I patted his head and asked him to go inside and start his homework, telling him that I wanted to speak to Daddy.

I walked around to the driver's side, asking, "What happened?"

Tony screamed at me, "I reamed his ass out. He is in big effing trouble. He's looking in the sky, not paying attention."

I said, "So you yelled."

"Someone has to yell. What you're doing isn't effing working."

I walked away. Tony left, tires screeching, giving me his famous departing gesture. In my home, I found Nick crying hysterically and apologizing as his arm lay limp on the kitchen table.

"Mama, I'm sorry. I can't do my homework. Daddy broke my arm."

I couldn't believe the words I'd just heard. I rushed over to him. "Nicky, what are you saying. Daddy hurt you?" I examined his arm. It was bending fine but I noticed the marks left by a strong grip.

Nick said, "Daddy hurt me really bad. He broke my arm, Mama," and then demonstrated with his hand how his father had also pulled his head back and forth. "Daddy pulled my hair and hit my head on the dashboard."

I was enraged. My hands trembled as I tried to reach Leona by phone. There was no answer. I called the police, hoping that this time I would get someone who would help us.

An hour passed before an officer finally arrived. He listened to Nicholas describe his experience, using the exact language that came out of his father's disgusting mouth.

"My dad said I'm lousy at everything I do. 'What are you shitting and pissing in your effing pants for? You won't see daylight until you are old enough to take care of yourself. And you're never going to see your best buddy Kyle ever again.'"

The police officer took no notes, just names, and said he would "talk" to Tony. I urged him to the point of pleading to call DCF and suggested he could most likely find Tony at JB's café.

Twenty-four hours passed. I heard nothing, so I called the police department and spoke to the officer's superior. He explained how he told the officer who came to my home NOT to call DCF until he heard what Tony had to say and he would have the officer call me.

The officer called me back about an hour later to explain that after he left me, he drove to Tony's and left a note on the back door to contact the police department when he got in. Tony went to the police department the next morning, asking what the note was all about.

His explanation for his behavior: "I was disciplining my son for swearing." Tony walked away again with no consequences for his behavior.

Clenching my teeth to fight back my bitterness, I thought, *This is bullshit! You saw and heard my son!*

This whole conversation infuriated me, escalating my anguish. I wanted to scream, "You useless, flaming idiot! So you drove right by JB's café and let Tony finish his night out drinking, go home to sleep it off, shower, eat, and present himself when he was good and ready!"

I hung up the phone, wishing the whole police department would just BLOW UP! Wondering, *What do they have to do? Find us dead before they do something about this abusive hell we were living?* I couldn't help but to repeat to myself, *BASTARDS, BASTARDS, BASTARDS! THEY'RE ALL BASTARDS!!!!!!!!!!!*

Upset After Upset

In spite of the mental anguish, the emotional rollercoaster of the continuous battle of staying safe, strong, and to protect Nick from his out-of-control father, I managed to complete a class at a local college for women on how to write a business plan. It was intense and quite a commitment, three mornings a week for twelve weeks.

Taking that much time out of my workweek frightened me. If I didn't work, no money came in, but my desire to improve my situation to be the best I could be was strong.

My plan was to sell my condo and move my business, Nicholas, and me to a house—a plan I thought would make our lives easier. I would have my salon on the first floor, and Nick and I would live on the second, eliminating a business lease and putting my hard-earned money toward my own mortgage.

I did well at school. I was proud of myself and felt accomplished. I was moving forward. I was thrilled the morning the office staff at the college walked over to my classroom to meet me and congratulated me on a job well done. One woman commented it was the best business plan she had ever read. Her words brought me to tears. I was barely able to choke out a "thank you." Wow! Someone was proud of me.

I drove home that afternoon excited, full of hope, feeling on track, thinking it was a miracle to have pulled this off. I started house hunting; I hired a financial planner, someone I knew through a networking group. She advised me to do this or that, and I trusted, I believed, I was doing everything right. All my ducks were in a row.

Months went by before I was finally able to move forward on a house that was in a great location for my business. The first floor was once a doctor's office with great potential for a salon. The backyard was small but adequate for Nicholas, as was the upstairs three-room apartment. I was willing to sacrifice our living quarters if it meant having my own building. A better life for Nicholas and wiser use of my money.

I hired an inspector, an appraiser, an attorney, and a real estate agent—everything I was advised to do—for it to become another chapter of horror in my life. The deal fell through. The money I spent on the appraisal and inspection was gone, and then I was almost sued for not selling my condo.

I couldn't sell the condo. Where would Nick and I live? The clause to protect me from this type of lawsuit was not in the sale paperwork. The attorney blamed the real estate agent, and the agent blamed the attorney. It cost me.

When I thought it couldn't get any worse, it did. At year-end, I was devastated to learn that I owed almost $4,000 in taxes! How could this be? My income was poverty level. I struggled to make ends meet.

With trembling fingers I called my accountant, believing he must have missed something. I expected to hear, "Oh, I'm sorry, come right down." But he gently explained that when my financial advisor had me move my little nest egg to her company, it was a taxable gain, and therefore I had to pay capital gains tax because the house deal fell through.

Thinking that this could not be real, I immediately called the planner. I shared with her what was going on, asking her how this had happened.

"I paid you $700 for you to advise me. I trusted you. I had no idea if the house didn't go through, this would happen. If only you had explained that to me, I never would have moved that money. Never, ever would I have moved my money knowing that."

I'll never forget her comment: "Well, that's why I am not a CPA."

Her cold words and nonchalant attitude cut me to my core. I felt so betrayed, defeated, and alone, and now I was broke and in debt. Where would I ever find the $4,000 I owed when I had trouble just feeding Nicholas every day? The little bit of money I had saved so I could improve our lives, to put me in a position to grow, was all gone. And I was still paying rent at work.

That sting of betrayal stayed with me for years. It reinforced my inability to trust anyone. In my naiveté, I thought hiring people from networking groups was much safer. I thought people in those groups had this unspoken pact to watch each other's backs, protect each other, help each other to grow and move forward. What a confused, silly little girl I was.

I couldn't shake the defeated feelings I carried twenty-four hours a day.

How will I ever crawl out?

Trying to accept and deal with all the financial upsets took everything I had left in me. Or so I thought.

Part II

Crawling Out

Just So Done

Only a few days after the incident with Tony hitting Nicholas's head against the dashboard after football practice, I started to cling wholeheartedly to the idea that this new police report to DCF was the link I was waiting for, the piece I needed to back up my case to stop the abuse and stop visitation. I believed it would lead to the end of the hell Nick and I lived. That gave me permission to think about other things than trying to stay safe and, hopefully, to move past dealing with the aftermath of the latest financial disaster.

At the same time, I began to be more aware of how lousy I felt. I was weak, so weak. I ached all over. Every move I made brought more pain. My heart raced, and I was so fatigued I could hardly crawl out of bed to crawl to work to crawl back home again. My doctor was concerned about my blood pressure and wanted to put me on medication. My thyroid was unbalanced once again, and my weight was like a yo-yo. I had acquired a habit of clenching my teeth, causing headaches to throb morning, noon, and night. I seemed to be sick to my stomach more often than not, always worrying how much longer I could go on living like this. What would happen to me? What would happen to Nick?

My reality was that I had to push myself to smile, to fake it, to keep going. Truly, what choice did I have? This stress made my fibromyalgia flare up. Bouts of pain were so severe, I felt like I had crashed into brick walls. Some days the pain was so intense as I stood behind my styling chair, it took my breath away.

My daily responsibilities of being a mom, a single parent, and a business owner and having to do it all under such stress took their toll on me. I cried more often than not. I hadn't slept through the night for years. I didn't remember what it felt like to be rested, energetic, and to face the day with joy.

In addition, the shame and embarrassment of what I felt I'd done so wrong all my life had become debilitating. I continually asked myself, *How did all this happen? How did it get so bad?* I had strived long and hard to have a normal life or, in fact, a normal anything. But to what end?

These thoughts brought me back to when I was thirty-five years old and first heard the word "dysfunctional." How devastating to learn that, sadly, Tony and I both came from dysfunctional families—those whose function was impaired or abnormal.

Wow! As I contemplated this new awareness, another slow-moving anxiety crept up, looming larger each day as I realized this was much bigger than I originally thought. A few sessions of therapy wouldn't move this mountain of confused wrong messages Tony and I had both received as innocent little children.

Tony looked at me as if I had three heads when I tried to share this new revelation with him. He wanted to hear none of it.

He commented, "If you want to go hang out with a bunch of quacks, go right ahead."

He certainly wasn't interested in going to any meetings or seeing any doctors. He was just fine the way he was. I was the one, he said, with all the problems.

Among all the frustrations, I remembered I read somewhere, perhaps in one of my Al-Anon books, that change begins with self. I know today you can only change yourself. Start there and stay there. Focus continuously on working to change yourself, your thoughts, to learn and to grow.

As my discernment grew of how dysfunctional my life and Tony's had been, so did the reality of how huge a problem it was. I started to see the domino effect that dysfunction had on all family members and how so many people around me were affected by this unspoken hardship and didn't recognize it. Each week, each month, my elevated awareness seemed to grow, becoming mountainous. And, my shame and embarrassment grew right along with it.

Hiding the full extent of the abuse I had suffered and what I came from made my exhaustion worse; it became even harder to pretend that I had it all together. After a while, I worried, *Do I have a sign on my back with big letters: "COMES FROM A DYSFUNCTIONAL FAMILY"?*

My days now consisted of smiling and pretending, my nights of crying and praying to exhaustion. It was truly a physical and emotional vicious cycle. All I could think about was that I had to save my little boy from this kind of life. *God, please show me the way.*

Not quite a week had passed since the night Nicholas was so incredibly brave, telling the police officer what he experienced with his dad at football practice.

We were in the car driving to the store when Nick blurted from the back seat, "Mama, Daddy also yelled, 'You know you learned those swear words at school. Stop being a stinking liar.'" After a short pause, he continued, "Mama, I didn't because we would have to go to the principal's office."

His worrying and innocence popped up often out of the blue, making it clear to me that even though he seemed calm and fine, he worried subconsciously. I did my best to assure him he was safe and please not to worry anymore.

I was clear on one thing: I was done. I was done being patient, done being the polite little Christian girl. I was done listening. I was done talking to and dealing with people who would not help us.

I was prepared to plow through the planet to find help to protect my child. As I said before, in my really angry moments, I wished the police department would blow up, just poof away for not being there to protect us.

It was one thing not to protect me, an adult woman, but not to protect an innocent child was inexcusable.

No More

Through this all, Tony assumed things would continue to be the same. I guess he didn't understand what "I am done" meant.

He didn't catch on for a while that I refused to let him see Nicholas. He would call, acting as if nothing had happened, asking questions about Nick's days, totally expecting to continue as he had in the past.

I quickly informed him again, "No more."

I simply stated, "You are done abusing him. I don't care what the authorities or doctors have to say. You are done. No more."

And I hung up the phone.

I wasn't surprised the following week when Tony was a no-show for the appointment at Nick's therapist.

The next week I finally had a chance to talk to another child advocate at the therapist's office. This appointment was just for me and the advocate. Nicholas was at daycare. This time the advocate backed *me,* saying Tony had no rights—no child support, no visitation—and she would help me find a lawyer. Those words had become a joke.

This therapist-advocate meeting lasted longer than I expected. Rushing to pick up Nicholas on time, I ran in to get him. I didn't receive even a "Hi, Mama." All he was concerned about was, "Did Dad come?"

When I responded, "No," Nick replied, "I know why, Mama. He's at the bar. He'd rather be with his friends. Besides, I don't want to be with him on Saturdays anyway."

I believe even Nicholas at his young age had a speck of hope that Tony would turn it all around and become the dad he longed for.

Time passed, and Tony's frustration at not seeing Nicholas escalated, as did his calls berating me for one thing or another. He still didn't realize how serious I was about being DONE with him and all he represented. Of course, his nastiness never subsided. I didn't care anymore. My son was slowly showing signs of improvement. He was more relaxed and he seemed less upset.

Angela and Jeff informed me that one night when they had Nicholas, he shared with them that he hated his father and that his father was very mean. A few minutes later, Nick finished with, "My Daddy says I'm a rotten little boy."

Angela reminded me that evening Nick said he had "a sick belly" and that he'd also had bathroom issues, making it clear to us there was a connection between Nicholas's worrying about his father and re-emerging emotional upsets. But, clearly, each day was better than the last, and it had been only two and a half weeks that I'd been able to keep Tony away.

I hoped that Tony understood he had pushed me to my limit. I felt like an enraged mama bear, protecting her cub. I would attack anything or anyone who came close. I had been patient with Tony, trying everything and every way I could think of, but none of it had worked. No one helped. So it was Nick and I, and we were done listening.

The rage I felt then was the same as when Teddy choked me with the vacuum-cleaner cord. As I thought about the strength I conjured up to pull that amount of hair out of someone's head, it was affirming to know that I did have limits, and I'd definitely reached mine again.

When I'm done, I'm done. No more vulnerable, frightened little girl, not when it came to my little boy. I was crazed with strength, almost afraid to think of what I could be capable of if I were pushed any more.

Nicholas Speaks His Truth

At Nick's next therapy session, his therapist asked him, "How do you feel about not seeing your dad?"

Responding rather quickly, Nicholas looked up at me and said, "I'm not sad anymore because I don't have to see my dad. I'm very happy and my belly button is orange."

I didn't know what he meant by that, so I asked him, "What does the color orange mean?"

Nick looked at me with a surprised, "why don't you know" kind of look and responded matter-of-factly, "Mama, it means I'm grateful."

The next weekend was a New England Patriots game that Tony had planned to take Nicholas to. Tony realized that I was serious when I reminded him once again that Nick was not going with him that day, not going tomorrow, not going anywhere with him, ever.

Tony was angrier than ever, telling me that I was effing starting trouble and that I would be sorry. His threatening words didn't affect me as much anymore.

I also no longer listened to anyone who said, "Nicholas needs his father." No one needs to be around anyone who behaves like that, especially an innocent, vulnerable child.

That afternoon, Nicholas blew his nose and commented, "The only good thing my daddy taught me was how to blow my nose. I don't ever want to see his face again."

I just hugged him, thinking how sad that was his only good memory. I made plans for us to stay at Michelle's house for the night.

Nicholas's teacher also kept a close, attentive eye on him, sending home weekly notes on his progress at settling down and focusing on his schoolwork.

I was grateful when Sr. Mary, whom I met with every week, told me of another single parent who was willing to watch Nick on Saturdays while I worked.

That interview went well. Nick seemed fairly comfortable. The only issue I had was that the house reeked of smoke. I was up front and asked Steve if he could smoke outside when Nick was in his house. Steve agreed but was a bit surprised that his immaculate home was that offensive.

Nick and I left shortly after the interview. I was thrilled knowing that we had just taken another step away from Tony and that Nick would be safe and have a little boy his own age to play with.

I laughed out loud when I recalled that in the middle of the interview with Steve, I'd thought to myself, *Hmm, just my luck. A single dad, but he's too old, too short, and not even cute.*

I had learned from Sr. Mary that Steve was a widower. Their little boy was only four when she passed away. In a sad sense, I thought the boys already had something in common—the longing for a parent who was gone, the longing for normal, the longing for family.

As Tony tired of my new rules, his phone calls annoyed me to no end and his demands became more absurd. Always a battle, I stayed consistent, but he continued his screaming, going so far one day as to say that Nick "needed a good ass chewing."

"Ass chewing"? Slamming Nicholas's head against the dashboard? What kind of parenting was that?

I reminded Tony that Nick was only seven. Tony rambled on about how he would never come to my defense, ever again. I foolishly tried to explain to him how he once again had twisted the whole situation from his own unacceptable behavior to Nick. Tony slammed the phone down in my ear. There was just no reasoning with him.

When Nicholas overheard this type of conversation between me and his father, he went right into disrespectful mode, mimicking his father's behavior. It frightened me to think of all the damage done by me listening to others as I struggled to find help.

I no sooner had hung up the phone when Nick started to demand that I come to his room. Four times he repeated, "Get in here!"

I concentrated on reminding him of proper words and respectful behavior. As we ate our breakfast, I asked him why he was speaking to me in such a way.

"All I wanted was for you to watch me make my bed."

I reminded him that the tone and words he used didn't work.

All he said was, "Dad does it."

While I drove him to school, I continued teaching him acceptable behavior, asking him if he saw our friends act like that. "Do you see Angela and Jeff speak that way to each other? Do you see Auntie Michelle and Uncle speak that way? How about your friend Kyle's parents? Do they behave that way? No, they show love and respect."

Nicholas agreed, "Yeah, Mama, they show us lots of love" and off he went, smiling, to enjoy his day.

I was pleased our conversation went so well, believing as I drove to work that I possibly *could* undo the damage that Tony had caused. With patience, time, and love, we would be okay.

That Saturday my neighbor helped me out by watching Nicholas; she noticed he was anxious and told me later that Nick said he was worried his daddy was coming for him. She said she did her best to assure him that his daddy wasn't coming and that he was safe.

The notes from Nick's teacher continued to arrive weekly. Each note expressed improvement. He was doing better and better, settling down even more. At home, I saw significant change, too. He sang while he played in the tub, participated in football practice, and was very lovable and respectful. Our days and evenings were becoming more peaceful.

Nick also stayed consistent about not wanting to see his father. It had been a full month since they had been together. Tony was furious with me and informed me that I was ruining his son by not letting him see his dad.

The Cover-Up Continues

I was getting antsy and annoyed with still not hearing from anyone from DCF. One afternoon I spent frustrating hours on the phone trying to get some answers.

I finally was transferred to a supervisor who informed me, "We have not been to your home because there is nothing in the police report that even suggests child abuse."

Not believing what I heard, I asked, "There was no mention of threats? None of swearing? Did the report mention the marks on Nicholas's arm where he was grabbed?"

"No."

"Nothing either about Tony hitting Nick's head on the dashboard or pulling his hair?"

One big "NO!"

My heart pounded in disbelief and anger. *No! No!* I thought. *This was such an important link. Why was this happening?*

The supervisor sensed how upset I was. I commented that I was going to leave work and go straight to the police department to ask why the report had been so vague. In an instant, she spoke up, warning me not to waste my time.

She said she "was from the same town" and that she had "horrific experiences with the police department. All it did was cost me money and a near nervous breakdown."

The feeling of defeated agitation was overwhelming. Her words crushed me to the point that I had to sit down, and I was sick to my stomach. My hands trembled as I continued to write down her advice. She finished our conversation by suggesting that I might consider "moving to another town so you'll have access to a different police department" and that "you'd be better off working with Nick's therapist and his school counselor."

As I drove to pick up my son from after-school care, my thoughts raced. I wanted to walk up to that officer who wrote the totally inaccurate report and punch him in the face, kick him in the testicles, then drag him to his house. Once there, I would have him live through the craziness that we lived with. Let him see what it was like to have some disruptive, mean drunk banging on his doors all hours of the day and night, screaming obscenities, and then abusing his child. Then let me file the exact, word-for-word report that he filed.

Then ask him, "What does your sorry, pathetic ass think about the situation now, you BASTARD!"

I did my best to calm down and compose myself so Nicholas wouldn't get upset. There was that headache again from clenched teeth. When I arrived home, I had a message on my machine from Tony.

As I pushed the play button, the sound of his voice sickened me more than ever. "Miss you, Bud. You know you're my best buddy. Mom has my phone number if you want to call me." At least this message sounded like he was sober.

Nicholas came running into the room with a frightened look on his face, raising his hands to his cheeks, screaming, "No! No! I don't want to!"

I told him, "I know you don't, honey. Don't worry."

As I picked up the phone to return another call, Nick fearfully asked if I was calling his father. He was so distraught that I had to hang up the phone to calm him down.

I did my best that evening to forget about the outside world. I broke the rules and let Nick have ice cream for dinner, play longer in his bath, and I held him while I read three bedtime stories.

I dragged myself to bed that evening without dinner and fell immediately asleep, totally exhausted, mentally and physically.

The Rollercoaster Continues

Tony kept up his efforts to creep back into our lives, unaware of his son's true feelings, and me too frightened to inform him for fear that if he got the chance, he would badger Nick. Afraid Nicholas would assume his therapist told his dad what he said in therapy, jeopardizing the trust that Nicholas finally felt with her.

Tony's next attempt was asking if he could take Nick to lunch.

When I refused, his threats started up again. "Why should we both spend $2,000 on a lawyer when I'm going to get him anyway?"

He tried to use my financial hardship to scare and manipulate me. And often he succeeded, even though I would never, ever show it.

Nicholas had several good weeks, no bathroom issues, no eczema flare-ups, all work completed at school. He was a happy, playful little boy, very loving and respectful. His Saturdays were going well; he seemed excited to go play with Josh, and Steve said the boys were doing great together.

I had an appointment with yet another attorney, hoping to find some real support to keep Tony away from Nick. The lawyer and I talked for about fifteen minutes, and I made another appointment to meet with her and her partner, at her request.

Nicholas was sick the next day. Luckily, I knew the phone number of my first client to call her and let her know I needed to bring Nicholas to the doctor's first thing that morning. I told her she could wait if she would like, but I had no idea how long I'd be at the doctor's. I packed up the car with Nick's pillow, blankets, and a favorite teddy bear, anticipating a long, rough day ahead of us. Dr. Chris said Nicholas was quite sick; he had a very high fever and couldn't go to school for a few days. He wrote out a prescription.

When we arrived at work, I found three clients waiting outside. I set Nick up with his things on the tanning bed, making sure he was warm and comfortable as possible, placing a trash can close by but hoping he wouldn't vomit anymore.

It was the most difficult day. I don't know how we got through it. I obviously started behind schedule with my clients. That lasted throughout the whole day, and needing to attend to Nick so often escalated the tension. To make things worse, Tony was on the phone numerous times trying to convince me he "didn't hurt Nicholas" and that he "should be able to be Nick's father any way he wanted." With absolutely no patience left for him, all I said was, "Not when you hurt him," and I hung up.

Tony's sober phone messages stopped one month and one day after the football practice incident. I started to record his mumbling, slurring, hard-to-understand messages on a small recorder, along with the messages from his father's girlfriend, in preparation for court. I felt the recordings would show who these people were and I could use these recordings along with the trail of people I spoke to looking for help.

Each day Nicholas's emotional and physical improvements affirmed I was doing the right thing, I was on track. Angela's comment that almost instantly when visitation stopped, Nick's happiness increased weekly and he became more relaxed confirmed my decision and calmed the voices in my head of who was right, who was wrong; what was right, what was wrong. She also repeated Nick's words at dinner one evening with her and her husband: "Did you know I have the meanest father in the world?" That evening after Angela and Jeff brought Nick home, he was such a happy little guy. He became silly, evidence that he was becoming less stressed by his father's actions.

His little life was certainly improving. His teacher's notes were consistent with, "He continues to have good days and he is cooperative at school." He was doing just as well at home, with no signs of emotional upsets and would randomly say things like "I don't even want to hear the name daddy ever again."

I prayed, *Lord, show me the way; give me more strength and courage. Help me know how to help him delete all those horrible memories; help me to know how to give my son half a chance at having a happy life.*

Nicholas silently continued to worry more often than I realized. Out of the blue, comments popped up: "Mama, I keep dreaming you gave Daddy permission to see me. Please, Mama, don't ever. I am really scared. I don't even want to hear Daddy." I understood perfectly. Tony's voice had now become an instantaneous trigger for my nervousness and high stress levels as well—that woodpecker banging away at my peace and sanity.

I reassured Nicholas that I would keep him safe, convincing him his therapist was helping, even though I was convinced of none of it.

Posttraumatic Stress and Triggers

In November I first met with the new attorney, the partner at the law firm I had recently been to, to talk about custody, no visitation, and Nick's well-being. Then I followed up with Nicholas's therapist, checking in on her opinion of where Nick was emotionally and whether it was a good time to start court proceedings. She threw a monkey wrench into the plan by diagnosing my little boy with posttraumatic stress. She claimed he was just starting to calm down, affirming what Angela and I had discerned; it was just too soon to start proceedings. Stating that Nick needed more time to heal, and starting legal proceedings would not be good for him emotionally or physically.

Terrified, I researched posttraumatic stress disorder (PTSD) as soon as I could. I learned that a person with PTSD typically develops behavior patterns after a traumatic event or a series of like events. Anxiety disorder can occur after something horrible or scary, after witnessing a stressful event, or that stressful event happens to the person.

Of course, I didn't pursue full custody. My son's health and well-being were too important.

Tony's abusiveness never altered, nor did his threats. Angry I wouldn't even let him speak to his son, he reminded me often what an awful person I was and that I knew all along that Nicholas "missed his dad so much," finishing his conversation with I should know he "made some noise at court today."

I simply hung up the phone, relieved his words or threats no longer frightened me to the extent they used to. I chuckled when visualizing asking him, "What did you do, Tony? Go knock on the court doors and start making some noise?" Really! And, of course, I still made copies of all his phone call messages.

I checked in periodically with Nick on his feelings about seeing his dad. At times, the words "he needs his dad" would torment me.

But Nick was consistent, always repeating, "I don't miss him. I don't want to see him. My body shakes when I'm with him, and my belly is scared. All he does is yell at me, Mama, and he says a lot of bad words."

I hugged my little boy, so proud he was doing so well and totally impressed he was aware of his feelings and how his body reacted to the situation.

He finished one conversation with, "Mama, if I had a good daddy, I would want to have the same name as him."

His words crushed me. I squeezed him a little harder, telling him he was a good boy and I was lucky to have him for my son. My thoughts went to the conversation when Papa's girlfriend matter-of-factly stated that I was keeping him a baby, laughing at the fact that I had him seeing a therapist. Well, Jean, that was no baby who just expressed himself so well, empowering me to continue building my brigade of witnesses against his unaware father.

I had grown weary of listening to Tony and his view of what had been going on, six weeks of how he was only sticking up for me. The whole incident at football practice had *nothing* to do with him sticking up for me. It was his idea of what a child should be doing on the field. It was about his abusive way of handling the situation.

I blatantly told him to stop calling and asking questions, suggesting that he get his life together, get sober, and maybe we could reevaluate. The same old caustic words came out of his mouth, speaking right over my words. He never heard me tell him his son was just diagnosed with posttraumatic stress. As I tried to get Tony to listen, in the next room, I heard Nick burst into tears. Just that quickly, overheard conversation triggered Nicholas's PTSD.

Going to him as I hung up the phone, he was in panic mode, nervous, claiming, "Daddy is going to yell at me; I'm afraid he's going to break in here."

Pointing out that the blinds were closed and the doors were bolted, I told Nick that we were safe, calming him down in the usual manner with a bath and a story.

Shortly after putting him to bed, Nick came running into my room to tell me he was having nightmares. He asked if I could come lie down with him. I got him back to sleep, only for him to be back in my room at midnight, telling me he was scared. Daddy was coming in his window. Could he sleep with me?

As he snuggled in my bed, I reminded him his bedroom was on the second floor, calming him by rubbing his head, telling him that no one could crawl in his window. In the morning, I found a baseball bat lying on the floor beside Nick's bed. The next night he slept all night in his bed but added a hammer to the other side of the bed. It broke my heart to witness his fears, knowing my words that he was safe didn't reassure him.

Casey Morley

On the Edge

That December, I was diagnosed with Reynaud's syndrome, a circulatory system disorder that affects your fingers and/or toes. It occurs when the small arteries that supply them with blood become extra-sensitive to cold and suddenly contract. This reduces the flow of blood to the affected area; with the lack of oxygenated blood, the skin becomes pale, often with a bluish tinge. When the spasm ends, blood flows back in and the paleness disappears, but then the pain starts.

The inside of my left small toe was affected. The color change went from white to bluish to a bluish red. Each step I took was torture. The doctor explained that a small ulcer formed under the first layer of skin, causing this horrific pain. He also hinted that it could have come from having frostbite in the past. He said to be sure to stay out of the cold and to keep my fingers and toes warm.

As I drove to meet my friend Nancy for lunch, a memory popped into my head. When the doctor mentioned frostbite, I thought, *How absurd,* but maybe it wasn't. Years back, on a cold Sunday evening, a bunch of us were at JB's café. We all had a great time until Tony switched from his usual drink to downing shots of vodka. It didn't take very long for him to become anal. He was on a roll; nothing or no one was getting him out of his malicious state centered on me. Upset, I left and decided to walk home. I wasn't thinking. I just wanted to escape that scene.

I had walked about a mile when I realized I was in trouble. The temperature that evening was in the single digits. My boots were more cute than warm, and I had no hat. I was freezing. My hands and feet started to hurt they were so cold.

Thank God, Harry, one of Tony's friends, came to rescue me. I couldn't thank him enough as he drove me the remaining four miles home. If not for Harry, I might have died that night.

If I had to guess, my walk that Sunday evening was when I developed frostbite. Now, years later, I had Reynaud's.

This new syndrome only added to the endless hell I lived. Each step I took caused excruciating pain, draining me even more, adding to my exhaustion.

I was eager to get home to research this new ailment as soon as Nancy and I finished lunch. I learned this disease might also occur as a secondary effect of conditions other than the cold. Five or six other possible causes didn't resonate, but one jumped out at me, "an emotional disturbance."

Intuitively, that made sense to me. *Well, I have certainly had plenty of them in my life. Did I get frostbite walking a mile that Sunday evening, or was the Reynaud's from all the abuse? Or both?*

Either way, I had it, and it was quite painful.

I was grateful that winter when my client, a massage therapist, suggested I take sulfur for the Reynaud's. She started me out with a low dose. There was no change. The throbbing was too intense, so when I had a chance, I elevated my foot. My client told me to increase the dose, and, slowly but surely, the ulcer cleared up.

The Reynaud's syndrome pushed me over the edge, even though I diligently tried to stay strong and focused, hopeful and positive. Life's challenges seemed to spiral this nightmare I lived out of control once again, beating me into the ground. I feared I was losing my mind. The mental fatigue and anguish never let up. I prayed passionately. *Please, Lord, help me hear you. Help me see you.* I questioned at times, *Can I even pray right? Can I do anything right?*

After one prayer session, in seconds, I had a clear picture in my head. I was living in a brown paper bag, clawing at the bottom of it, trying to get out, but all I had to do was turn around.

I felt God sent this revelation but wasn't quite sure what to do with it. I was sure of one thing, though: God revealing this picture was a divine message, a true, clear, divine message that there was a way out of where I was. I swear I even heard the words, "There is another way."

As I processed this vision, I had no idea how to get out of survival mode and one day live my life in peace and love as I hoped to, not in fear and drudgery, thriving instead of surviving. At the same time, I feared I wasn't going to make it. I worried that what I was going through was going to start to show. The struggle was too enormous, and I feared being exposed. I didn't want anyone to know that I wasn't as brave, smart, or strong as so many thought me to be.

I clung to my daily prayer readings. They helped me think about something other than my worries and helped me build my hopes and my faith. God was my only constant, my only link to breath. If I hadn't trusted and believed then, I know I would be dead today.

Tony backed off for a while; his phone calls came in less often. I knew his pattern only too well. Let me calm down, let some time pass, and then swoop in with some irrelevant conversation in his sweet voice, pretending nothing had ever happened. He counted on my giving heart to forgive and forget his behavior, hoping we could "play house" again until his next vulgar, abusive explosion.

Meanwhile, Steve, my Saturday babysitter, began to enjoy my company. He started to ask Nicholas and me to stay for pizza on Saturdays and then inviting me to lunch weekly. We had long talks and shared our daily struggles as single parents. I started to feel it was okay to open up a little, to think maybe there are safe men in this world. For a few hours a week, I had a sense of normal. We were becoming friends.

Steve started sending me cards, cute ones, suggestive ones, and, then, slightly *romantic* ones, arriving as often as every other day. I didn't recognize he was gently romancing me until the slightly romantic cards turned into plain ol' romantic ones. He was attentive and thoughtful.

Nicholas was safe. That was all I saw.

That Mother's Day Steve surprised me with an invitation to dinner. He thought of everything—a roasted chicken dinner with all the fixings, a nice bottle of wine, flowers on the table, even a gift for Nicholas to give to me. The boys got along great. It was a beautiful day, a pleasant change. That evening he kissed my cheek. The next week he kissed me passionately.

We started to feel like a family. We went to church together every Sunday, then out to breakfast. Steve started to talk about what type of house we would need, saying we should build, assuring me not to worry, he had built before. He looked at me endearingly, often speaking of how he admired me for all I'd done on my own. He tried to identify with my life, repeating he couldn't have done it if he couldn't have retired when his young wife passed away. I often spoke of how quickly you learn what's important and how to prioritize daily, sometimes hourly.

Almost weekly on Saturday afternoon, we relaxed on his back porch just before pizza time. He held my hand one afternoon, asking, "How did your faith become so strong?"

Without hesitation I said, "Adversity." I paused a second to think and finished with, "Yes, Steve. My faith grew through all the adversity." Tears welled up in my eyes as I thought for a moment of all that I endured in my life.

Steve looked lovingly at me, hugged me, and said he wanted to be there spiritually with me someday. As he walked back into the house, he looked over at me like a sixteen-year-old boy in love and said, "I never thought God would give me another chance."

Spending a few hours here or there with Steve and the boys was like a bunch of mini-vacations. Unfortunately, those interludes only held my reality at bay for a while.

One Baby Step at a Time

Another one of my-take-my-mind-off-my-fears practices was to go through the catalogues that arrived in the mail. I would circle all the things I would like to purchase when I had more money. One day I came across an ad for the book *Heal Your Body A-Z* by Louise L. Hay. Beneath her name it read, "The mental causes for physical illness and the way to overcome them." I learned that Hay is a metaphysical lecturer and teacher and best-selling author of many books that have been translated into twenty-five different languages and sold in thirty-three countries.

Totally intrigued, I ordered the book that contained a brief view of Louise's work. This simple little book fascinated me and gave me lots to think about.

Reading it turned out to be like the first day at a new school. In the introduction, Hay shared one of the reasons she knew that dis-ease (Louise's spelling) could be reversed simply by changing mental patterns. She offered a brief background about being raped at five years old, being a battered child, and being diagnosed with cancer "in the vaginal area." A teacher of healing, she believes that cancer comes from a pattern of deep resentment that, held for a long time, can literally eat away at the body. With lots of hard work between her mental and physical cleansing, in six months she was cancer-free without any invasive treatments. Her beliefs and her teachings certainly grabbed my attention. And this was just the introduction to the book!

In reading further, I learned both the good in our lives and dis-ease are the results of our thought patterns that form our experiences. She explained that good, positive thoughts produce experiences we enjoy, and negative patterns produce uncomfortable, unrewarding experiences. The mental thought patterns that cause most dis-ease in the body are criticism, anger, resentment, guilt.

Louise believes *criticism,* indulged in long enough, often leads to dis-eases like arthritis. *Anger* turns into things that boil and burn and infect the body. *Resentment* long held festers and eats away at the self and, ultimately, can lead to tumors and cancer. *Guilt* always seeks punishment and leads to pain. Anxious to see whether any of my issues resonated with her beliefs, I hurried to look them up.

- High blood pressure: probable cause was a longstanding emotional problem not solved
- Aches: longing for love, longing to be held
- Thyroid: humiliation, "I never get to do what I want to do; when is it going to be my turn?" and frustrated creativity
    - Hyperthyroid: rage at being left out
    - Hypothyroid: giving up feeling, hopelessly stifled

My fingers raced through this information. I couldn't help but be amazed at the connections.

- Goiter: hatred for being inflicted upon, victim, feeling thwarted in life, unfulfilled
- Lower back problems: fear of lack of money, lack of financial support
- Poison ivy: feeling defenseless and open to attack

Then I read that the throat represents our ability to "speak up" for ourselves to ask for what we want. When we have throat problems, it usually means we don't feel we have the *right* to do these things. We feel inadequate.

Thinking, *Oh, my gosh! This is my story!* I immediately flipped through the pages to look up Nicholas's issues. Probable causes for Nicholas's bathroom issues: fear of parent, usually the father; his eczema: breathtaking antagonism, mental eruptions.

This small, spiral-bound, 122-page book was a huge part of the beginning of my crawling out. Eager to learn more, I found myself ordering all kinds of material from this Louise Hay.

One of the next lessons I learned from Louise's teachings is that the very person you find it the hardest to forgive is the one you need to forgive most. Louise reminds us that forgiveness is *not* condoning their behavior; it is simply letting go, no longer letting that behavior hurt you or affect you. She taught me that everyone does the best they can with the *understanding, awareness,* and *knowledge* they have at the time; they are in pain as well. I'd work on that one.

The *Course in Miracles,* published by the Foundation for Inner Peace, says that "all dis-ease comes from a state of unforgiveness." And that "whenever we are ill we need to look around to see who it is that we need to forgive." Reading this from two of my new sources started me down the long road of forgiveness I had in front of me.

Another practice I began around this time was to create more time to sit quietly with my Lord. I subscribed to a daily-reading booklet that arrived once a month called *Science of Mind: A Guide for Spiritual Living.* These readings took my mind off the fear and slowly started to change my mindset, helping me to hang on, helping me to learn a more peaceful way of looking at things, one baby step at a time.

Our Time in Court

During the preceding year, Tony and I had spent one day each month in child support court. Neither of us had lawyers; we couldn't afford them. The court would mail me my court date and I would have to rearrange my clients and close my business for the day. This made me anxious and furious. Money was still tight and the day in court, long and boring, waiting around for our number and names to be called, only to be told after just a few minutes with the judge, "See you next month."

Each month the process was more grueling than the last. At every hearing, we had a different judge, so we had to start all over again explaining the situation. Tony had one excuse or reason after another why he couldn't pay his court-mandated child support—either he had no job or he was laid off. This time around, he was hurt. We had to wait for doctor reports, which was why we kept hearing, "See you next month."

I started bringing some reading with me. I began to learn and understand more about thyroid issues, for example, from Ridha Arem, M.D., *The Thyroid Solution.*

> Thyroid imbalance under active or over active generates a myriad of emotional, mood, and cognitive effects and weakens the ability to cope with stress. Agitated emotions inevitably create new stress; under stress the brain emits chemical messages that trigger major responses of the endocrine system...

With chemical imbalance in the brain, too much of this chemical or too little of that can make you prone to depression and panic attacks when you experience too much stress. If you experience stress for a long time because of major setbacks, trauma, upheavals, the endocrine system becomes chronically challenged and causes health problems. Dr. Arem claims that if you suffered from stressful events in childhood, you are more fragile when dealing with stress later in life and more vulnerable to *depression, anxiety, panic attacks, and posttraumatic stress disorder.*

The events in my childhood could certainly be responsible for this dis-ease and all the other escalating medical problems I lived with. I started to understand that a mild disturbance in our system triggered by one stressful event is manageable, that most systems can recover from it rather quickly. In my case, the ongoing, incessant stressful events and physical traumas produced a cascade of continual autoimmune disruptions, making it difficult for my system to ever recover. It is my belief that if my thyroid condition had been diagnosed soon enough, maybe my system might have been able to heal itself.

On September 11, 2001, the court-appointed days ended. The judge declared Tony disabled from his fall the previous winter when he hurt his neck. In just a few minutes, the day's appointed judge dropped Tony's child support of seventy-eight dollars a week to zero and erased $12,480 off the records—more than three years of court-ordered child support that I'd counted on.

I was speechless. "Did he really say that?"

The judge looked over to me, asked if I had anything to say. Before I could respond, he slammed down his gavel, said, "Next."

Too late, I tried to say something. My thoughts racing, a bailiff took me by the arm and escorted me out of the court.

No! No, wait! Wait! I have something to say, Judge. Please! Please listen to me, I screamed in my head. *Please let me have another turn. This has gone on too long. No! This is not right!*

Judge, please take a minute to think about what life has been like without that money. Don't take that money away from me. I need it to raise my child.

Please, sir, that was 160 weeks he missed. Just to wipe the record clean isn't fair. I have had to stand in line for energy assistance. I eat cereal for dinner. I had to fill out paperwork after paperwork to prove I need assistance for day care, after-school care.

Wait! Please let me speak! What about healthcare insurance? You didn't say anything about the health insurance Tony was court-ordered to have on his son. He hasn't done that either.

Please, somebody, help me! I need that money. That $12,000-plus was enough money to pay for many months of health insurance for Nicholas. If anything, order Tony to pay something, even ten dollars a week, on that back child support. Those forty dollars a month could buy milk, bread, *or even school lunches. Don't just let him walk away with no penalty for being irresponsible.*

Awareness Continues

Court appearances one day a month for a year were draining. The decision, devastating. Overwhelming. Until it was rendered, I clung to my prayer life, looking for the strength to maintain, to keep my sanity, to hold my life together for Nicholas's sake. After the decision, I read anything I could get my hands on that dealt with physical or emotional health. Slowly, I began to sense that things would be okay.

Then, one more burden. A letter from my landlord told me I had to find another space from which to run my business. After the initial panic, I started thinking out of the box. I decided to go around town to other small businesses that complemented my services and offer to join forces. We would share space; share overhead expenses; keep our own identity, our own phones, our own appointment books; and just give each other's clients a bigger menu to choose from. What a great idea! Excited, I started on my new plan.

Six months of setting up appointments and meeting with other small-business owners didn't go as smoothly as I'd hoped. I couldn't understand why they all said it sounded great but couldn't move forward on implementing my idea.

Most of my clients knew of my frustrations. One day, as I styled the hair of one of my sweet weekly clients, she asked me to share with her husband who sat in the waiting area the trail of events I had experienced in trying to implement my new plan. I told Doctor E. every detail and conversation.

When I had finished, he looked at me for a moment or two, a knowledgeable, grandfatherly expression on his face. In that moment of silence, my heart started to race. I found it hard to swallow. My face felt flushed. I worried that he thought I was just a foolish dreamer and wondered what I was doing in business for myself. Then he said in an authoritative voice, "Do you know what your problem is, young lady?"

With wide eyes and a shake of my head, I answered, "No."

"You think like a man, scaring the crap out of these women with your creative thinking and your 'I know who I am and I know what I want' powerful mannerisms."

At first I thought he was telling me I was doing something wrong. Quickly, though, a proud smile came on his face, the kind I suspected his own grandchildren witnessed, and I knew he was giving me a compliment and the greatest pat on the back I'd received in a very, very long time. It felt wonderful. It felt like family, like Sunday morning sitting around the breakfast table discussing our plans. They loved and respected me, admired me.

It was as beautiful a moment as it was sad. I hadn't experienced that sense of family, sense of support, since living with Mr. and Mrs. B. For the moment, I wasn't alone. Somebody cared about me and my problems. The doctors' hugs goodbye that day comforted me. Their words of encouragement and pride were a wonderful gift that I'll treasure for a lifetime.

His words didn't fix my dilemma, but that support from a wise, well-educated, successful man carried me.

I eventually found a sister team to complement my services, and we moved one mile down the street. The sister team and I pulled it off. We blended our services and successfully completed a major renovation. In just five short weeks, I negotiated a contract and signed a lease. We framed rooms, rewired the building, built walls, and put in proper plumbing. We painted, hung a new sign, and moved in. All the while, I ran my business at the other location, ran my home, and raised my son.

We certainly deserved a pat on the back for a job well done. I know we amazed many with all that we accomplished in such a short time. We were blessed with great contractors and lots of loyal, handy friends who went above and beyond to help.

During the move, I learned that two years prior to receiving notice from my former landlord, he had put the plan in place to move me out. He had negotiated my leased space away to another tenant, agreeing to let that tenant expand into my space when he hit his second anniversary. It boiled down to the landlord being able to get more money for the space from the other tenant. Simple as that. Business is business.

My business move went well. I finally could balance my everyday life because the sisters shared overhead expenses.

Nicholas was now at the YMCA for weekday after-school child care and was happy there. The staff was wonderful. He was in a safe place and he had plenty to do, hanging out with other children his age. The finance department at the Y was just as great. They always worked with me on child-care expense, allowing Nicholas to even enjoy summer camp. God bless them all.

On the outside, my life seemed a little smoother. But in reality, I became more and more aware of childhood messages that I had stuffed deeply inside. For a short while, though, teaming up with the sisters let me put those new awarenesses on the back burner, allowing me to continue masking my abandonment issues, to continue making light of the nagging internal voice that told me that I was not good enough, was unworthy, dismissed.

But, Louise Hay and the rest of my new authors had taught me that through years of abuse, I had lost my power and I needed to learn how to grab it back. It certainly wouldn't be handed to me. The time had now come to deal with all those stuffed messages.

Casey Morley

The Foreman

December 2003, two months after I moved my business, someone new walked into my life.

A client who loved playing around on her computer had an appointment. I asked if she could help Nicholas and me out and look at our home computer; we couldn't figure out what was wrong. She called a friend. After a brief introduction to the problem, she handed me the phone. Her friend asked me a few questions and we hung up. Before my client left, she told me her friend was a construction foreman and they met at a computer class. "He's just a wiz at them." Right after lunch, the Foreman showed up at the salon with a stack of papers that he thought would assist me with the problem.

My first thought was, *You've got to be kidding me.* I politely thanked him but knew instantly that wasn't going to help. With my limited computer skills, I might as well try reading a foreign language. Frustrated with the whole situation, I decided I'd just have to make the time to drag that machine back to the store.

The following day, as I was closing up the salon, the Foreman walked in, inquiring how I made out. I decided to be up-front with him and explained my dilemma. Before long, he was at my house checking things out for us. I couldn't allow him to stay very long that afternoon. Time was moving quickly and I needed to get ready for a date.

The next day, a Sunday, I felt like I was getting sick. I was grateful to have the day off, and the snow gave me permission to stay in. As the day went on, I felt worse, and decorating the Christmas tree just didn't happen. I spent most of the day on the sofa. Nicholas had never seen me this inactive. He stayed close by all day, quietly keeping himself busy.

Evening was fast approaching. The snow was piling up when we heard the snow blower. Thank goodness something was being done—it was a blizzard out there.

Nicholas kept peeking out the window, giving me a play-by-play description. "Our sidewalk is done. There is only one worker, Mama. Now he's cleaning off our car."

What is he talking about? I thought, as I pulled myself off the sofa. *Why are they cleaning off my car?*

Peeking out the window around our full, undecorated Christmas tree, I sensed this wasn't the cleaning crew. I realized it was the Foreman. Too sick to go outside in that storm, I called one of the phone numbers he left with us to express my appreciation for his thoughtfulness. I left a voicemail and offered him some homemade soup to go. Shortly after that, he called back to refuse the soup because he was going to help some other friends.

On Tuesday I was still under the weather and struggling with getting through my workday. I decided to end my day a little early and perhaps get a start on decorating that tree. I was determined to at least put the lights on to start to make it festive for my son.

I was home only a few minutes when the phone rang. It was the Foreman, disappointed I had left work and concerned about how I felt. We chit-chatted about this or that for more than two hours.

I finally ended the phone call, anxious to get the lights on the tree before I had to pick up Nicholas. I worked at it for about a half an hour when the doorbell rang. There stood the Foreman, bearing gifts. I didn't consider him a good-looking man, but at that moment, standing there, so meticulous in a sharp black overcoat and a big smile, he was handsome. He had asked so many questions during our phone conversation. He totally surprised me by ordering our favorite foods.

I was speechless. He explained he only wanted to make it easier for me, knowing how sick I'd been. He started to help me put the lights on the tree, but soon it was time to pick up Nick. As we walked out, he asked if it would be okay to come back later and help finish the decorating. Oh, that would be wonderful. *What a break,* I thought. I was tired of doing it alone all those years.

I had no sooner cleared away the dishes and cleaned up after dinner than the Foreman was back. By that time, Nicholas had started his homework. The Foreman jumped right in to help. We ended up taking turns with the vocabulary words. At one point while I looked up a definition, the Foreman came looking over my shoulder. In seconds, we were cheek to cheek. I could feel his warm breath at the same moment he brushed his finger against mine, sending a chill through me. That was when I thought, *Hmm! I think he is interested in me. So that's what this is all about!*

Nicholas went off to bed that evening without any hesitation or procrastination. Perhaps it was a sign Nick thought this guy was okay.

The Foreman and I continued to get to know one another, and as the evening went on, he appeared to become more comfortable. Leaning against the kitchen sink, he asked if he could give me a hug. "Are you sure you want to do that after how sick I have been?" He assured me that he was a warrior when it came to not catching anything.

I had never experienced such a hug. It was warm and gentle; it felt like our hearts leaped out at each other like old souls reuniting. I didn't feel like I was hugging a man I had known only a week.

Steps Forward

Over time, I started to call the Foreman his given name (not given to protect his anonymity). That sounded much nicer to me, and I was the only one who used it. I liked that. It felt special to me.

The Foreman now knew my given name and preferred calling me Kathleen. At first I was uncomfortable with it; I had not used it since that day in the doctor's office when I was fifteen and I jumped at the chance for another identity that the name Casey represented. Over time, the Foreman said Kathleen with such love and admiration, even I started to think it was a pretty name after all these years.

As we got to know each other and the Foreman's story came out, he seemed broken when he talked about how women in his past had cheated on him and how poorly they had all treated him. *Wow! How sad,* I thought. *If I help him with only one thing, it would be worth it.*

As the Foreman told me about his life, I began to relax and open up a little about mine. I shared a story about meeting Tony at a local restaurant during the first week of Lent. I had decided that year I wasn't going to follow the old tradition of giving up sweets or wine or whatever. Instead, I was going to give up the past and all that went with it, beginning with Tony.

I asked Tony to meet me, and we sat at the bar of his choice. Tony ordered his usual drink and I had water. He kept saying, "Let me buy you a drink for the good ol' days."

I was sickened and saddened; nothing had changed for him except his appearance. He had aged; thin, just plain old and beat-up. He'd lost height; gray-haired and balding, and very unsteady. The only evidence of the man I once loved with all my heart was those gorgeous blue eyes that now had a sadness to them.

I got right to the point, informing him why I wanted to meet with him. "I am here to forgive you for all the pain." His eyes filled up as I continued, "To forgive you for all you have said and all you have done."

Tony was emotional as he assured me he had not and would not ever again hurt anyone like he had hurt me. Tears streamed down his cheeks. He wanted me to know that he paid the price, daily, for losing his family.

Tony was right. He had lost everything. It was sad to witness his brokenness.

I asked if I could ask him a question. I got a quick nod and asked, "Why didn't you ever come home?"

It was incredibly sad to watch his expression and hear his words of regret. He spoke of the times he met his dad at their favorite taverns and how his dad would always ask, "What are you, pussy whipped?"

I thought, *What a price for a child to pay in search of some love or some kind of approval from his father.*

After a deep breath, he said, "Kathleen, you were right." There was a silence.

I asked, "About?"

"You always told me if I didn't catch on and get it together, I was going to die a lonely old man. And that's exactly how it is going to be."

For the moment, I forgot I was sitting next to the man I couldn't stand looking at, the man whose voice I never wanted to hear again, the man I couldn't tolerate for one minute, the man I had come to hate. I saw a broken little boy longing for love and acceptance. Filled with empathy, I was able to bring myself to kiss him on the cheek and say goodbye. I walked out of that little place feeling great about what I had just done for him—and for me.

The Foreman thought I was the sweetest, most loving woman he had ever met. He often sat close to me, telling me he loved my calmness and how I had raised my child. He said he spoke to his friends and therapist about how wonderful he felt when he was with me.

Not long after I shared the Tony story with the Foreman, he asked, "Was there anyone in the past other than Nicholas's dad?"

I told him a little about Steve and how we started. The Foreman was surprised when he learned that Steve just… stopped one day. He stopped being who I knew him to be, he stopped being so thoughtful. The cards were fewer and cold.

When I asked him to talk, to tell me what was going on, his words were, "I can't do this anymore. I guess it's… too much would change."

I wasn't prepared for such an abrupt switch in his behavior. I stood there, speechless, while he finished.

"Oh, it's not that I don't love you. I guess it's that… I'm selfish."

I never saw that side of him, never saw anyone turn off feelings like you would turn off a switch.

I was crushed. I felt robbed, abandoned again, angry at myself for letting Steve in, and angry I wasn't smart enough to see it coming. I asked myself, *How did I get here, from too old, too short, and not even cute?* I was grateful it didn't take me long to realize I wasn't mourning Steve at all. I mourned the loss of a sense of family, the loss of the picture Steve drew for us.

The Foreman was also curious why Tony wasn't in Nicholas's life. I wasn't comfortable going into that much of my story, so I chose to share with him the part about how one month after I decided to not allow Tony into Nick's life, I went to a lawyer to set up what would happen if I were to pass away suddenly. Where Nicholas would live, who would care for him, and who would decide financial issues. As I shared the story of the infamous football practice and what had occurred since that evening, I ended our discussion with what transpired at the attorney's office. Attorney Sal asked, "How long has it been since Tony saw your son?"

"It's only been a month," I replied.

With raised eyebrows, Attorney Sal responded, "'Only a month'?! He already looks bad in the eyes of the court. Go home and raise your son. Let him take you to court."

For once, an attorney told me something positive. I started skipping again. I felt safe and empowered. I felt for the first time that Nicholas and I would actually get through this. Through the grace of God, we would get through this, and all would be well.

I welcomed the Foreman's words of praise, and his admiring looks felt wonderful. It was astonishing to hear someone noticed and enjoyed my calmness and inner peace. I thought to myself, *If you only knew all the work it took to arrive on this square.*

I had explained to the Foreman that a while back, I started to see decision making as standing on a square. When I had to make a decision, I learned to stop a minute, even thirty seconds, to ask myself,

If I am standing on this square and I decide to do this, or that, will I be going forward? Will I be going backwards? Will I be only side-stepping or standing still by deciding to do nothing for the moment? Just taking that little bit of time to think helped me tremendously. The thought of going backwards was just not for me.

I sensed he felt better about his own story when I told him it was okay to make mistakes if we learn from them. The Foreman wasn't sure what I meant by that, so I tried to explain we all learned many things from the people we were around as little children. As adults, we tend to recreate the environments we grew up in. It is common to mimic or recreate the exact type of relationships we witnessed in our young worlds, even subconsciously.

The Foreman was angry and bitter when he shared parts of his story. It was a new concept for him to try to remember not to condemn anyone, that everyone does the best they can at any given moment.

I shared with him that when we know better and have more understanding and awareness, we will do things differently. I told him how Louise Hay also taught me that blame is one of the surest ways to stay in a problem. When we blame, we give away our power. Our past is our past, and our future needs to be shaped. We need to remember that people who did all those terrible things to us were taught to live that way and most likely were just as frightened and scared as the rest of us.

The Foreman's interest in what I had to say seemed to increase as we got to know each other. He seemed to feel better about his past when I told him I thought our days on this Earth are just a lifetime of going to school. I assured him that I thought he had plenty more days left to learn. I know I gave him something to think about, even though the concept I was trying to teach him baffled him. But, he was open to listening. He commented one night, "If that is how you got where you are, this stuff must work."

Life Was Sweet

A few weeks after Christmas, the Foreman asked me out on a date to celebrate my birthday. To my surprise, I was excited about the whole idea. It was fun to prepare for the special evening. He arrived on time, dressed to impress, with a beautifully wrapped gift, my first cell phone with his phone number already programmed. I didn't need it, but the Foreman was excited about it. When we arrived at my favorite restaurant, we were escorted to our reserved table, where a dozen red roses waiting for me. How sweet. And so romantic.

The Foreman and I started dating after that impressive evening. He was charming, funny, attentive, clean, and neat. He liked my calm, peaceful manner. He often spoke of our first conversation over the phone, referring to how sweet my voice was and how he just had to meet me.

He also frequently commented how nice to see there were still some good old-fashioned girls left, Suzy Homemaker kinds of girls. To me, it was a compliment because I had worked very hard throughout my life to create a calm, peaceful, welcoming home. He was always so appreciative of any meal I served him. Frequently mentioning how he admired my parenting skills. What a polite, respectful child I had. Always adding what a wonderful relationship Nicholas and I shared.

All my friends loved him, adored our relationship, and cherished watching our romance blossom. I heard, "What a nice guy!" just about weekly from someone.

Valentine's Day was the next week. Everywhere we turned was a reminder to "remember your sweetheart." The Foreman and I had known each other for ten weeks, but I was comfortable with him and, most important, I felt safe. He was always a complete gentleman.

We decided to inquire about a Valentine's Day special offered by a luxurious inn that included a beautiful suite, a bottle of wine, chocolates, and dinner specials for sweethearts in their restaurant. The Foreman and I didn't get much alone time. I thought this would be a great opportunity to see what it would be like to be with him without buffers. The Foreman assured me he understood it would be a platonic adventure. He was clear that in no way was I being suggestive or promiscuous.

My friend Wendy offered to stay at my house for the evening. Her son was the same age as Nicholas, and the boys were thrilled to have a sleepover. Movies, treats, and sleeping bags were right up their alley. I had to warn her of the possibility that Tony could appear—out of the blue—drunk, on my doorstep, frightening the boys, especially Nicholas. Tony wasn't to be let into the house for any reason.

Since everyone seemed to be content and happy, the Foreman and I packed our overnight bags and headed out early. We planned to take a nice drive to the eastern side of the state to poke around a country store before we headed to the inn.

As we drove, the Foreman seemed tense and irritable. He complained about Francine, his housekeeper. He had mentioned earlier that she was baffled that someone from his computer class called him about my computer initially, that he wanted to bring me that stack of papers rather than sending her. Now he complained about his housekeeper overstepping her boundaries with her curiosity over his personal business. His voice and words were agitated every time he repeated her questions about where he was going and who he was going with.

I couldn't help but inquire, "What concern is it to your housekeeper, errand girl, or whatever she is?"

The Foreman ended the conversation with, "She has no life."

I had spoken to Francine only on the phone, but at that point, I couldn't help thinking, *Oh, the poor thing.*

The countryside was beautiful. The Foreman and I took a walk, held hands, and had great conversation before we headed to the inn. As we unpacked the few things we brought along, I smirked at how comfortable I felt with him in that situation, and not for a second did I think I couldn't trust him.

It was cute to watch him place his belongings about the room. At one point, he placed packets on the bench at the bottom of the bed. My first thought was that he must not be feeling well and had brought Alka Seltzer. I walked over to the bench and picked one up to read what kind of medicine he was taking. It wasn't until I felt the round, disc shape enclosed that I realized all those packets were condoms. He had set me up, watching me all along. He roared with laughter as he repacked them. He said watching my expression was worth its weight in gold as he held his sides laughing.

The Foreman and I had a few cocktails while we got ready to go to dinner. The restaurant was loud and overbooked. We barely made it through our appetizers when we decided to have our meals packed up to go. Back at our suite, we watched a movie while we ate our dinners. I lay in his arms as we talked the night away. I must have drifted off at some point.

I was nudged awake by the squeaking of the door. The Foreman had plenty of hot, fresh coffee, a big smile, and a "Good morning, beautiful!" We sat up in bed, drinking our coffee and flipping through the cookbook we'd bought at the country store the day before. He was cute when he picked out things he wanted us to make together or that he would be brave enough to try on his own the nights I worked later than he.

Our relationship was going along smoothly. We were comfortable together and grew more attached every moment we spent with each other. We shared many dinners, laughed a lot, hugged, and held hands. I loved the fact that he was romantic, thoughtful, and full of compliments.

The Four of Us

The Foreman's youngest child, Danielle, was a few years older than Nicholas, but the two got along quite well. Early in the relationship, I could sense they both enjoyed having a sense of family our little four-person unit made. The four of us often shared Sunday breakfast at my home. The two children gulped down their food, anxious to read what movies were playing at the local theater.

One particular Sunday, with the children and their friends off to the movies, I started right in preparing a big meal for our company. The Foreman sat quietly working on his crossword puzzle, listening to the beautiful romantic music that played in the background.

When I had everything in the kitchen under control, I took the quiet time to discuss his talking about our future in front of our children. I felt it was much too soon to be sharing with the children that he wanted to marry me or to talk about *our* future home together. I didn't want to set anyone up for a letdown. He assured me he would hold back discussing his dream of marrying me and doing things with Nicholas and Danielle together as a family.

Later, as I stood at the stove stirring a huge pot of spaghetti sauce, the Foreman came up behind me and started kissing the back of my neck. His breath was warm, his kisses soft and gentle. Goose bumps rose up all over my body. I loved when he did that attentive part or sweet little peck as he passed by. This time, though, his kisses were different, more urgent, as he brushed my hair away from my neck. He turned me toward him and his soft, warm lips met mine. I could feel his heart pounding through his chest, each kiss more intense and passionate than the last. He started to caress my breast. I could feel his throbbing manhood against my leg.

Thoughts of *I should stop this* raced through my mind. I wasn't sure I was ready to be this intimate. I'm not the type to jump into that. I thought it was important to take my time and watch for the true person to show up. Not rely on the best behavior stuff that goes on at first. Of course, there was also that Catholic upbringing that tormented me from time to time.

"Honey, we have company coming and the clock is ticking. The children will be back soon."

He ignored my words as he became more heated and passionate. In that moment, he swooped me up in his arms and carried me to the sofa.

I whispered, "The sauce will burn," as he continued with his kisses, his hot lips now kissing my exposed breast. In that early afternoon of passion, we made love for the first time. I was sure while we all sat around the dinner table that afternoon, everyone knew by my flushed cheeks what had occurred earlier in the day.

The Foreman grinned like a little boy, "They don't know. Stop being so silly. I love you."

To refocus thoughts, I switched the conversation to Danielle and her upcoming birthday. She was thrilled that her dad and I were going to give her a party.

Who's the Child?

On the day of the party, I worked hard to make it a nice time for everyone. We had plenty of good food, kids' treats, birthday bags, games, and cake. The adults watched as the kids chased each other with water guns. At one point, Nicholas got the best of Danielle in the water gun fight and she screamed at him, "Eff you!"

The Foreman was so embarrassed. He immediately wanted to take her home to her mother. It took a lot of talking on my part to convince him to teach her what was acceptable and what wasn't and then to accept her apology. Exasperated by the whole situation, he left.

At first, I thought he was going for a short ride to calm down. I finished up the party with cake and presents, cleaned up the kitchen, did the dishes—the Foreman never returned. This disturbed me. What kind of behavior was that? He acted like a child, stomping away to pout.

When he finally showed up the next morning to help finish cleaning up the backyard party mess and to take down the tent, his behavior was worse than the day before. He angrily went about his cleanup with a cigarette hanging out of his mouth. The smoking was supposed to have ended weeks ago.

He never thanked me for all I had done for his daughter. Instead, he treated me like I was the enemy. I offered him a cup of coffee. His grumpy, "No!" sent me back into the house. On my way in, I let him know this was no way to treat me. I told him, "This is not how people behave when they care about someone."

As I finished up my work inside, I started to think about all those stories he had shared with me when we first met, the stories of how the women in his past cheated on him, stole from him, lied, and just treated him poorly. Perhaps his horrid behavior was the result of that treatment. We were able to talk it through later in the day. The Foreman thanked me for my patience and understanding, admitting he acted poorly.

Disturbing Observations by All

The Foreman was immediately back to his old self, and our love continued to grow. As the year went on, we felt even more like a family. His older sons visited often. We shared Sunday dinners, sat around talking and sharing cups of tea. Nicholas and Danielle got along famously, acting like big sister and little brother, loving it most when we watched movies together and ordered pizza. Our first year together was fun and exciting, and we all looked forward to preparing for Christmas.

Christmas Day was wonderful. We couldn't ask or want for anything more. The Foreman took the children shopping. They had fun purchasing gifts for their mothers and were excited for us to open them. The Foreman spoiled me as well with many gifts. We had a joyous, love-filled day and looked forward to sharing the New Year.

The week between Christmas and New Year was very busy, and that weekend was my turn to host our monthly gathering with our friends.

We had a great time as usual. Right after the gift exchange, Noreen squeezed through the now-crowded kitchen with the gathered-up Christmas wrappings. She asked the Foreman, who was closest to the back door, to take the trash out. He snarled, "It's Nicholas's job." The room went silent for a moment. Because it had snowed all day, I suggested it could wait until morning.

Right after dessert, everyone decided it was best to get home before it got too cold and everything started to refreeze. The Foreman left right behind the other guests. I cleaned up my kitchen for a good half hour when I decided to trudge through the snow with the trash.

Concentrating on my footing as I approached the trash container, I looked up to see the Foreman's truck parked and running, the windshield wipers swooshing back and forth. Approaching the driver's side window, I saw him sitting behind the wheel, sleeping. The door was locked, so I pounded on the window, yelling, "Hey! Hey! What are you doing?"

He eventually opened the window and said, "I'm letting the truck warm up."

In disgust, I told him he needed to get home, that he had been sitting there for more than half an hour.

This scene was unsettling to me, especially knowing Nicholas watched it. Over the next few days, one by one, my friends called to thank me for a wonderful Christmas celebration, and all of them commented on the Foreman's snarling and how much alcohol he had consumed. I was so busy being hostess I hadn't noticed what he was doing. No one pointed a finger. We all had cocktails. They were just concerned over the amount he drank and his sudden attitude about "Nicholas's job."

I was disturbed about our friends' observations and shared their words and concerns with the Foreman. I had no reservations telling him, "I can't and won't go down that road again." He assured me it was just a one-time thing. He said that we had all overindulged at one time or another. I trusted and believed him, since I hadn't witnessed any of this type of behavior from him in the past.

Where Are We, Anyway?

Except for the trash incident, for the next six months, our relationship stayed consistent with our wonderful first year. Life was good. The second half of the year, not so good.

That summer I started to feel the Foreman wasn't always honest about where he was or who he was with. He started not going home, staying at friends' houses all night. On those nights, his "good night" or "good morning, sweetheart" calls never happened. He also became lax with his business commitments. I tried to discuss my discomfort with his new so-called friends and his behavior with him. Reminding him again that I would not live this way. It wasn't healthy, and it needed to stop. I told him to make a choice.

I started to feel my unconditional love had led me to indiscriminate love. I began to think I had seen qualities that were not there. Did our leaping hearts fool me?

I also started to wonder whether our first conversations about his ex-wives or ex-girlfriends were a bit distorted. Questioning, was he really so beaten up emotionally by the women of his past? I had learned by that point that what we bring to the table through our thoughts, actions, and efforts impact our experiences in life.

As I took an honest assessment, I quickly saw that I needed to restore some balance in my life. I also realized that at least a dozen things had happened in the past six months just were not acceptable. The picture was becoming clear as I watched more closely what the Foreman brought into his life. I felt like I loved him for what he used to be and was waiting for him to become that man again.

A Stranger Knew My Secrets

That fall, I went to a Hay House You Can Do It weekend conference. Louise Hay, one of my now-favorite authors, holds these conferences annually. It was thrilling to be there, and I was excited to meet some of the authors I so enjoyed learning from. I had signed up for all I could possibly squeeze in, thirsty for knowledge, anxious to take in what they had to say.

As my friend Shelly and I tried to decide where we would sit, I noticed a woman at the end of one row working on another woman's neck. I was curious whether she was working on the woman's thyroid. With some hesitation, I walked over to them, hoping to slip in close enough to listen or to get a turn. In a minute or two, the first woman looked over at me. When I asked whether she was doing thyroid work, she nodded yes and said she was doing some energy work on the gland.

Shortly after that exchange, Gloria, the energy worker, turned to me. I shared my thyroid issues with her and my concern about Western medicine and its approach to "killing" my thyroid with radioactive iodine, especially after my horrific experience years back with the surgery. Gloria started to work on my neck. What seemed like only a short time later, she said, "I did a soul retrieval. Parts of your soul left from all the abuse you have been through."

I was taken by surprise; my reaction at first was embarrassment. *Oh, no. She knows my secrets.* I wanted to quickly get away from her.

People were starting to settle down, so we ended our brief encounter. I took one of her business cards.

Her final comment was, "You will start to remember things."

Feeling very exposed and embarrassed, I went back to my seat.

All through the conference, I remembered Gloria's words to the point of distraction. I couldn't help but be intrigued. I kept asking myself, *How does a woman I never met in my life, who lives at least ten states away from me, know I've been through so much abuse? And, what's soul retrieval, anyway?*

With such curiosity, and my list of questions building, I was grateful I grabbed one of her cards.

That evening, as I rummaged through my treasures from the day, I found in the thank-you-for-coming gift packet the premier issue of Dr. Christine Northup's newsletter. In it was a section called Body Wisdom featuring guest columnist Dr. Mona Lisa Schulz, a noted neuropsychiatrist, neuroscientist, and medical intuitive. By knowing only someone's name and age, she can "see" the state of their physical body in her mind's eye, regardless of their distance from her. More important, she can tell how a person's beliefs, thoughts, emotions, and moods contribute to their state of health, good or bad, and help them change the areas of their lives that contribute to illness.

Dr. Northrup's front page: "Women all over the world are discovering that true health is only possible when we understand the unity of our minds, emotions, spirits, and physical bodies." The article continued, "Self appreciation is the foundation upon which health is built."

As soon as I got back to Connecticut, I called Gloria. Happy to answer my questions, she explained that she asked the energy around me, "What is missing? What happened?" She said that was when "pieces of you left like a bouquet of balloons. Parts of your soul just left. The abuse was too much to bear."

I wanted to know about soul retrieval, so I Googled it. According to what I read online, following trauma, we subconsciously choose to give up or separate ourselves from bits and pieces of our "soul self" (our light, power, consciousness, love, intelligence). This ongoing dissociative process may happen instantaneously for protection if the trauma was severe enough, such as childhood physical and/or sexual abuse, or progressively over many assorted traumas accrued over many different levels.

My research further explained that on Spirit's side, this soul retrieval healing work involves a great deal, but, basically, your personal space needs to be first cleared out before any part of your soul self can come back, for the soul cannot return, in whole or in part, if anything occupies that space. (It's the principle that light and dark cannot occupy the same space at the same time—one or the other has to give.) So it's not about calling one's soul back in, but also removing from your energy field (on one level or another) all that is not of you that blocks the reintegration process.

My readings indicated that some symptoms of soul loss are depression, a sense of incompleteness, an inability to move forward on some issues, and feeling not in control of your life. In some cases, the soul part will return on its own, but a soul retrieval practitioner helps when the soul doesn't know how to return or when it's safe to do so.

I next found myself making an appointment with Dr. Mona, fascinated by the concept that someone can intuitively assess your health and well-being over the phone. That hour with Dr. Mona was the fastest, most amazing hour I had experienced in quite some time. She spoke of people around me and aspects of their lives or personalities, telling me that the stress I felt was brought on by them and their ways and was keeping me sick. She scanned my body from head to toe, suggesting ways for relief.

The most important piece of information in that hour was when she talked about why I chose to be around people who abused me and why I selected men who didn't listen to my voice and who certainly weren't marriage material. Dr. Mona suggested that I find a cognitive behavioral therapist.

Her reading moved me forward on my recovery journey. This insight helped me leap to another square. It all fit together.

More Promises

The Foreman and I were in the middle of a disagreement. The relationship had started to feel like a project. The days of love and laughter were farther and farther apart. I had become impatient and felt we had hit a roadblock; we showed no real evidence of moving forward. I was distraught and becoming more frustrated as time passed.

The Foreman behaved as if we were just at a crossroad, and he was waiting for me to catch up and see things his way. He believed our relationship was fine and that I was the "love of his life."

In the midst of our argument, I blurted, "You need to get some help!"

He jumped right back at me with, "You need therapy!" asking, "Why do you need to be loved by every man?" a typical out-of-left-field question he always threw out to avoid talking about his issues. Followed by, "All you ever want to do is get everybody's first names." He always resorted to this argument when I brought up something I didn't like or understand concerning his words and/or his actions. He was a pro at deflecting attention away from his issues.

I was so tired of hearing those words. To me, they were irrational. I was in business for myself. Getting someone's first name is the beginning of making a relationship and a potential future client. It was as simple as that.

I could never get him to understand that it was just a skill I learned back in the day at one of those build-your-business seminars. It was a simple business-building tool. The Foreman saw it as me being too friendly, flirting; that I needed attention from all the men. He never acknowledged the women I spoke to.

My friend Noreen referred us to a couple's therapist whom she highly respected. Four weeks into this stage of the relationship, in the last two minutes of our session with Dr. Lori, the Foreman blurted out his news. With trembling hands and shaking voice, he told us that he had done some research and discovered that he was an alcoholic.

With dropped jaws, Dr. Lori and I looked at each other. I don't know which one of us was more shocked. We both were speechless. Being that it was in the last minutes of our session, the Foreman and I had to leave. I walked out of Dr. Lori's office numb; I didn't even look at the Foreman. I got in my car and drove home in a daze.

His promises started almost instantly. In just a few days, he was back to the man I fell in love with and promised to take care of his drinking issue.

That stage didn't last very long, but the promises continued, more excuses, more denials, and more hiding. He played his mind games again in his attempt to maintain control, to hurt me, calling me a flirt, telling me I needed so much attention. It was his way of taking the blame off himself and throwing it back onto me. Yet it was he who had ex-lovers who were still a part of his everyday life in one form or another.

We had taken a step as a couple by going to therapy, and I had followed up on Dr. Mona's suggestion. I already had my own appointment with Dr. Amy, a cognitive behaviorist, to help me understand why I chose to be around people who didn't listen to my voice.

The Foreman and I had another argument the morning of my first session with Dr. Amy. He was on the phone continuing his absurd, unreasonable, finger-pointing. *His* woodpeckering. The simple but constant having to know every move I made—"Why'd you go to church? Who'd you talk with? What time did you leave work? Where'd you stop on the way home?"

I had had enough. I was at my limit. My whole body shook, tears streamed down my cheeks. I was exhausted. I heatedly shouted as clearly as I could, "You need to do a 90/90"—an Alcoholics Anonymous expression for needing ninety days with no drinks and ninety consecutive days at AA meetings. Somewhere deep inside, I knew this was really a beginning, not an end.

I never shared with the Foreman the reading I had with Dr. Mona, knowing all too well that he would have just found a way to demerit her and her work. Knocking me again to take the focus off himself and the fact that he was neither keeping to the changes he agreed to nor choosing to move forward and start his healing work.

On my fourth visit with Dr. Amy, she diagnosed me with posttraumatic stress disorder (PTSD). Mother and son with the same diagnosis.

The next twenty-four hours of my life were the most profound I have experienced. One half of me was filled with joy. *It* had a name. Dr. Amy acknowledged my pain, and it was real. I was not a baby, or weak.

Dr. Amy had already taught me that even though my conscious mind told me I was a good person, my subconscious mind told me the opposite. It only knew the messages I was sent as a child. Those two parts—my conscious mind and my subconscious—set me up for the lifetime battle. Was I a good person, worthy of love, or not?

Her words "you've been through a lot" made me feel like a thousand pounds had been lifted off my chest. Dr. Amy elaborated on how incredibly strong I was and shared that women who had been through as much as I had could end up with multiple personalities, commit suicide, or develop addictions.

The other half of me was angered and frightened. I felt an incredible anger when I thought of the hell I had been subjected to during my lifetime, and the reality of what could have happened to me if I were not as strong a person filled me with fear to the point of tears.

Once I was home, the tears seemed like they would never stop. I cried and cried, hysterical, sobbing tears, but I knew deep inside that my tears were healing. The rollercoaster of emotions seemed to just bring more tears—tears of joy, tears of anger, tears of gratitude, acknowledgment, relief, but most important, tears of permission to shed others' shame and guilt. The years of hiding were over. *What had happened to me* ***wasn't*** *my fault.*

To calm myself down, I started to pray, hoping it would take my mind off all these emotions. Next, I decided to do an angel card reading with one of Doreen Virtue's oracle cards called *Healing with the Angels,* another tool I used often to try to cope.

The first card I picked said to expect unexpected things. In seconds, the phone rang. It was Tony. I couldn't disguise how upset I was. He expressed his concern over my shaking voice, tears he couldn't see still streaming down my cheeks. He probed long enough for me to share my diagnosis from that morning. Without any hesitation, he took ownership of the part he had played in all this. NO excuses or denials. He just said, "I know I'm part of it, and I'm sorry."

I found myself talking to him as if he were my best friend. For the moment, his honesty brought me back to when we were young. He was once again the man I fell in love with. He was sweet and compassionate, and his heartfelt ownership seemed to put the past in the past for the moment.

I felt numb—to what I was living and to what was going on over the phone. I wondered, *Am I really hearing these words?* I felt totally exhausted and told Tony I needed to hang up and rest. All of emotions of the day—the validation, the crying, Tony's ownership and understanding—had brought on a killer headache.

Nicholas, who by now had not spent time with his father for six years, watched me in my turmoil, reading quietly nearby, close enough to be loving and understanding. He never said a word, just allowed me to process without questions or judgment. He came over to me to give me a hug when my phone rang again. It was Tony. He said he needed me to come outside for a minute. To my surprise, he was sitting in my driveway. As I approached his car, he handed me a bouquet of fresh flowers, revealing how upset he was to hear me cry like that, promising that he would cut the head off whoever was making me cry. He repeated those words, adding, "And shit in his neck." A sweet gesture, but his words so true to form. He indicated he thought the Foreman had some part in all this.

Tony went on, "Don't ever let anyone make you cry. You've cried enough in your lifetime. I want you to know that I'll love you forever. I'm sorry I did terrible things to you, and I promise you I will never and have never done that to anyone since." He reminded me that he pays the price daily for losing his family. But he couldn't help himself, adding, "Don't get a big head because I'll love you forever. I tried to love others, but I can't love them in the same way I love you. And I thank you again for my beautiful son."

I thanked Tony for his kind gesture, turned around, and went back inside with the flowers, only to discover that Nicholas had watched the exchange from his upstairs bedroom window.

As I closed the front door behind me, Nicholas appeared on the upstairs landing with a slight smile on his face, asking, "What was that?"

I kept it brief, responding, "Daddy knew I was upset and crying and he wanted to make me feel better."

In a strange, silent way, I knew it was a small step toward healing for Nicholas to witness his father show a human, sweet side of himself. I don't think Nicholas had many memories, if any, of his father's kindness. Nicholas would be thirteen the following month. I prayed his wounds would heal, allowing him to experience true peace and the ability to see that not all men behaved the way his father typically did.

Healing Begins

That day of validation in Dr. Amy's office gave me permission to start my work of grieving. I felt an immediate sense of strength. I was empowered and determined to learn and understand. Identifying the events and conditions that caused such pain and fear, all the wrongs and hurts, being allowed to say it out loud began another step in the healing process.

And, this step—breaking the denial process and no longer minimizing what I had endured—was huge. Those beginning days of my work to end self-doubt and to stop diminishing myself, discounting my needs, and rationalizing represented major steps, though small, toward reclaiming my power. Dr. Amy taught me that exploring the past and feeling safe enough to talk about it openly would help me move forward to enjoy a normal, healthy life with normal, healthy, unconditional relationships for the first time ever.

I began to understand that with loss comes shock. We become numb. I had developed somewhat robotic reactions to what occurred in my past, disbelief, and was paralyzed by anxiety. Shock can lead to denial when the pain is too much to acknowledge out loud. It is a way to survive until you're ready to deal with the truth. Sadly, many go through life never ready to deal with yesterday's pain.

My emotions of anger, guilt, shame, embarrassment were a continuous battle. Dr. Amy helped me understand that my emotions were *false guilt*—remorse or regret for someone else's behavior and actions. True guilt is regret or remorse over something you personally have done. I began to understand for the first time in my life that I was not weak and I wasn't being a baby. It was okay to mourn the loss of what I had never known or never had. In fact, it was healthy and healing.

Each week I told Dr. Amy more of my story, sharing my feelings and confusion. Being allowed to cry without judgment in a very safe environment allowed me to continue my healing journey.

The shame and guilt started to subside. My wounds slowly started to heal. My thoughts were less confusing. I began to delete the old, incorrect "truths" and reprogram the messages that I knew to be true, learning what really is normal and, oh! No more secrets!

I was grateful for the sessions with Dr. Amy. They gave me an emotionally safe square to stand on for at least one hour a week, a square that offered gentle guidance and support through this very difficult process of walking back through the pain, sharing my vulnerabilities. It wasn't easy; it took time to trust Dr. Amy. I kept waiting for the betrayal and judgment for what I shared.

But that never happened. She stayed consistent and assured me that in time, I would learn to trust and be able to recognize an abuser. She taught me how important it was to be around safe, supporting people who loved me. She added that I should never allow anyone to criticize my process. It takes as long as it takes. Those words gave me permission to not allow people to judge me.

She constantly reminded me that I was courageous to start the healing process and that we don't remember everything all at once. My memories and feelings would surface when they were supposed to. She told me to respect the process.

I started to become aware of the triggers: people too close in my space; loud noises or loud claps; tones of voice; certain looks and sounds, like certain cell phone rings; even being held too tightly. Nicholas used to hug me tightly to express his amount of love. I started to recognize it made me feel "held down" and trapped. I asked often for him to hug lighter. One afternoon he forgot and hugged me tight. I lost it, flew off the handle, escaping from his hug. I went to the kitchen and started slamming cabinet doors, screaming, "You can't do this anymore. You have to stop. You have to stop!"

I soon realized I wasn't even talking to my son. I was yelling at all of *them*, for yesterday's pain and traumas. For a minute, I felt like a toddler having a temper tantrum, inside my body hearing, *No more! No more!*

I got control of myself and apologized to Nicholas as I hugged him and explained what a trigger was. He was just wonderful, loving and understanding once again for one so young. After that, Nicholas tried to be cognizant of his actions, trying hard not to upset me, knowing it's tough enough on me to experience those flashbacks.

Yes, It Took Fifty Years

As I continued my sessions with Dr. Amy and became more familiar and comfortable with the process, I worked to not repress anything any longer. I didn't have to pretend any more. I had lost much and had a right to be angry. My tears were now healing tears, and I knew that nothing bad would happen to me by exposing all I had been through and all I had kept hidden.

My sadness was very real, not a sign of weakness. Sometimes my tears were heavy. At other times, I felt awkward, sitting in front of Dr. Amy, struggling to control them. I felt then that they would never stop, and, still, a piece of me feared looking like a baby and inadequate when I tried to make sense of it all. My sessions were difficult, exhausting work.

Dr. Amy's constant assurance that I kept making great strides and her repeated reminders of how incredibly strong a woman I was kept me adamant about staying the course and on track.

Chronic loss and abandonment issues popped up consistently. Dr. Amy also helped me understand how the absence of a nurturing environment and the conditions I lived with as a child had a cumulative effect on my life. My awareness grew. Things became clearer. The messages I had received as a child—what I was taught to feel or not to feel—were distorted. I learned children *do* have rights. "Stop being a baby" and all the other wrong messages I had received needed to be deleted. Not being supported by my parents was just wrong.

I started to understand that being emotionally abandoned—given no direction or offered any solace as a child by any adult—had a great impact not only on my sense of self-worth, but also on that of my brothers and sister.

The unrealistic adult expectations placed on me at such a young age were too much for such a young person. They had left me, in a sense, physically abandoned as well. While the hours of caring for our mother's house and my siblings helped me negate my fears of abandonment, my boundaries were violated by physical, emotional, and sexual abuse. I became an object, not a treasured gift.

It is a birthright to be around responsible people, to be loved, nurtured, and protected. A parent's job is to make sure his or her child is not violated physically or psychologically. Not being protected made me believe that I had no value, caused me to always strive for acceptance, ache to be good enough, long for love and approval.

With Dr. Amy's help, I wondered no more why I felt so helpless and ashamed about my childhood. I had become a master at minimizing and pretending things were not so bad. Learning to speak my truth and not fear a consequence or punishment, plus eliminating the belief that no one would believe me, took a long time to get into my head. The unknown was quite frightening compared to what I knew. Dr. Amy made me aware that my habit of understating and discounting my feelings had gone on for so long, it had become a way of life, what I thought was normal, and that making the best of what I was dealt was not the right way to live.

As a child, I came to realize that the harder I tried to go above and beyond, to reach the unrealistic expectations I held about acceptance, love, and acknowledgment for a job well done, the more evident it became that I wouldn't get the pat on the back or "Good job!" It was just what was expected of me.

My emotional isolation and the lack of joy in my childhood formed my perception of my choices and my unrealistic thinking, setting me up for feeling never good enough, never accomplishing anything well enough. I internalized the sense that something was wrong with me. I always tried to quiet that inner voice that told me I was inadequate and damaged goods that, in turn, promoted more feelings of alienation and defeat. All my life I felt alone in this world, wondering why I didn't feel safe and why so many around me were so judgmental. Asking myself what would it be like to be loved unconditionally.

My sessions with Dr. Amy helped me to break through my sense of inadequacy and to understand the reasons for my emotions and beliefs. My world became less distorted.

I learned it is okay to ask myself, *What do I want?* or *What do I need?*—something that had never occurred to me. My inner being quieted when I remembered that I didn't need someone's approval or have to care what people thought of me. I realized that, over time, my self-validating would get easier, allowing me to be less dependent on others' opinions while I witnessed my growth on this path of recovery.

At one point, Dr. Amy thought it would be a good idea to put together a support team to delete the abuse team. For the next session, I invited one friend and one family member to share an hour with me at Dr. Amy's office. Before we got started, my brother asked, "Why now? Why all of a sudden this comes up? She's in her fifties."

Dr. Amy said, "Let's just hear what she has to say."

I did not go in with an agenda. I just shared whatever parts of my story came up. The hour seemed to be over in a blink. Before ending our session, Dr. Amy asked my guests if they had any questions.

My brother responded, "All of this is quite overwhelming. Some friends and family members believe she's an exaggerator and belongs in Hollywood."

Dr. Amy's comment was brilliant: "And you wonder why it took her fifty years?"

Another Chronic Illness

Shortly after that meeting, I was diagnosed with adrenal fatigue, something also referred to as hypoadrenia, a deficiency in the functioning of the adrenal glands, part of the endocrine system. In my research, I learned that the adrenal glands typically release a precise and balanced amount of steroid hormones into the body. Because the adrenal glands are designed to be so responsive to changes in the body's inner physical, emotional, and psychological environment, many factors can interfere with this well-tuned balance. Meaning too much physical, emotional, and psychological stress can deplete them.

I also read that the thyroid is another endocrine gland sensitive to the effects of stress. My physical, emotional, psychological story was starting to become clear. My list of symptoms, in hindsight, made sense to me, and it was no wonder I struggled through so many of my days. It was just another piece of the puzzle that added to my frustration and discouragement.

As I learned about this syndrome, I thought back to the days of exhaustion I experienced. I am grateful that I never gave up the effort to reclaim my health and my life. I now had one more clue of how my life had affected my health, and I was more determined than ever to do something about it.

Who's the Crazy One?

After working with Dr. Amy for a while, I realized that validation was important to my healing process. Speaking my truth and telling my story, naming things, helped me move forward. To have weathered the storms in my life, I had shut down, become robotic. I was weak from exhaustion and too overwhelmed to hear my God.

As my therapy sessions progressed, the stronger and clearer I became and the more I emotionally left the Foreman. He saw it as me pushing him away. In reality, I was only trying to stay safe. His increasingly diabolical behavior triggered memories of past abusive situations.

His continued irrational behavior was torture. Some days he would call me thirty to forty times with a barrage of emotions. One minute with a soft, sweet voice expressing how much he loved and missed me, the next minute, a snarling, angry voice telling me how wrong I was.

He often asked the same question, "Are you dating?" then hung up. Two minutes later, another ring. "Are you dating?"

This went on until I was half-crazed.

When I answered, "NO!" he would go into, "Are you seeing someone? Are you seeing someone?" It was like Tony's phone calls all over again except with a different message.

"Oh, my gosh! Stop! Please! This is crazy," I would try to break in. "Leave me alone." All day and night, he never let up, never listened, never heard my words about his irrational thinking being the cause of his (and our) problems.

This endless battle brought me again to a point of a sick stomach and trembling body. Most of my energy went toward keeping calm to do my work and to keep thinking clearly. Every phone I owned flashed with the Foreman's messages.

I was so distraught, I recorded those messages on that little tape recorder I used back in the Tony days and brought the recorder with me to a visit with Dr. Amy. All I thought was, *Please, someone, tell me I am not crazy.* I was so tired of looking for people with whom I could share what the Foreman was up to so I could watch for their reactions to know if I was nuts or if he was. Their initial expressions spoke volumes.

In Dr. Amy's office, I sat filled with anxiety as I pushed play. After listening to only a couple of the messages, she assured me it was abuse, pure and simple. How deplorable that I could not figure that out on my own. Despite my progress, I still struggled and lived with not knowing truth and seeing clearly. The Foreman worked on me so that I was in a state where I couldn't decipher anything and be clear on it. I needed HELP!

To those who ask now, "Why didn't you just get out?" I ask you, "How do you get out of something you don't know you're in? How do you recognize normal when you don't know what it is?"

With continued therapy, the physical abuse had become clear. The Foreman's emotional abuse was subtle. It snuck up a little at a time. I thought, *Since he never hit me, I just didn't understand him.* Again, my thoughts were, *What's wrong with me?*

The Foreman was so good at manipulating everything and everyone. Every person in his life either did not recognize it or was too frightened to say anything for fear of being belittled or further manipulated. I fell into the first category for a while, then the second, but eventually regained my power and after months, was able to fight my way clear of him.

Then there was the continuous battle over the housekeeper. He always complained about her behind her back, and I never got answers to my frequent questions. "Why does she stay all day when there is nothing left for her to do? Why does she stay nine hours every day, with no pay or for mere pennies? What's wrong with her? What's wrong with you?"

The Foreman would always answer, "She has no life," griping about her putting her nose where it didn't belong, having no boundaries. He'd mumble something about needing to get her a boyfriend to get her out of his hair.

I always told him, "Use your words (with her)."

He always replied, "They fall on deaf ears." What a dysfunctional mess.

I did get the chance to ask Francine why she continued to show up daily when there was so little to do. Why she continued to let her years of uncashable paychecks sit on the desk collecting dust. Surely she could find a job that paid her.

Francine tilted her head over to her left shoulder and said, "I'm stupid," with a whine in her voice. I walked away, thinking, *What a sick situation.*

Still Searching

Sessions with Dr. Amy did help me but were just not enough. I needed to learn or to know more. I wanted more clarity, so I made an appointment with Grace, another therapist. Thinking back to when I first met the Foreman, he spoke of how wonderful Grace was.

I was led to believe that she was a couples' therapist and that the Foreman saw her for the horrible treatment he had experienced at the hands of other women. I wanted to meet her, I think, mostly to see if he had lied about her as well.

I started my work with Grace with a few Reiki sessions. I was drawn to her and intuitively knew she would help me move forward. The Foreman *had* lied. She wasn't a couples' counselor. She was a substance abuse counselor and a hypnotist. When I learned this, I knew I had to see her more than once.

The five or six times I met with Grace were difficult. But my agenda was knowledge, and I kept my appointments with her for what she could teach me. I found myself learning about alcoholism. At times, I felt a bit sneaky, for she had no idea I was connected to one of her clients, but the knowledge I gained was lifesaving and worth the psychological discomfort.

Simple questions about alcoholics during our sessions brought me the answers I was looking for, but I wasn't prepared for all I learned about them and how they operate or think. As Grace taught me about alcoholics and their behavior, I cried. In fact, I spent much of my time with her in tears. What I learned applied to all men in my life, so Grace had no reason to question my tears.

It hurt to hear such truth. It hurt to finally understand how the Forman had played me all along. I was sickened to know that our relationship began with *betrayal.* He started with a lie, and he ended with a lie. My heart broke at the reality of what was exposed. I gave him my all, my heart and soul, my friends and family, my home and life. His deception crushed me.

My abandonment issues surfaced once again. I feared losing love all over again. My parents were not able to love and protect me; Tony loved the bars more than Nicholas and me; and now the Foreman was not willing to address his problems, not even for our love. How worthy or valuable was I? That question never left my thoughts.

The Forman's words, "You're the love of my life"—how precious were they when his vodka was his real love? I felt like a fool when I thought of how I had struggled with leaving him behind. Now I felt like I had left a broken little boy.

Initially, all I wanted to do was to teach him what I had learned. In hindsight, I know we were drawn to each other to move forward in our healing. I moved forward, but he chose not to, chose to stay in denial, to continue drinking and pretending he had it all under control.

Each session with Grace, as she spoke in general, I learned a little more about alcoholics. In just a short time, I had made a list that I used often to remind me of what I was really dealing with.

- Alcoholics are charming and manipulative.
- Alcoholics often think their partners are mean to them, often due to not remembering their own actions.
- Alcoholics don't know they are where they are.
- They live in a blackout state most of the time.
- Loved ones often don't recognize a blackout state.
- Two drinks can put alcoholics back into an alcoholic state.
- Alcoholics are capable of driving a car and doing other tasks while in a blackout.
- Alcoholics don't see or say it like it is.

People who live around alcoholics become hostages to the way alcoholics think. It started to become clear to me that all the Foreman's friends and family members were certainly held hostage. I now saw for myself how it just crept up on me. I became a hostage to avoid his irrational, jealous, insecure accusations. My little list clarified so much.

Something as simple as going with friends to weekly singing bowl meditation at a local church caused him to overreact. I explained repeatedly how relaxing and soothing the process was. We all laid on our yoga mats with blankets in the candlelight with a beautifully voiced facilitator.

Again, he didn't hear me, repeating the usual questions. "Who were you with? Where were you? Do you expect me to believe that?"

Each time I answered his questions honestly. Each time he repeated his questions until he drove me wild. I gave up my night out with the girls and invited him along.

Of course, after he experienced exactly what I spoke of, his comments were, "How dumb," and "I didn't get anything out of that."

The Foreman's paranoia continued. I started to leave the damned cell phone, which now *felt like a leash*, at home or in the car. If I shut it off, there was a problem. If I didn't answer it, there was a problem. When I chose to answer it, his questions about my whereabouts or whom I was with reeked of paranoid control, insecure jealousy, just plain bizarre behavior. I tired of this way of life and started ignoring him more, which only caused his actions to escalate, making him even more insecure.

It took me a long while to get Grace's words through my head. "No one can have a relationship with an alcoholic. No relationship with an alcoholic is healthy." She explained, "Something happens to their brains. Never will you get through to them. Never."

I struggled so with "never will I get through to him." I kept trying; it took me more than a year to understand it and get it. Until then, I couldn't help myself. I continued to explain to the Foreman that his behavior was destructive, even though Grace's words, "Don't even try until there is one year of sobriety at the very least," lingered in the back of my mind. For some reason, I continued to think this time would be different.

Beat Him at His Own Game

When I started working with Dr. Amy, the Foreman often told me that she was the wrong person for me to work with. In his sweetest voice, he'd tell me, "Honey, let me help you. You're crazy. You need help."

He called my friends and family members behind my back to inform them that I was in trouble. Claiming I was very fragile and that they needed to help him rescue me from those people who were bad for me. As he stated his love for me to them, he claimed he didn't know what else to do. I was crazy and he needed their help to protect me, to get me to the right doctors.

If he thought his actions wouldn't get back to me, he was wrong. I was livid! Even at that, I understood by that time how diseased his thinking had become. One last time, I went to him for some closure, still trying to leave him on a positive note with respect and no accusations. True to form, he became angered and manipulative.

I wasn't as composed as I thought. I realized in minutes of being in his company that I wasn't strong enough to combat a pro manipulator. Emotionally shaken, with trembling hands, I pulled out my list from Grace that I carried to read daily. I started to read what I learned; in the middle of the list, he sat untouched by my words and said, "I said it before and I'll say it again. You're with the wrong person." He repeated his words a few more times as I attempted to finish my list.

In my head, I knew this was crazy and asked myself once again how I got in this position when my intentions were so different. I got more upset and my body shook at the reality that he got me again. I was engaged—even if it was negatively—when I talked to him. So upset with the whole situation, I blurted out, "Grace taught me this."

The Foreman's expression was of shock, but he recovered quickly, responding, "Grace was good at nothing. She had no expertise. I saw her to quit smoking."

Our conversation became more heated. I reminded him she was the woman he raved about when we first met. All of a sudden she had no expertise?

For just a few seconds, he became enraged, with an expression on his face I'd never seen before. With clenched teeth he asked, "Are you trying to make me hate you?" He hated being caught at his own game.

I turned and walked out, relieved to be out of there, but proud, remembering Grace telling me that most women wouldn't have taken on the challenge. As I got into my car, I felt strong and empowered, thinking, *That's right. I am* not *most women.*

No Boundaries

I tried to tiptoe around the Foreman to the people in his life to perhaps have an intervention. My attempts fell on deaf ears. I realized then that all of them knew all along—they had all become accustomed to shoving the problem under the rug. I felt it was cruel of them to act as if there was no issue all this time, sucking Nicholas and me into their dysfunctional web. I was learning to listen to the Foreman's actions and not his words.

Five months after my PTSD diagnosis and I still struggled to get away from the craziness. The stages of awareness of the disorder are just that—stages—and the work is very difficult. It's normal to expect confusion and some back and forth as you delete and reprogram a lifetime of confusing messages. When you feel crazy, know that you are not. For me, it was a laborious process to do PTSD work while still being emotionally abused by the Foreman.

Despite the abuse, though, I continued to heal square by square, and I became more aware of what Dr. Amy meant about me being an incredibly strong woman. It truly is a miracle that I am *not* crazy; through the grace of God, I made it through some horrific storms.

I started to recognize that the Foreman had no boundaries, and it wasn't only about the drinking. I thought back to the day when I walked into his home unexpectedly; he never locked his door. He was sleeping in his bedroom, the door wide open, his body sprawled across his bed, his testicles exposed. The aroma of something baking was in the air. As I found my way to the kitchen, Francine sat at the table having a cup of tea. She informed me that the Foreman had been sleeping for an hour and he was exhausted from working through the night.

This whole scene sickened me. He tortured me with his accusations, and, clearly, he had different rules for himself. Behind Francine's back he would tell me how annoying she was. He really didn't care that she was trying to escape her own story. As a woman, I knew the housekeeper cared for him more than she let on and was only waiting her turn. It had nothing to do with cleaning his house.

It was clear the Foreman took advantage of her loneliness and her willingness to do things for him. Pretending she was in charge and the lady of the house irritated him, but he fed that dysfunctional behavior when it was to his benefit. They used each other and never caught on that that very behavior kept them so unhappy.

Vicious Cycles

My time with Dr. Amy was draining. I remembered more and more of my childhood traumas stuffed deep within me. One day I realized that all my life, my friends picked me. I always felt worthy and special when people I thought were nice wanted me to be their friend.

I know now that isn't the case at all; it's the law of attraction. You attract people who mirror the square you stand on. If you replace anger with happiness, you will no longer attract people who are angry. You will not need all that rage. If you replace fear with faith, faith-filled people will show up in your life, and so forth. Change is not easy, but without change there can be no growth.

Life stirs and invites us to change and grow every day. Look around at nature and, clearly, you will see the joy in change. I have learned to replace fear most of the time with faith, sorrow with joy, and have remembered to replace anger with peace. I understand now that I attracted the Foreman into my life to conquer my fear of abandonment, but it has been incredibly difficult taking my life back as well as my power.

The first graphic illustrates my constant, cyclical internal battle about who I was. Deep within me, I wanted to be worthy and loveable, but most of the evidence of my life disproved that, according to my self-perception. The second graphic shows my life in the other direction—the physical—where I dealt with myriad triggers, some subtle, others, blatant.

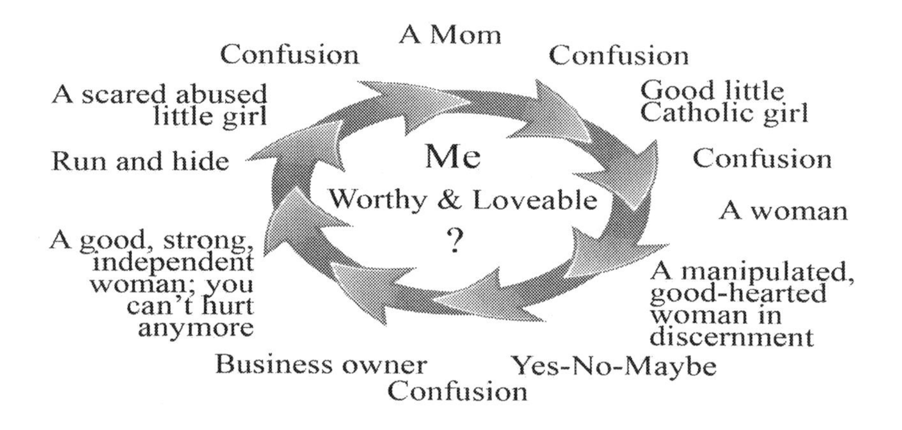

What's right? What's wrong? Who's right? Who's wrong?

What did I learn? What do I know?

Where am I going? What am I doing?

What am I deleting? What's the new program?

Grace's words, the Foreman's words, Dr. Amy's words, 24/7.

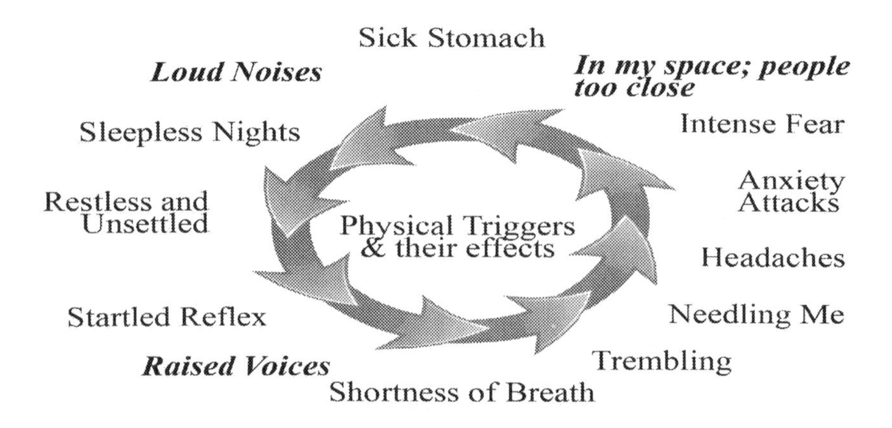

Once I understood that I was caught again in the contradictory, explosive world of alcoholism, I knew I was back in survival mode. I also knew by now that I had learned quite well to ignore my wants and needs. That is exactly what I was doing again before my breakup with the Foreman—making the best of what I had.

In the process of wanting the Foreman and me to work, to be good together, retrieving the goodness of our first year, or what I thought was a good year, I stood by him, supported him, tried couples therapy, even when he dropped the bomb that he was an alcoholic, despite my longtime, subconscious knowledge of his problem.

After my work with Dr. Amy, I came to realize that the Foreman's words that I needed therapy for wanting to be loved by every man I met were actually him speaking about himself on some level. It was he who had unhealthy connections with past women. It was he with the ex-lovers in his life. I learned somewhere that what you don't like about someone is really what you don't like about yourself. Like I said, we tend to mirror each other. And, of course, what we do like about someone is also what we like about ourselves.

Knowing My Triggers

Learning my recognizable triggers wasn't easy at first. I never knew when or what was going to take me back in time. Everyday things scared me—a loud clap, a knock on the door, the size of people, or how close they were to me. I felt trapped, vulnerable, and sick to my stomach. The stuffed memories kept coming up and out, and it was a miracle I had held it together without medication or hospitalization.

One evening when the Foreman and I were happy together, my brother Brian was visiting, and I was making dinner while we waited for the Foreman. I was at the stove checking on dinner when we heard a knock at the front door. Immediately Brian asked, "What was that?" I thought he was referring to the loud bang when, in fact, he was asking about what he'd just witnessed. As the Foreman entered my kitchen, Brian shared that I had a startle-reflex reaction and Nicholas ran and hid—all over a knock at the door. My brother's comments disturbed me. I didn't even realize my body reacted to a louder-than-normal noise, and I couldn't see around the corner to witness Nicholas's reaction.

The Foreman and Brian both concentrated on what was wrong with Nick and me. I tried to explain that it was a trigger, and that for Nick, it had become an automatic response since his father had frightened him so much. Out of Nicholas's hearing, I shared some of what Nicholas and I had been through with Tony.

The two responded, "He's not here now. He is old and bent over. He can't hurt you, so stop carrying on like this."

Nicholas's and my reactions were silly to both of them. They were both cold and clueless; the more they couldn't understand the severity of what we'd been through, the angrier I became.

I ended our evening early, escorted the Foreman out, and told my brother that he had no idea what our history with Tony was. That his assessment of Tony being old and debilitated had nothing to do with it. In those next ten minutes, I told Brian the boiling water story, how Tony punched me and knocked me out more than once. I explained how Tony tormented and abused Nicholas, adding "There are many, many stories like this. Do you still think that man would never hurt us?" Furious, I told him that you don't just wipe those memories away.

Brian said he'd had no idea. With a sick stomach and pounding head, I repeated his words, "That's right. You have no idea. I dealt with this hell all by myself because of the shame."

Still angered with how the whole evening went, I reminded him of the day he said, "I kind of thought you were a dipshit." His words had always puzzled me. I couldn't imagine why he thought such a thing of me. Obviously, they still bothered me enough to bring them back up after all this time. After I asked him to please go home, my last words that evening to Brian were, "If I were such a dipshit, I wouldn't be standing here today."

As I locked up the house, I thought, *Wow! Brian really has no idea who I am. But in only a few seconds, I spoke up about my reality. Truly, no one knows who I really am, only my maker, my Lord.* I wondered, *Will I ever feel safe enough to allow anyone to know the whole me?*

After Nicholas fell asleep later that evening, I called the Foreman, letting him know in no uncertain terms if he couldn't be kind and supportive of Nick and me as we try to overcome our triggers, we didn't need or want him in our lives. I was tired of never being heard, as a child and as an adult. "No more. I'm done." With simply no patience left, I hung up the phone. The Foreman must have realized that I was very angry. Days went by before he was brave enough to call.

In the next few weeks, things seemed to settle down with the Foreman and me. One calm evening, I suggested that his trust issues were part of our problem. If he dealt with them, his fear and jealousy issues would stop. I asked him to please get some help. I told him how grueling it was to live with such a vicious cycle.

"I can't share my days with you with complete honesty because I never know what will send you off into a jealous rage or what angle you will take to try to control things. Just think of your reaction to the handyman."

Within a month of meeting the Foreman, when talking about our day, I told him that my handyman asked if he could buy me a glass of wine someday.

The Foreman had asked, "Are you going to?"

I had shrugged my shoulders "maybe."

He pulled his hand from mine and pouted like a child—a red flag I wished I had paid attention to.

I was more aware of the problem those days but still believed that the Foreman would do what it took to be healthy and happy. After all, he wanted to marry me, and he knew I wouldn't marry that problem. The good little Catholic girl struggled with boundaries, but it was clear to me even then that I was distancing myself. I was disengaging, emotionally detaching. I had given so much of me that I had lost a part of myself. I wondered, *What is my identity?*

Lured in Once Again

The Foreman the manipulator was very good at what he did; he kept sucking me back in with his simple, everyday needs. I ended up helping him find a new place to live, helped him work through some of his money fears. He always needed something else. "Please help me pick out carpets." "…lighting." "…cabinets." The list went on.

I once asked, "What's wrong with Francine? You let her overstep her boundaries."

The Foreman's crude reply, "I don't want that bitch to be part of this; she already knows too much of my business."

I realized he didn't see the part he played in that dysfunctional mess.

I made the mistake of thinking that he and I could be friends. The Foreman's words, "Please help me with this," continued until his manipulation snuck up on me once again. It started to feel like we were boyfriend and girlfriend. There were more conversations and sharing, a meal here and there without the romance. Four months passed before I realized he was creeping back into my life, only moving slower.

Panic rushed through my body. I had worked too hard and had come too far. He hadn't changed. He hadn't done what he said he would—he just hid it better. I went back to my notes from my work with Grace, reread what life would be like living with an alcoholic. Life repeated itself.

I wrote the Foreman a letter explaining that his emotional abuse was making me sick, triggering old memories about my dad and Tony. I had made great progress with Dr. Amy, and it was essential that I be around people who treated me well.

I finally told the Foreman that his paranoid accusations needed to stop immediately, or I would take legal action. I realized I was still trying to reason with him while I was reprogramming how people treated me. I wasn't aware of how abnormal his actions had become.

Gentle, supportive, loving friends were what the doctor ordered. The Foreman did not fit the bill.

As I think back on his strange behavior and how it crept up on me this time, I wonder at my naiveté. I shrugged it off with "Oh, he's just having a bad day." Which seemed to be more often than not the preceding six months. When I read back in my journal, I realized I was too close to see how often those red flags popped up. It became a battle to figure out if what came from his mouth was truth or a game. I compulsively looked for clues to stay strong and clear.

My friends started to become just as disturbed with what they witnessed with the Foreman, often repeating, "He's just a different guy lately." At one time or another, they made a point to talk to him one on one, asking, "Where is the guy we know and love? We miss him." They all witnessed the repetitive words, the bizarre accusations—the progression of alcoholism. Discouraged that they couldn't reason with him, they admitted that he had fooled them as well.

The Breaking Point

In just a few weeks, we had a wedding to attend. The invitation had come more than a year ago. The mother of the bride, Tammy, was a client of mine who adored the Foreman. I called her to decline at the last minute, saying that things were very unsettled between him and me. He had become out-of-control jealous. Tammy talked me into still attending and said she would make a point of meeting with the Foreman before the event.

At that meeting, Tammy saw how difficult it was to reason with him. He worked on me for so long after that—his sweet talk, the flowers, sliding in that Tammy didn't know what she was talking about—I finally gave in just to end the discussion.

When we were apart, other things and people were more important to him.

The night before the wedding, we were to have dinner with some friends. That day the Foreman helped some friends of his, who also happened to be partiers. One thing led to another supposedly. The Foreman never got home to change for dinner and arrived to pick me up late. There he sat at dinner in a lovely restaurant in picnic clothes.

During dinner Bob and Donna took turns trying to reason with him about his thought process and bizarre accusations. They sensed I was disgusted with him and surely had a slow burn going as I bit my tongue not to lose control. If I dug deep inside, I would have realized I was madder at myself for even sitting there.

The Foreman just became more arrogant, repeating the same old accusations, speaking over everyone. The more people tried to reason with him, the more he carried on. In the middle of all this, I kept asking to be driven home. I didn't care anymore about ruining the evening. The Foreman had already ruined it. Please just take me home.

The drive home was silent. I couldn't get into my home fast enough. I fell into bed, dreading what tomorrow—the wedding day—would bring. Obviously, I still struggled to do what was best for me but didn't want to disappoint Tammy.

At the wedding the Foreman couldn't have been more attentive or more a gentleman, telling me how grateful he was to be given another chance. I wouldn't describe it as another chance; it was only to get this wedding commitment over with.

The other women at our table looked at us as if we had the greatest relationship. They envied my position, longing for their husbands to be so sweet. The Foreman looked at me with admiring eyes, showering me with sweet little kisses as he held me ever so close as we danced. He always attended to my chair as I approached the table, just plain treating me like a princess.

But things were finally different for me. All day long I couldn't help but to think about his behavior the day before, the choices he had made, and how my evening turned out. I didn't believe anything he said, didn't trust him anymore. I realized I had had enough. This was not anything I wanted. It would be too much work, with nothing in it for me.

Reaching My Limit

Two days after the wedding, we had two different funeral calling hours to attend. Both deaths were people close to us whose families did not know we were not together. One funeral was late afternoon, and the next in the early evening. Out of obligation, I felt I could get through the pretense of still being a couple.

The Foreman refused my calls most of the morning. He was pouting again. I had to woo him out of his mood. It felt like bad parenting, like giving chocolate to a toddler to stop his tantrum.

We went to the first calling hours and returned to his home around 4:00 p.m. to freshen up. I wasn't surprised to find the housekeeper just sitting there. For some reason, I could only image why, she left with an attitude. "What's up with her?" I asked. No answer. A few minutes later, I asked again, "What's Francine upset about?" Again, no response. The Foreman played people against each other. Typical behavior, controlling, manipulating—doing what he did best.

On our way home from the second calling hours, we called a local restaurant to order some grinders. He left his cell phone in the car when we went inside. When we returned to the car, he had two messages, both of them from ex-girlfriends. One needed to be rescued from a flat tire and the other just plain missed him.

"Okay. Is this behavior normal? You see nothing wrong with this situation?" I asked.

I waited until the next day to talk to him about how unsettling our mess had become and my decision that I'd had enough.

The Foreman went into attitude mode once he realized I was leaving him permanently, ignored my questions, then started playing his games, first asking me to be with him on Friday. Then, when I gathered up my things to leave, he didn't know what he would be doing on Friday. One minute he was having lunch with his boss, the next, he was having dinner with his boss.

Later, in a brief phone conversation, I could hear the ice cubes in the background each time he took a sip. His words switched from reasonable to unreasonable.

I hung up and decided to take a bubble bath to calm down and hopefully get a good night's sleep. Only minutes passed. The phone rang, and I let it go to voicemail.

"I guess you hung up on me because you're too busy for me. Do you see your behavior and how bad you've been treating me?" So it was my fault again.

I was crazed. I wanted to take a baseball bat to the phone so I would never have to hear that voice again.

He's crazy, that's all it is. He's lost his mind.

I shut off all the phones so I could get some sleep.

The next morning, I no sooner reconnected the phones and he called. He started in right where he'd left off the previous evening. He had himself in a such a state, he repeated himself to the point my whole body trembled. There was that woodpecker again.

I drove to his house ready to explode. I couldn't get there fast enough. He wouldn't answer his door. I was furious—enraged at this point. I wanted to tell him off and give him the good-bye letter I wrote in the early hours of the morning. I could have unlocked the damned front door with my key, but deep inside I feared what I might do being so angry. I left the letter in his truck.

Back home, still very shaken, I called the telephone company to change my phone number to unlisted and unpublished, a huge step that told me I finally decided to get off the back-and-forth square. I was finally leaving him and moving forward. I had learned some very hard lessons at last.

All day the Foreman left message after message at the salon, one minute sweet, next minute angry, interrupting my business. I turned the answering machine volume down. That leash—the damn cell phone—tucked away in my lunch bag underneath the receptionist desk rang all day as well. I arrived home to eighteen more messages. All forty-two messages that day were *exactly* the same.

That last week with the Foreman was nothing but a nightmare. I felt like an internal switch had finally turned on. I would never again accept what I DID NOT WANT. I was really done. It had taken many months to understand the deeply embedded messages of my childhood and the role they played in my choices.

I had done a lot of very hard, difficult work. My battle of what was best for me and in my highest good was over. I was clear that I would never allow myself to be abused by another human being, even if it meant I stood alone as I always had.

Who's the Fool?

Leaving the Foreman physically and emotionally was a long and exhausting process.

I thought about my struggle for sanity. What was right and what was wrong? Who was telling the truth? Who was lying? Tony was just who he was. He liked to hang out at the bars and drink. When he worked, he worked hard. When he didn't, he didn't.

The Foreman fooled me. He didn't hang out at the bars, and he worked every day.

I was surprised to learn only two percent of alcoholics don't work, and most repeat themselves when they've consumed a lot of alcohol, one way they try to keep you in the relationship. That explained all of the Foreman's messages left on my phones. Alcoholics pretend to think something about you that pushes your buttons—that compels you to defend yourself—to keep you engaged with them and keep the battle going. I just kept trying to show I was not to blame, something I had felt since I was a little girl. And the Foreman knew that was one of my buttons—that's why he kept pushing it.

He pretended to believe I was seeing someone else to keep me engaged. He didn't care if it was a negative response or not—he had my attention. The more I defended myself and my actions, the more he pretended I was pushing him away. He was very clever with his manipulation, and I, in my vulnerability, continued to try to get through to him.

By now Grace had figured out I was involved with an alcoholic on some level. At my last session with her, I asked, "As a woman and professional, what can you leave me with?"

She said, "You should believe in what you know, and you must remember that you are not to blame."

Grace then went through all that she taught me on how alcoholics behave. As she finished summarizing our work together, I said, "I know all that, but I still feel like he played me for a fool."

She quickly jumped in with, "You are no fool. The alcoholic plays himself for a fool."

As I struggled to really leave the Foreman, I would share more and more of what I learned with him. The rule about absolutely no communication for a year didn't go over well. He tried to work me, telling me that Grace never really said that. Then he wanted to know whether the year was from the last drink or the last drunk. When he heard it was from the last drink, he again diminished Grace's professionalism and knowledge on the subject. "Why a year?" he asked.

I reiterated Grace's words, "Alcoholics are charming and manipulative. Their voice will suck you in, and you're right back where you started, and nothing has changed. Also, memories of the good times and places can help you to forget the bad stuff." That was exactly how our last year played out. I was heartbroken over the good times, over losing what I thought we had together.

The phone messages started again, trying to convince me we both made mistakes. He told me we should learn from them and stop living in the past. I wanted nothing to do with it. I knew only too well, just another attempt to manipulate me. And nothing was going to change for him.

Setting Limits

As I chipped away at the reality of what I came from, I became more and more aware of specific beliefs I had internalized, some helpful, many hurtful. Learning to feel comfortable asking myself questions like, *What do I need? What do I want? What will I accept or not accept?* felt foreign at first. Once I learned to identify my wants and needs as an adult, they didn't seem to be much different from the wants and needs of my childhood—to be safe, to play and jump with joy, to be held, to be loved, and so on.

I started to tiptoe around setting limits and boundaries, concepts and skills that were new to me. I wasn't very good at it at first. I was unclear how to define my separateness. I had to unlearn what had been, to me, normal, though hurtful, behavior and become able to recognize abnormal behavior. These were difficult lessons at first. Where was the line, and how did I draw it?

As I started on this new road, I got confused, became overwhelmed. As I struggled to stand up for myself and insist on change, my body would tremble. I cried, became so upset that I had to call Dr. Amy to help me stay clear and strong.

Each time I found myself in this type of battle, Dr. Amy would ever so gently remind me that I made a choice—to live a happy, healthy, normal life with happy, healthy people around me to love and support me. Her next question always was, "What do you need to do to achieve your goal?" Her words always reminded me to go back to my what-square-am-I-standing-on process.

Some days I would worry, *Will I get through this?* I had so much work to do and so much to learn or figure out. I now see that even when I felt I was going in circles, spiraling downward, I was still making progress and moving forward, one gentle, divine nudge at a time, healing and growing at every turn. I began to believe there would always be another way, another friend, another job or opportunity. My alternatives were limitless and open to divine guidance.

My friend Tina, the founder and director of SOUL (Source of Unconditional Love) Center, was of great solace to me that year. Our lengthy conversations about my inner growth were comforting and supportive. She often would suggest that I burn pink candles to change negative energy into positive. She helped me to see my options, always reminding me all that I was going through was a normal part of the process of change. She constantly repeated, *"No more abuse,"* showing me it had only stopped my growth.

She often reminded me to pay attention to what my gut was telling me. She taught me to slow down, breathe, and bring any idea to my solar plexus, where I should feel—feel the joy, fear, uneasiness, or whatever came up—something I had lost along the way. I was too busy simply fighting to survive. In addition, she taught me to repeat, "I am now in the process of..." and to fill in the blanks with whatever I needed to do.

Through her, I continued to learn how to regain my power. I learned not to rush into yes or no answers, to sleep on it, to keep my vision, put it in writing, and then visualize some more.

I started to learn to take time for myself and to allow myself to attract people who were harmonious with my wants and needs. She counseled me not to fear another abuser, to trust that I would recognize one much sooner than in the past.

I found that taking care of me first and not giving up my power was not easy.

An important lesson for me was to stop thinking I had to help everyone who needed or asked for it. Tina taught me that I don't have to invest anything to deserve love. Sharing love is not about giving or taking or keeping track. It's just for the sake of sharing. She helped me see that many people in my past had other agendas. She said it well. "Don't worry about the people in your past. They are not in your future for a reason." That was huge! I'd outgrown them and decided to move forward to become a better person. I don't have to rescue anyone. It's okay for people to struggle. That's how they learn, how they help themselves.

Tina always said that I could help and teach others by sharing my story, basically, my "been there, done that." Those words took on a new meaning. I no longer saw them as "How horrible." I now add to them, "And take a look at me now!"

Taking My Power Back

My heart was beginning to open up again. I was letting go of the wounds one at a time. My emotional baggage became lighter with every step I took. My shame and guilt left me as I worked through my abandonment issues. I started to believe that I did have worth, that I did matter.

In the nine months that I had worked with Dr. Amy, she had remained consistent, reminding me what an incredibly strong woman I was as she continued to walk me through my story. I could now see that being vulnerable didn't mean being weak. I felt like I was walking on less shaky ground. Validation was like opening a door, with one new form of awareness appearing after another. Even with all the hard work I'd done, I knew the work would be lifelong and was necessary for healing to occur.

The reality of all that I had lost or that I'd never been given was shocking. Some days, I was numb with disbelief; other days, I was angry as hell. Some days, I fought hard not to stay on the this-isn't-fair square. I knew too well that would only make me go backwards, and that was not an option in my new world.

Speaking my truth stopped the denial. No more secrets. Grieving became essential. As my grieving process continued, I became less dependent on others' approval. I began to trust my own perceptions more and to feel stronger and empowered. I wasn't crazy after all. Chronic loss is chronic loss. Wrong is wrong.

With more knowledge and understanding, I did things differently, just like Louise Hay taught me. Remember, she says, "We are all victims of victims. Our parents could not possibly have taught us anything they did not know."

As I became stronger, clearer, and more balanced with peace and joy in my heart, I looked forward to experiencing the life I deserved. Changing one thought after another.

As my healing became evident to me, I started to think about how my relationship with a long-time friend had changed. We had seen less of each other over the past year. She had so many changes in her working world, and I was busy with my sessions with Dr. Amy. I decided one morning that since I had worked so hard in therapy, I would give my friend a call, try to get back on track. I missed our once-a-month lunches and just being girls together, talking, laughing, shopping, whatever.

My friend was distant and cold with a sharpness to her voice that I didn't understand. Still, she agreed to meet me for lunch the next week.

We sat down and started with some general catch-up small talk when my friend abruptly jumped in with, "Let's do what we came here to do." Then she started in on me. I had hurt her, she said. She had a list of my wrongs, a list she'd kept for years. Each item she called me on left me more puzzled than the one before it.

Startled, I thought, *Who am I talking to? Who is this person sitting across from me, pointing and waving an accusatory finger at me, at times only inches from my face, that nasty look on her face and a growl in her voice?*

Her list went on and on. I was wrong for this thing or that—holiday and birthday celebrations handled incorrectly or not at all, business moves bungled.

This was how our lunch played out. I was more confused than anything and spent most of the time trying to figure out how all this had become so bizarre. Where was I when all this anger developed? Wondering, *Am I really hearing all this craziness?*

In my disbelief, and trying to process what I was in the middle of, I knew that this was the first time I would speak my truth and stand up for myself. I was quite upset, but I moved forward anyway.

My eyes filled with tears, my voice trembled, my hands shook. I wasn't prepared for this attack, but I had intuitively brought along one of my daily readings to have as a crutch in case I needed it. I knew I didn't have the words yet to express what I needed to say, and it was the perfect message for this situation. It was about how the "I'm telling you this for your own good" argument—used in anger and resentment—serves that person in a negative way and does not help their growth.

I believe my friend's intention that day was self-serving and without compassion. She was closed to hearing anything I said before she even sat down. Her body language expressed that as well, along with her rolling eyes. She didn't understand that I didn't know how to take care of myself yet and wasn't brave enough to express what I felt in my heart. I wanted to tell her, "No! You can't do this to me anymore!" But I still didn't have the strength to do it on my own and had to use someone else's words.

So based on my daily reading, I tried to tell her a story about a young woman who was excited about her growth and how she had changed for the better. Later that same woman was frustrated and depressed. When push came to shove, she repeated some of her own mistakes from old beliefs. She complained, "I thought I knew better."

My friend was clearly growing impatient with me. I continued anyway, telling her, "We all contradict ourselves, forget our intentions, and wander off our path. Take one step forward, two steps back. It's all good. Progress is not linear, not a straight line from A to B. We may all make new starts, only to fall back again. But we learn from both the forward and backward motion, and from each movement, we are wiser.

"I've been to hell and back, some days to the point I could hardly breathe. But I know I am a good person who would never intentionally hurt anyone, never mind make a list of their so-called mistakes behind their back for years. I need to be around people who love and respect me and support me, not judge me."

Her last words were, "I don't know what to tell you."

By that time, I had my composure back and with a strong voice said, "And I don't know what to tell you." We paid our lunch bill and departed.

I walked to my car, feeling free. I had spoken my truth without worry of a consequence or a price to pay. I had been rejected in some form all my life. I refused to allow anyone or anything to make me feel like that again. I felt wonderful, like I was on top of a mountain, and not for a moment did I think, *What did I do wrong?* I had lived fifty years thinking that way. No more! I am no longer willing to carry around pain in response to someone else's actions.

I did spend the next week, though, analyzing and processing the bizarre events of list making, harboring grudges, finger pointing. I talked to Dr. Amy about it. She said it is always a good thing to validate feelings. I did attempt to validate my friend's feelings by letter. I said I was sorry she walked around for so long thinking those things. If she had only spoken up, she would quickly have learned it was only our perceptions were at different ends of the pole—not wrong, just different. I wondered why she thought her needs from me would be the same as my needs from her—she had a partner and a mother to love and care for her. I had neither, ever.

My good friend Catherine always says, "When faults are thick, then love is thin." I know no one ever walks this Earth without some lessons to learn, and I'm sorry my former friend saw things as she did, but I believe it really had nothing to do with me. If I were so horrible, she would not have been a friend for so long.

Some Peace

I did my best to calm down and try again for a more settled life. Struggled to get back to the life I lived before the Foreman walked into mine. I had so much work to do; it saddened me to realize what square I was on and how much of my life I wasted trying to reason with another alcoholic.

I asked myself continuously, *How did I get in this situation again? How did I not see through all that charm?*

I was angry at myself for trying so hard, for being so gullible, for being kind and supportive to a man whose main agenda was to hide his alcoholism.

Each break-up with the Foreman helped me detach from him emotionally but only gave him the desire to work me even more. Now, without his constant pecking at me, I slowly started to find some minutes of my day where I was not in anxiety mode.

Nevertheless, just seeing his phone number on caller ID or hearing his voice in a message triggered PTSD symptoms. I spent much of my time analyzing my everyday moves and decisions. It was a battle to stay clear and focused, to find my way to reach my goal. I fought an almost-constant, overwhelming urge to speak my mind to him. I needed to remind myself constantly that it didn't matter what he said or what he thought. You can't reason with an alcoholic. I wouldn't get hooked again.

When I changed my home phone number, he had the new number within twenty-four hours and left those tormenting messages again. I thought, *What was the use of having the number unlisted and unpublished?* I immediately called to have it changed again, explaining to the phone company it was given out. I didn't receive a call at home for two weeks. What a pleasant change. Home was finally becoming a peaceful haven.

He Didn't Hook Me

Even though the phone didn't ring, my inner battle was still a constant. Blame was the next message to delete. With Dr. Amy's help, I continued to work hard to teach myself that I wasn't to blame for everybody's dysfunction, toxic lifestyles, their problems, my childhood, etc. That my history couldn't hurt me anymore. That I deserved harmony in my life and was worthy of nurturing relationships. If I could accept those ideas, I wouldn't feel so trapped.

Just one day after I changed my home phone number the second time, the Foreman called my cell phone eleven times. As I deleted his repetitive messages, he pulled up and parked in front of my business. I couldn't control my bodily reactions. I immediately went into a panic. My heart raced, pounding out of my chest, my body shuddered. I thought, *Would I be able to care for myself being face-to-face with him?*

Breathe, I whispered to myself. *Breathe. You can do this.*

The next minute he drove away. I sighed one big breath of relief.

The day after, as I locked up the salon for the evening after a long day, I turned to walk to my car and there he was. He appeared out of nowhere, scaring the daylights out of me, and followed me to my car. He started in again with he loved me and wanted to help me. Help get back on track. He tried to come closer to hug me.

He asked, "Can I kiss you?"

I put my hand out. "Just stop!"

He continued to plead with me, "Let me find you different doctors. You're getting worse by the day."

All along, Grace's words swirling through my head as I attempted to appear in control. *You can't reason with an alcoholic. They're charming and manipulative.*

The Foreman told me that I was too close to see how much I had changed, to see how sick I was. Everyone was talking about it, and everyone kept asking him, "What's wrong with her?"

Anger flooded my whole being. I wanted to hit him, pound on his chest, knock him down, kick him. Anything to just get him away from me. Or me away from him.

"You bastard! How dare you sneak up on me in the dark, scaring me like that? Get away from me." He didn't budge, so I started shouting, "Get away from me" over and over.

He stormed to his car, yelling, "You're crazy!"

I quickly got in my car and locked the doors. As I calmed down and caught my breath, he drove away.

I wished I had more composure and control, but I still took a step forward, awkward or not, and reminded myself that change is incremental—it happens a little at a time. But I was tremendously proud of myself! He didn't hook me. That was what was most important. For now, just let me get home.

Slipping Backwards

In the middle of cleaning a few days later, I came across an incredibly loving message in a card from the Foreman. For a moment, I went back to when things were good between us. I wanted to call him.

No, I told myself. *Stop. Remember all you learned. The man you long to be with is not there—and never was.*

I was exhausted emotionally. Learning to fill the void, the emptiness, the feelings of being abandoned again roared through my body. My head told me, *Yet another person didn't want you.* Even though I knew enough to know that wasn't true, the thought was there. My battle to crawl out hadn't ended when I broke it off with the Foreman.

Three and a half weeks after I changed my phone number the second time, I felt like I was starting to make progress taking my power back again. I was finding some peace. My body was calmer. When your belly is calm, it's a sure sign you're on the right track.

Then I received a call that one of my brothers was in the hospital. Without thinking, I called the Foreman. *Of course*, he was ready to help. With his sweet voice, he told me to come right over.

Only moments after arriving at his home, I knew I had stepped backwards. *What was I thinking? What was wrong with me?* No, wait. That's just it—I wasn't thinking. What could he possibly do to help? Just looking at his face, my body reacted as if it were in danger.

Get out, I told myself. *Get out fast.* I did.

Once I was home I cried for hours, tears of joy because I recognized how close I had come to crawling back into the mess with the Foreman, tears of sadness for what was, and tears of worry for my brother.

I just let my tears come, and they were healing. My next few days were better. I felt that I was moving forward. I had fewer conversations going on in my head. I felt like rejoicing. I had more peace in my life, even though the struggle of disengaging from the Foreman was ongoing.

Almost Caught Me

It was Labor Day weekend. Even though my friends were close by, loneliness surfaced in bits and pieces. When you are used to sharing with a significant other, you are bound to feel emptiness for a while, but I knew true happiness starts within.

I was doing my best to heal and take care of me, but I still reeled from the hurt of the Foreman's betrayal. It was like a knife stuck in my side, a knife I just couldn't seem to pull out.

I no sooner had gotten a full night's sleep than he was back with his "sweet" agenda. The next morning, I discovered a note on the windshield of my car. He offered the use of another cell phone because he canceled the service on the phone he gave me for my birthday. The note went on that it was "just a friendly gesture" and he wanted nothing else. Yet he *wanted* me to contact him; he was looking for Dr. Amy's phone number. Or to have Dr. Amy call him because he *wanted* to get Francine to go see her. The Foreman commented he knew I was home and was only avoiding him. Adding, if we were in love, we should be able to talk this through and things would be different. The last few months he had felt ignored. "Let's talk and work this out. I love you. You're the love of my life."

As I read the note, I now recognized his manipulations. My blinders had been removed. Despite that, his invasion infuriated me.

You crazy bastard, I thought. *Your logic and reasoning are totally absent.*

This was his sick attempt to try to engage me in any conversation at all. Besides, he kept trying to compare the old us to my married friends, and we were not married. Who taught him this behavior is okay? It's abusive. How many other women live this kind of nightmare?

His next move was to stick a newspaper clipping between the doors at the salon. It was an ad for help with "your defiant child" and getting back control of your family. Stop the arguments and the tantrums. The ad talked about bipolar and ADHD children.

Oh, my gosh! You BASTARD! Now attacking my son!

But soon I started to doubt myself. Worried, *Was I too close To see any of this with my son?* The Foreman's gall leaving such an ad at my door shook me. I had to be sure!

Nicholas's vice principal, who happened to be a client, was due in that day. I showed the ad to her since she had kept a motherly eye on Nick for me while he was in school. After one quick glance at the article, she assured me that he was a well-adjusted child, adding that whoever left it was way off base. Oh, the relief.

My frustration soared. I would not allow this man to make me feel crazy any more. Or make me question my own awareness and judgment. He almost caught me again.

I continued to call Dr. Amy when I was confused or upset. Her calming words once again, "You're choosing a good life, not an abusive one, starting now."

One Little Thread at a Time

As I calmed down, I affirmed to myself that, yes, that was exactly what I was doing. I remembered an article I had read recently by Dr. Phil. The main message, "Don't accept anything you don't want." That became my new mantra. I posted it all about, in my bathrooms, in my prayer corner, at work. My vacillating emotions seemed to subside when I remembered it.

I had spent so much of my life unconsciously trying to prove I was not to blame for whatever was wrong. I did it as a child, with Tony, and now with the Foreman. My fear of abandonment, sense of unworthiness, and fear of not having enough added to my long struggle. But I did hold on to a sense of pride that my past struggles had not left me bitter—only better. And this too shall pass.

I spent an enormous amount of time trying to figure out what the Foreman and I mirrored in each other. What aspect of him was an aspect of me? Some of his traits frightened me. Could I also be a master manipulator? Could I be so jealous and insecure? These questions tormented me. I had to know so I could continue to break from my past.

Over time, I understood the true mirror. We had lost our power, or it was taken from us. We were two broken, little children in adult bodies looking to be loved and valued. We just chose different ways to deal with it, or not deal with it.

The clearer I became that the Foreman was an abuser, the shield of loving him now removed, the more abusive he became. He was scared and had no boundaries, and he took my new boundaries as me ignoring him.

His bizarre behavior crept up on me. Despite my need to break away from him, I still felt compelled to try to help him. I hadn't completely moved off that square yet, even though I knew he had to do his own work. I was too busy being supportive and trying to help him do what he needed to do, being the good little Christian girl again. Without realizing it, I became a hostage again, a little more each day, one little thread at a time.

The Foreman kept trying to get his point across about how sick I was and that I was getting sicker by the day. He saw my PTSD symptoms as getting worse, when, in fact, Dr. Amy assured me that it was normal, very normal, for these things to happen—that the triggers, the jumpiness, the old, suppressed memories popping up when you are ready to handle them is a normal part of healing. I wasn't getting worse. I was getting better, and more aware. I was finally healing on many levels.

It became quite evident the more I was around the Foreman toward the end, the jumpier I got. His mannerisms became a trigger while I was working through my past traumas. His behavior brought my body back to that frightened little girl hiding in closets or sleeping with a knife under her pillow.

For the few months that we still had any interactions, I stayed clear with my decisions, no matter how many angles he used or how many promises he made to get back into my good graces. His lies continued, along with his vacillating sweetness.

"You're the love of my life" didn't work anymore. That infuriated him. I stayed strong. I was exhausted but determined to end the struggles and take care of *me*.

My peace only lasted a short while. Since the Foreman didn't get anywhere with his new promises, he started leaving nasty messages again on the machine at work. Now, I was the liar. I'd said we'd always be friends and we would always talk. He was angry that I had cancelled his hair appointments, asking me, "What does that say about your image?" He called the machine twenty-six times from the early afternoon through the wee hours of the morning with the same question, except that with each call, his words became either more slurred or more mumbled. He said I should look in the mirror, then dredged up the single and flirt accusations. A broken record.

To aid in my healing, separate from Dr. Amy, I started to meet once a month with HEAL: Healing Emotionally Abused Lives. At first, it was difficult to sit there and listen to everyone's story without feeling, *Oh! I can help them.* Eventually, I figured out it wasn't my job.

I'm not a victim anymore, nor was it my job to fix anyone else. I'd come a long way.

The next thing I'd know, I was choking with guilt over leaving the Foreman, as if I were to blame for that mess. Eventually, I'd remember that I was just living my life. Can you imagine feeling guilty of that.

Compassion Gone Wrong

Thanksgiving morning, as I went to Mass, I realized I was grateful for all I had been through. My spiritual director's message repeated in my mind, "We have to go through what we go through to get where we're going." There are no wasted moments or wasted experiences. I felt a great sense of relief. At this moment of prayer and peace, the Holy Spirit poured into me like an ocean wave, bringing me to tears, big, beautiful tears of gratitude at how far I had come. It was a memorable and beautiful experience. I felt so much at peace.

The rest of my morning was a little tougher. The Foreman kept calling on the cell phone, playing heartbreaking songs that would make anybody cry, with each call begging me to please call him. I had a difficult time with him being so alone and upset, being that it was a major holiday. Distancing and disengaging aren't easy. I discussed inviting him for the day with Nicholas. Nick showed some hesitation. Even at his young age, he tried to protect me.

My compassion for someone alone on a holiday got the better of me. I found the Foreman crying, drinking, and still listening to that heartache music. It was a sad, pathetic sight. He was still so unaware of the part he played in his loneliness.

He didn't appear drunk, so I invited him to Thanksgiving dinner, making it clear to him that it was just a meal, so he wouldn't have to be alone. He assured me he was very clear with the stipulations and expressed his gratitude.

I treated the Foreman with respect as I would any guest at my home. Danielle arrived around the same time as the others. We had a nice meal and shared our holiday. The Foreman was the last to leave, and Danielle was coming back the next day to help make Christmas cookies. It was something she looked forward to doing with us.

Friday came and went. Danielle did not make it over to the house like she had planned. Later that evening, though, she called me. She was upset, crying hysterically, and talking so fast I couldn't make out her words at first. I was able to calm her down enough to finally understand her. She explained that her dad just called her a lowlife and told her she wouldn't ever amount to anything. All because she didn't show up to make cookies as she promised. I assured her she was a lovely, sweet young lady, to shut her cell phone off, and go enjoy her night like any sixteen-year-old should.

I couldn't sleep. I kept waking up with Danielle on my mind, knowing all too well what she was living. I identified so readily with her. I was that little girl no one protected, listened to, or helped. Danielle didn't have a brother to give her a knife or any support to keep her feeling safe.

Saturday morning the Foreman showed up at my salon with a thank-you card. He wrote in it that I made the family happy by having him over for Thanksgiving dinner and to remember, I was family. He also brought me some homemade clam chowder. He invited Nick and me to come over to help teach his older children how to make clam chowder like their dad. He had no idea Danielle had called me the evening before so upset over his abusive words to her.

I was angry when he walked in with that ridiculous attempt to trap me again hidden behind the thank-you card. He thought that if he were a gentleman, I would forget his past behavior and just shove it under the rug. I let him know once again that I would not stand by and watch him abuse his beautiful daughter.

Between clients, I connected with Danielle, checking in with how she was doing and how her night went. I asked her permission to speak to her mom about our phone call. With a sigh of relief, Danielle said she would like me to do that and then shared more of the story.

Her dad blamed her for me and Nick not coming over that night to make chowder. I tried to console her by explaining that none of that was true, that it was actually all about her dad's choices. I told her, "Please don't ever believe those words." I assured her that I loved her. I spent much of the rest of my day in discernment over what I would say to her mom without stepping over anyone's boundaries.

This situation with Danielle and her father was clear to me. I couldn't just sit and do nothing. Knowing that another child was living with such confusion brought my blood to a boil. I wouldn't be a bystander. I wasn't a bad little girl, and neither was Danielle. These messages were and are just wrong. No child should be subjected to such inappropriate messages and then have to spend a lifetime figuring out how to crawl out.

One More Child

I knew I was taking a chance meeting with Danielle's mom, but for the Foreman to blame his daughter and to speak to her in that abusive manner was just not acceptable. I could only hope her mother would be strong enough and open enough to do something to protect her.

I met with Stephanie right after work that day. I shared the phone experience her daughter and I had the night before. I was clear with my view this behavior wasn't healthy for a young lady who was at such a vulnerable, impressionable age.

Stephanie seemed to understand and shared her thoughts about why she thought the Foreman's older children made the choices they made. She believed it was due to their parents' history and how they related to that. Stephanie shared some of their story. She then opened up enough to go into some of her own story and spoke of the people who have put her down. One relative did as soon as she entered a room.

I had to ask, "What do you do to take care of yourself?"

"Oh! I just ignore him," with a nonchalant shrug of her shoulder.

Do you, I thought. With the little she shared of her own story, it was evident to me that she got and was still getting the wrong messages. She didn't see it happening in her own life, so how could she recognize it in her daughter's?

Unfortunately, her words and actions during my visit proved to me this was everyday life to Stephanie, and she really didn't see a problem. Before I left, I shared three numbers with her—for the local social services, Alateen,[4] and Dr. Amy, suggesting that perhaps one of these places would be a good start and a safe place for Danielle and, maybe, for her, too, to find someone to talk to.

On my way out the door, Stephanie told me she wasn't even aware I had received such a distressed call from her daughter. She decided to tell me about a message from Danielle she saved on her answering machine at work, insinuating their likeness.

I couldn't help but to ask, "When was that?"

Her response, "Oh, four or five years ago."

I left, my gut wrenched, to know Danielle had lived that way for at least four years and no one recognized it. I had to assume this abuse probably had been going on her whole life. And this was their normal.

Poor Danielle. Another child getting the wrong messages. How much pain would she have to live through before she figured it out? Again, how do you get out of something you don't know you're in?

---

[4] Alateen, part of the Al-Anon Family Groups and an age-specific Al-Anon group, is a twelve-step program specifically for young people affected by someone's drinking.

I headed over to pick up Nicholas. On our way home, I had to drive right past the Foreman's house. I struggled. I so wanted us to be part of the chowder-making gathering. For a moment, I even put it on Nicholas, asking, "Do you want to go?" I caught myself. I started to repeat my mantras and searched for Dr. Amy's words, "You are choosing a good life." Grace's words, "Remember what you know."

I took a deep breath. No. I refused to take a step backwards and enter that home pretending that everything was all okay until the next incident. That would mean I accepted the way the Foreman treated his child. Even though I longed for the family piece I so wanted to experience again, I drove home to make Nick and me a nice dinner. Knowing for now, the two of us were all the family I needed.

The Truth as He Saw It

I prayed for continued clarity and strength to choose what was best for me. I closed my eyes and envisioned a pretty pink bucket embossed with lace. A girly, frilly container sent from heaven full of strength and courage. I let the contents cover me like a cozy blanket. The warmth reminded me that I was strong and well.

Once emptied, I used the bucket to send back all that was not working for me to God to transform, asking, *Please, Lord, take this hell from me.* At times I laughed out loud, envisioning the angels pulling up my bucket, saying, "Here comes another one!"

I crawled into bed that evening, grateful I made it through another day without stepping backward and only sidestepping a short while.

That evening was the third night in a row I woke up at 1:33 a.m. Doreen Virtue writes when you continue to see the same numbers, it's the angels trying to get your attention. I looked up 133 in her book, *Angel Numbers*, written with Lynnette Brown: "The ascended masters are supporting your healing work by helping you have positive thoughts, intentions, and affirmations. They're whispering divinely guided ideas of love to you, so be sure to notice your musings and insights." What a comforting message to read in the middle of a night of restlessness and discernment.

I became accustomed to leaving the cell phone in my car to avoid being disturbed or upset. That particular evening, the Foreman left five messages. Angered I didn't show up to make chowder, he rambled on with the usual: He didn't make me cry; that nut doctor I was seeing did that to me. He wasn't the problem at all. I was the one who was sick.

He just kept on, telling me that I lied, that Grace never taught me the rule of one year sobriety before you even think of having a relationship. That having him over for Thanksgiving was just a joke. That I was no different than Phyllis [one of the women he spoke of when we first met who supposedly treated him so badly]. That I should think about how nice Thanksgiving was and how I was throwing it all away.

When I was emotionally stable, I should let him know, because he needed to find someone more stable. My childhood issues were my problem, not him, and thank God he wouldn't be around for it. All in one message. Arrghhh!!!!

Now that's a very stable, sound-minded man who really wants the "love of his life" back! I thought.

His next phone call went off on a different angle. Nicholas and I were the only two not present at the family gathering. His brother stopped by and was shocked we weren't there. The Foreman stretched my once-a-week session with Dr. Amy to three or five, saying all those sessions did nothing.

I wasn't allowed to be around Danielle anymore because I was so sick. I wasn't to contact her, and if she called me, I wasn't to answer the phone.

What?

The next message was back to how nice a day we had on Thanksgiving. I couldn't help but to say to myself, *Make up your mind, crazy man.*

He couldn't believe how much Nicholas had grown. Couldn't I see how happy Danielle and Nick were when they were together? What the eff was wrong with me, ruining the family like I was? I seldom heard the Forman use the eff word. He must have really been crazed.

He said friends told him to run as far away from me as possible. His next sentence, "How can I help you?"

Next breath, he said that he would explain to the family how I blew it, how I was so crazy I needed five sessions *a day* with Dr. Amy. I was breaking his heart, Nick's heart; the whole family was heartbroken.

A new breath: "You must realize what you have done to everyone. My family needs to stay away from you. I'll let them know how crazy you are. Remember to stay away from Danielle," he continued, "because you only think of yourself."

He told me I was fragile and distraught. He knew the family wanted to see me and wanted to see us together. He and Danielle were family, and I was robbing the children of having a sense of family.

He told me that I needed help. That he loved me, absolutely loved me like he had never loved before.

The message ended, "Please, please, call me."

A Huge Step

I was quite upset, because letting my heart go out to him on Thanksgiving morning when I invited him for just a meal had turned into more abuse, a string of tantrums when he didn't get his way. I was certain he was in such a state because his controlling, manipulative expertise has lost its effectiveness. I visualized him taking a sip, pacing the floor in a panic, thinking, *Wait a minute! Wait a minute! Why isn't this working anymore?* I calmed down at the thought. It meant I had reclaimed some of my power.

To control my reaction to his string of messages and to avoid responding to his out-of-control thinking, I spent the day saying my affirmations addictively. I searched for all I had learned. I clung to my notes and prayers, reading and rereading them, hoping to come across the perfect words to guide me back to peace. I finally remembered, *I'm choosing a good life.* I was able to let go when I concentrated on the fact that life with the Foreman in it would not be good.

My mantras that day:

- It is done unto you as you believe.
- I am moving forward, even when I am in between.
- I am at peace.
- I attract nurturing, peaceful people.
- Peace is all around me.
- I'm grateful for the courage to embrace the unknown.
- I am doing my best to break the patterns of my life that no longer serve me.
- I can take care of myself as I allow myself to grow and move forward on this journey called "my life."

I continued to take my power back by consciously making choices to create a better life. I reminded myself that every thought and decision formed my future. I can and will rise higher; I won't take the easier path by staying within what is familiar. Lasting change begins within. It takes a lot of work deleting the old, especially when emotionally abused at the same time.

Through the grace of God, I did it. I often reflected on the day in Dr. Amy's office when she had to tell me the Foreman's messages were pure abuse and how I marveled at how quickly she recognized it. How sad she had to tell me. For me, Danielle, and many others, that's our normal.

Nine months had passed since I started my work with Dr. Amy, four full months since the day I was done with the Foreman for good as a partner. I now focused my attention on what I wanted rather than on what I didn't want.

I had learned so much. I was like a sponge and had intuitively picked up material to aid my growth. Stronger, clearer, and more balanced each day, validation of the injustice I lived did wonders. I stopped seeing the Foreman in the same way. I no longer felt I abandoned him in his time of need. That was a huge step in my healing process.

Validation

Just days after the emotionally draining Thanksgiving weekend with the Foreman and my lunch date where I learned about the list of my perceived wrongs, I received an email from Tina from SOUL that made me smirk. She had no knowledge of what I just experienced. Her email said, "Be kinder than necessary because everyone you meet is fighting some kind of battle. And, again, don't worry about people from your past—there's a reason why they didn't make it to your future."

Two days later, someone else, again, with no knowledge of my lunch date emailed, "Should you find yourself the victim of others' bitterness, ignorance, smallness, or insecurities, remember things could be worse. You could be one of them."

I thought then that these emails were just coincidences. I don't think so now. I believe deep in my soul these unexpected messages were gifts from heaven sent through my friends' computers to let me know I was on track and divinely loved. I work hard each and every day not to assume anything.

Doing Something About It

Doing some housework one afternoon, I came across a basket filled with old children's movies. Stuffed between them was a small book I used daily during the Tony days when I attended Al-Anon meetings to stay strong, *Courage to Change: One Day at a Time in Al-Anon II,* published by Al-Anon Family Groups, Inc.

Flipping through it, it occurred to me yet again how wonderful it is to speak my truth without worrying about the consequences or what price I would end up paying. I still might hesitate or speak with a shaky voice at times, but my words do come out. I know eventually I will articulate my truth and act fearlessly and not experience the symptoms of such a traumatized body while doing so.

I'm quicker to notice cues from my body now, to remember to breathe and feel what I'm feeling. I now have the ability to recognize when I'm at the mercy of someone's mood, fears, addictions, or manipulations. I learned that from David Richo in *When Love Meets Fear: How to Become Defense-Less and Resource-Full.* Over time, a person living with chronic stress of someone else's alcoholic behavior loses touch with his or her own inner cues, needs, beliefs, and desires. Children especially need security and healthy modeling of emotions to understand their own inner signals as well as to help separate their thoughts from their feelings. In a family environment filled with violence or chemical, emotional, physical, or sexual abuse, the child will focus solely on the outside, over time *losing* the ability to generate self-esteem from within. Without a healthy inner life, that child as an adult tries to find fulfillment on the outside. I learned that within a relationship, a partner who fears love may become abusive toward the other partner, either emotionally or physically. I started to understand how my life reflected my upbringing.

Tony's physical abuse, the Foreman's emotional abuse, their wrong messages mirrored my wrong messages. I endured such a life because of my buried fear of abandonment. In some ways, I was subconsciously attracted to them to avoid the pain caused by my childhood issues.

Who taught me to endure that? Who taught me I had no right to happiness? That words didn't matter? That I should make the best of what I had and not complain? Who taught me that was normal?

Confronting my fear was taking a stand—doing something about it. Unconditional love was and is not allowing myself to be abused. Unconditional love with conditioned adult boundaries is my goal. This type of thinking will help my psyche heal and my body will be empowered to continue to fight the battle.

Richo says, "When your body hears, '(abuse) is unacceptable and you still going along with it,' you crumple up, defenseless and without resource." I am proud I was so courageous all my life. I'm proud I allowed myself to find my peace. I'm not lonely. I'm content. I have learned now that I can not and will not live with or be around anyone who refuses to do their work. I don't have to pay a price for anyone's love, friendship, or respect. It's my birthright. That was a long, hard lesson to learn.

Our friends are a good gauge on how the world sees us. Positively or negatively, they reflect some part of who we are. I see friends of the past as growth. When I changed my thoughts and actions, some fell away. And soon I attracted people with my new perceptions. The more I valued myself, the more I attracted friends who valued me. No finger pointing or judgmental views, just lots of love, support, and respect. What an inspiring change, and so comforting to my soul.

I would like to wear a sign, "If you're going to keep track or judge me, let me know at the beginning of the game." Let me decide if I want to play the game with an open heart or not at all. This way, I will be more aware and not so shocked when you drop the ax and start your finger pointing.

Awareness is a wonderful gift, pain and all. And to think I prayed for more of it.

The Pure One

I started helping a friend at church one night a week as her assistant teacher for first-grade religion classes, a fun and quite rewarding experience. The children were sweet, innocent, and loved to hear the age-appropriate Bible stories. They were a joy to watch and teach. The experience helped the little girl in me heal a little more.

I learned my given first name, Kathleen, means "the pure one." With that knowledge, I felt bathed in purity. All the filth I had endured washed away. What a gift.

Often, I found what I said to the children was good for me to hear as well. I started to take care of myself as if I were a little girl. I was sure to get adequate rest, intentionally chose not to be around smokers, ate healthy foods, and limited sugar. Balance appeared more and more in my life, along with the peace of mind that so many had robbed me of. A newfound patience helped me to see my prayers were being answered every step of the way.

What You Think About, You Bring About

As Christmas approached, the self-doubt demon came back. The rollercoaster was a wild one this time. My emotions were all over the place. Annoyed, exasperated, irritated, grouchy, feeling like I lost my power. The next moment I was sad, crushed, defeated, disappointed, distraught, and lonely. I was jumpy, trembling; had a lump in my throat; was sick to my stomach, cold, hot. Extremely emotional, tense muscles, gritting my teeth, tired, run down. Shame and guilt would creep in. I was exhausted!

This was a tough week, but the good news was I didn't step backward. I stood still and worked through the rollercoaster with every tool I knew of. One night before I fell asleep, I thought, *Look at me. I did beat the odds. Fifty years of abuse in one form or another, and they didn't win. Amen.*

In one of Dr. Doreen Virtue's books, I read that our whole experience here on Earth is a classroom in hindsight. There are no real emergencies. They are only opportunities or, let's say, God inviting us, to grow. Not an easy thing to remember when you're in the middle of it all.

Breathe. Conscious breath helps to stay connected to God. If I quiet myself long enough, I can hear Him.

My days continued to be unpredictable. I never knew when a rollercoaster of emotions would occur or how long it would last. I knew now, though, that in time I would heal. I would be clear that the past was the past. That it was okay to have fun, to be silly, to spend money. It was okay to let new people in. I was capable of recognizing safe people.

I bumped into a client who moved away some twelve years before. After our initial joy of seeing one another, she asked, "Are you just as spiritual as you ever were?"

Her question took me back for a moment. What a sweet thing to remember of me and a great reminder that, even when I thought I was losing, I was still hanging on. I just about skipped away from that pleasant reunion, gratefully aware of God's daily gifts.

I was learning to start my days with *I wonder what I will learn today? What surprise will show up? Who will I help today?* Or, maybe, *How will I grow?* Perhaps, *What will I give?* Or, *What will I receive?*

The more I healed through my traumas, the easier it became to protect myself from others' hidden agendas. Simultaneously working to be more aware of all my thoughts and decisions and how they affected my life. It's more work than anyone can imagine and a lifelong process.

We do create the good and the not so good in our lives. What you think about, you bring about.

What Did I Do Wrong?

The next day was totally different. The rollercoaster dipped over the top of the rise and plummeted. I wondered, *Will I ever be able to lower my defenses and still feel safe?* Any little change in the lives of those around me sent me right to the questions, *What did I do wrong? What part did I play with all this pain around me?*

I started to beat myself up again for believing the Foreman's words, "I love you so much," when he wasn't willing to take the steps for us to be together. Still lurking in the back of my head was the idea that I was not good enough. Somewhere along the way, I had learned that when words don't match people's actions, it means *I* wasn't worthy. If I were worthy, the Foreman would have gotten sober.

The longer I chose to stay with the Foreman hoping he would get well, the more consequences I created. My days and nights were more painful, and it became harder to protect myself. In a sense, limiting my time with him was like when I was a little girl hiding from the bad men. When I hid, they couldn't get me.

The Foreman and I reacted to each other's fears. He feared me leaving him, and I feared I couldn't take care of myself because I couldn't see I already had all those years.

How sad two hearts that loved each other with so many wrong messages. At one time, I believed that if the Foreman got into therapy and a program, we'd still be together. We could have healed and grown up together, reprogramming with love and acceptance. No more running away from what we believed. No matter what we came from, life could change for the better. Silly me. I thought the same with Tony.

Leaving the Foreman behind was difficult. Acceptance of what is was very tough to handle.

What a Christmas!

On Christmas 2006, it was just Nicholas and I again, the first without Danielle and her dad. They wouldn't be at our door early that morning. Our quiet morning just reminded us of our longing to be part of a regular family and was an unspoken sadness.

As we prepared to gather our things to spend our Christmas Day with Catherine, Nick's godmother, and her family, the phone rang. Nicholas answered and came to me, saying it was the Foreman wishing us a Merry Christmas, adding, "Mom, he sounded weird."

Almost instantly at Nicholas's words, I felt sick to my stomach. I tried to reason with myself, *Oh stop!* I kept repeating it, but that small voice wouldn't leave me alone. I sensed something was wrong. I couldn't ignore my gut; it frightened me.

I dialed the Foreman's phone number from my cell. As soon as I heard his voice, I knew what Nick meant. The Foreman claimed he was on his way out and would be gone for the day.

I no sooner hung up than that feeling grew stronger. Something was wrong. Again, I just couldn't ignore that eerie feeling. It started to haunt me.

Against all I had learned, I decided I wouldn't be able to shake this until I went and checked on him. I found the front door locked. He never locked his doors. I peeked in through the little side windows to the left of the door. The house was dark, the blinds shut. I rang the bell several times. My heart started to race. It was Christmas morning, and it looked like death in there.

I walked back to my car to get the key the Foreman had given me long ago, anxiety building, fearing what I would find. Once inside, everything was just as I suspected.

He was home. Sitting on the sofa in the dark, listening to that same old tear-jerking music he played on Thanksgiving morning. He had a drink in front of him, a cigarette in his hand.

The house was a total mess. Days of dirty dishes piled high, dirty glasses about the house. Things looked like no one had picked up for days. He had not showered or shaved and was crying.

As I asked, "What are you doing sitting here in the dark?" he got up, came over toward me. He tried to kiss me and hold me. He was repulsive. He stank of body odor, cigarettes, booze. So disgusting. I had never seen him like this.

As I pushed him away again, I asked, "What are you doing?"

He started with he loved me. I was the love of his life. I was so beautiful. All this as he wobbled back and forth.

"Just stop! Your words don't mean anything to me anymore."

The whole scene broke my heart. For a second, I thought of telling him to take a shower and come with us. Oh, no. That would only promote another Thanksgiving nightmare. I wasn't signing up for that again.

As I turned to leave, I saw it—the gun on the coffee table next to his drink. How had I not noticed it when I walked in?

At first, I didn't know what to do. Nicholas walked into the house that moment.

Oh, my God! What danger did I get us into? What did we walk in on?

My adrenaline increased by the second. The danger I put Nick and myself in shook me, not knowing what the Foreman might do.

To distract the Foreman, I asked for a glass of water. As he left the room, I picked up the gun with one of his dirty socks lying on the floor. I rushed to the master bedroom and threw the gun under the bed.

I couldn't get us out of there fast enough. I knew the Foreman was in no condition to look for the gun. He was out of danger for the moment, and, hopefully, he would just pass out.

He must have realized right away the gun wasn't on the coffee table. I was only four miles away when he started leaving voicemails on the cell phone, warning me to be careful with it. I had no experience, and someone could get hurt. Next message: Be careful how I drove. If I got stopped, the gun wasn't in my name. Even drunk—or, especially drunk—he still tried to manipulate me.

I did my best to carry on Christmas Day for Nick as if nothing had happened. By early evening, I dropped Nick off back at home so he could get snacks out for our friends. I went on to pick up Danielle and her friends to celebrate our Christmas. On my way, I stopped to check on her dad. I found him passed out on the sofa, but alive.

My next three days of discernment exhausted me. What did I do with all of this? I called our local police department. Asked some questions. I called Grace. By now she knew I was one of the Foreman's ex's. I met with her for the confidential end of it, knowing she couldn't share what I shared with her. I worried. I lost sleep. I didn't want to overstep boundaries or get involved, but I had to do something.

I thought that he had lost his mind.

I called and made an appointment for the Foreman with Grace, hoping I could urge him to see her. He fought me tooth and nail. He wasn't having any of it and was going nowhere.

In the middle of that disturbing conversation, he told me the gun wasn't even loaded.

You bastard! You staged this sorry-ass, pathetic scene? I thought.

To make matters worse, he started to laugh, and laughed even harder when he told me about the enjoyment he and Francine got at my expense when he told her about me taking the gun away. He quoted her, "I knew you wouldn't do anything when you called me on Christmas morning asking where your guns were."

I was totally enraged. "You sick people! You both need help! This is funny to you? Your game playing is sick—very sick—behavior. Nothing but a huge, controlling, manipulative power play. What did you think, Foreman? This neurotic behavior would get me to take you back or let you spend Christmas with us?

"Your sorry ass makes me sick. I lost sleep for days worried about your well-being and what was the best way to handle *your* problem. And all along you and your housekeeper, sister, mother, babysitter—whatever the hell she is—were having a good laugh?" I screamed. "You're both sick, sick assholes!" and stormed out the door.

What fools the two of them are. They deserve each other! I ranted to myself for the next five minutes, questioning which one was sicker or just plain more stupid. I was annoyed that I allowed myself to get sucked into their dysfunctional story again. I was grateful for the ability to quickly turn my annoyed, angry thoughts to those of gratitude. Grateful I recognized the Foreman's ploy for what it was and got out. Clearly, I was grateful their problems were not mine. And I couldn't help but wonder, *Was the gun really not loaded?*

Games the Foreman Played

As soon as I returned home, I switched the television on, thinking it would take my mind off what I had just experienced. At first, I had no idea what the show was about. The woman's words stopped me in my tracks: "All addicts are liars, and all addicts ruin the lives of everyone around them."

Just that quickly—an affirmation that I was on track and I was not to blame. It was a clear example of divine guidance. I couldn't help but think my angels were working with me. I smirked and chuckled out loud, amazed at how blessed I was and how quickly God spoke to me. I loved where I was and I love where I am going.

I had worked hard and would continue to do so to protect myself when it came to the Foreman. That experience was another example of how he played people against one another. His behavior indicated he certainly seemed capable of doing something stupid. Who in their right mind sits in the dark on Christmas morning crying, drunk, unkempt, with a gun—unloaded or not—in front of them?

I have learned firsthand what the Foreman does behind the scenes to paint different pictures to different people. Even in the middle of my own trauma work, I had figured him out and was able to see beneath his empty, sweet words and his game playing. He just wasn't a safe man.

I wondered what side of his personality he showed Francine that Christmas morning. I'm sure it was the exact opposite of what I witnessed. Their lives went on as normal; it was I who lost four days of peace of mind and much sleep. They deserved each other. Let her bake her little muffins and be his free errand girl. The emotional incest goes on.

I ended 2006 barely hanging on, physically and emotionally. Clarity was difficult. Making the best choices all around was taxing. *I will not give in to old habits,* I repeated to myself. *I am learning a new way. I am learning what I should have been taught many years ago.*

Don't Let the Bisque Fool Ya!

At 3:30 p.m. New Year's Eve day, my doorbell rang. Standing on the front door step was the Foreman, clean, showered, dressed like he stepped out of GQ, just like the first time he knocked on my door, with food, with a gift, a container of lobster bisque.

He almost got me. I almost bit the hook of his "I'm only trying to make a nice gesture" move. He left as soon as I said I was busy. Only to call back asking, "Did you see how much lobster meat it had?" It had none.

About a half hour later, he was back to add the lobster. Adding it cost twenty-one dollars a bowl. How ridiculous. Who buys lobster bisque, only to have to add lobster to it later?

He hung around, waiting for an invite, curious what my plans were for the evening. I could feel he was hoping I would forget everything that had happened and start over.

He was behaving like the man I knew in year one. Silently I repeated to myself, *He refuses to do his work. His words don't match his actions.* He refused to understand that I'd crawled away from his distorted thinking. I wasn't confused anymore about what it meant to be loved and cared about.

But I did start to fall backwards. I struggled with not giving in. My thoughts and my affirmations raced through my head, getting all mixed up, a silent battle going on. *I am deserving of the best life has to offer. I won't be tricked again. Nothing has changed.*

The Foreman's next words smacked me back to reality. "I only meet sick women. Why do I get involved?"

I wasn't sure I'd heard right. "What did you just say?"

He was wise enough not to repeat his words, so I did, "You only meet sick women. Do you really think that?"

He stood there, speechless, almost afraid of me. He sensed then I was not the same woman.

"You need to leave."

I'm surprised I didn't pour the bisque over his damned head. Trying to reverse the role and put the blame on the women he met once again. Gee! This story sounded familiar—pretty close to the stories he told me when we first met. Oh, yes! Poor, poor abused man! And the bullshit kept coming.

I was very aware of my sidestepping over what real love is. Oh, so much to undo, to figure out. Deleting was a job in itself.

The bisque was delicious. I slept well that evening and felt great in the morning. I got out of bed very early, settled into my rocking chair to spend some time alone in prayer. My home was warm and quiet, Nicholas still sound asleep. The lighted candles and the lights from the Christmas tree made the room peaceful and inviting.

Before long, I was led to the basket by the side of my chair. I picked up *Divine Prescriptions* by Dr. Doreen Virtue at random, a book I hadn't looked at for quite some time. By chance, I opened to page 59. The heading, "Prescription for Addiction." Again, I found these happenings amazing. I giggled. Certainly, the reading was a message to keep me on track. I read about the epidemic of drug and alcohol abuse and the destruction and suffering they caused. I also read about subtle addictions I never thought of such as compulsive spending, risk taking, gambling and, even more subtle, easy jobs, fine dining, television, etc. I also read somewhere that addictions numb the heart to pain but they also diminish the capacity to love.

Consequences, of course, are far worse for drug and alcohol addiction. Their stakes cannot be underestimated—literally a destruction of society, according to Dr. Virtue. Tens of millions have had their careers; families; finances; physical, emotional, and spiritual health; their lives destroyed by substance addiction, and the numbers continue to climb.

I stopped for a moment, prayed for the people I know and don't know affected by it and who, sadly, don't realize it themselves. I thought, *How scary to be on that square again, involved with another alcoholic's crazy world. And to think I never saw it coming.* Tears streamed down my cheeks as I thanked God it didn't take me as many years this time to see it. Not that it hurt any less, but this too shall pass.

Learning from Dr. Amy and Grace was a precious gift that helped me to see truth, to be clear about who I am, and to know that I am an incredibly strong woman. Through the tears that New Year morning, I read that the angels say addictions and obsessive-compulsive behavior spring from inner feelings of emptiness and being cut off from God and his all-encompassing love. The self-deprecating thoughts learned from parents and society make most people think they are bad or unworthy. And that blocks them off from God even more.

What a wonderful, positive way to start my new year. It affirmed all that I had learned in the past twelve months. I had worked very hard to forgive my abusers and all the people who pointed fingers, to not be held back by them anymore. I thanked them, for I have learned many lessons from them all.

To help me understand more, I read that because of their addictions and/or controlling behaviors, people look for something outside themselves to fill the emptiness or dull the pain. It's only a temporary fix, for soon they experience feelings of self-loathing for wasting time and energy in futile, shameful behaviors, only intensifying the original feelings of emptiness, continuing the unproductive behaviors. A vicious circle.

I saw this reading as a reminder that I'm okay and to breathe through my loneliness. Yes, I was on track and moving toward my highest good. No matter what anyone else may have thought. I allowed my tears to stream down my cheeks, for it was in that moment I was reminded again of my need for someone to be proud of me. I sat with that awareness for a bit and went on to look up personal loss.

According to the angels, when one sees with grief-filled heart, the person in pain measures past time against present time and compares how things once were before all the changes. It helped me see that I spent too much time trying to get back what I never had with the Foreman. I focused on the past, a key factor that delayed the joy that comes from embracing the new.

The angels continued,

> When the spring thaws from winter, does the tree grieve
> the passing coldness? When the blossoms fade and turn

> to fruit, does the tree's bosom heave with heaviness? You are as much a part of evolving nature as the tree, and we ask you to view each passing change as God readying you for newness and growth.

I ended my prayer session with, *God, please help me remember this lesson,* knowing life would be less painful.

The next morning, upon awakening, I remembered three clear visions from a dream. The first was of an angel statue I own. Called *Courage,* she stands strong with her arms raised above her head. The second vision was our Blessed Mother's face, and the third vision was a horse.

I looked up Mother Mary in the angel cards. The card read, "Have faith that your prayers have been heard and are being answered." The back of the card notes, "Mary is known as the queen of angels and she is with you. Your faith will illuminate your way to take whatever steps are necessary. One small inkling can pull you out of the darkness of despair, which could be the light that illuminates someone else's hopelessness."

I then looked up horse in a book by Ted Andrews, *Animal Speak.* The horse is rich in lore and mythology. What I went away with is that it's a symbol of freedom and strength. The horse brings with it new journeys, and it will teach you how to ride into new directions to awaken and to discover a new, deeper freedom. This horse vision to me represented that I was free from the alcoholic crazies and the hostage role. I felt like I was galloping forward, moving on, asserting my freedom and power in all areas of my life. I sat in quiet peace, enjoying the trail of signs I'd received to assure me I was going in the right direction.

The next day I had lunch with my friend Priscilla. I discussed my desire to write this book. She listened attentively to all I had to say, patient as I was excited one minute, the next, a bit overwhelmed. She gently settled me down, telling me she thought I had something to say and what she liked best was she believed I would make my book unique.

She was supportive, encouraging, and helpful, willing to assist me, declaring it would be a labor of love. Another gift that afternoon that I will treasure was she believed in me!

As I walked to my car after that lunch, I felt like I was floating in air. To think that someone I held with such respect, someone intelligent and wise, who was great at what she did, who had a great sense of humor, believed in me. I knew we would be guided, doors would fly open, and the help would be there. This I prayed in Jesus' name. Amen.

January 9, 2007. The Foreman walked in at work to ask me out on a date. He wanted to take me to the movies for my birthday. He wanted us to just be together. We would hold hands, he told me, ending with, "We won't even have to talk."

He continued his attempt to lure me back into his life, always pretending he was on track and doing well. I was way ahead of him.

Free Information

During my readings, I learned about Stockholm syndrome, in which kidnap victims form emotional bonds with their kidnappers. It gained much press attention during the kidnappings of Patricia Hearst and Elizabeth Smart. Research has suggested that Stockholm syndrome also helps explain certain behaviors of survivors of more commonplace types of abusive relationships—battered wives, incest survivors, and physically or emotionally abused children.

I self-diagnosed myself with this. I convinced myself that that was my real inner battle—I had created bonds with all of my abusers and had received so many conflicting signals from all of them, I never really knew what to believe. Even when Dr. Amy or Grace told me something, I still had to prove it to myself that it was true.

So although I was determined to leave the Foreman, I had one more struggle to work through—I had to convince myself that he truly had stopped drinking. Obviously, somewhere deep inside, I still hung on to hope by one slim thread that he would do his healing work and we might have a future. Or, was this a mini-battle between rational thought and Stockholm syndrome?

I discovered his new hiding place for his bottle. I watched it daily. One morning it was half empty, the next morning the half gallon was empty. The next morning another full bottle, the next half empty. A quart of booze in one evening became his norm. He still tried to convince me he quit when I asked, "What's that bottle in the garage?"

"Oh, it's out there because I threw it out." He had no idea that I was on to him. He had no idea things were clearer and clearer.

On one of those bottle-checking visits, I chanced to see his phone bill laid out on the kitchen table. Sure enough, Phyllis's phone number was there, numerous phone calls back and forth to each other daily. Lie after lie.

That weekend, at the last minute, I changed my plans to walk with Catherine. It was just too cold, especially with my Reynaud's. I decided to go to a yoga class instead. All through class, I thought I recognized two women across the room. *How do I know them, and from where?* Just before class ended, it came to me. They were the Foreman's ex-wife Deborah and her sister.

As people started to depart, Deborah and I simultaneously headed toward each other to say hello. She was warm and friendly, asking how I was. She quickly moved into talking about her children that she had with the Foreman and how they were going to their dad's house for dinner. By her words and mannerisms, she didn't know I had left him. "Deborah, I would have thought the boys had told you I left the Foreman months ago."

She must have felt that gave her permission to open up to me, and she started to share some of her life with him before the divorce. She said they had two sons and was pregnant with their third child when he arrived home very late from work one evening, full of hickeys. Her words: "By the time the master manipulator was through with me that evening, I was in tears, begging him to forgive me for thinking such a thing." As we walked to our cars, she hugged me and said, "The Foreman is going to regret losing you."

I left yoga class that cold Sunday morning, thrilled that I had received another message of truth, surely answered prayer. The bottles of booze, the phone bill filled with Phyllis's number, and now Deborah's words taught me this man had had thirty years or more of this game-playing life even before he met me. My inner peace was profound. I fell asleep that evening without a care in the world. I was content. The truth was exposed. I no longer questioned my sanity, even though Tony and the Foreman continued to try to suck me back in with their alcoholic crazies. They just never stopped tormenting us.

The next morning I went to work at 5:00 a.m. to pick up some things. The answering machine light was flashing. At first I thought I would tend to it later, when I came back to start work. For some reason, I pushed the play button anyway.

I was stopped in my tracks. It was Phyllis, the Foreman's girlfriend before me. The one he said cheated on him, stole from him, had him arrested. Blah, blah, blah. Phyllis asked me to call her; she said she was tired of the Foreman effing with her, effing with me, and effing with Stephanie, Danielle's mother. "Please call me," she said, "and I'll tell you what that bastard's been up to the last four years."

I never returned Phyllis's call. She couldn't have shared anything with me that I needed to know or that I hadn't learned already. I refused to get sucked back into their ongoing, impaired, unhealthy hodgepodge.

The Foreman was a very sick man. I wished I was more cautious of someone trying to meet all of my needs all of the time in the beginning. I believe his fear of rejection led him down a path of not being responsible for himself.

The trust was gone. Who was he anyway? Did he even know? I didn't care. I didn't love him anymore.

All Is Well

Today more than ever, I'm proud. I beat the odds, I didn't become a statistic. I might have had many horrific days, and I'm sure that there'll be more to come, but I still managed to be a loving mom, a good businesswoman, and a great friend. I made it through only by the grace of God and the belief that my Lord would continue to give me the strength and courage or would carry me when I couldn't take care of myself. I have done a lot of hard work for a very long time. I am grateful most for the courage to move out of denial and face what I came from. Many do not.

Tony and I came from dysfunctional homes and were offspring of broken people who should have never had children. Some days, acceptance of what is can be difficult, but when I remember not to take anything personally, no one's negative behavior affects me. It's a reflection of his or her consciousness, according to Don Miguel Ruiz, in *Four Agreements.* There is no need to engage in defending myself anymore. Just let it go, bless them, and walk away. Learning this has helped me build up immunity against negative vibes.

Today I feel bad for all who have hurt me. They are in pain, stuck, afraid to move forward and heal. I pray for their well-being. I am sad to leave them behind and trust wholeheartedly that God is making room for stronger, healthier, more loving relationships to come to me. All is well in my world. I often giggle with excitement, watching and feeling all the new and good that are coming to me.

It's my birthday today. I spent a little time pondering my story thus far. I thought about all the hurts, losses, disappointments, and the grieving. The worst is over and it's time to rest. It is time to focus on the beauty all around me. I'm taking a different type of responsibility for myself. Yes, I was derailed again by alcoholism and unawareness. As I said, it snuck up on me. Luckily, it didn't take as long to recognize the Foreman's façade. Lurking behind the scenes was a controlling, manipulative liar.

I know my future is bright and trust I will receive whatever I will need to stay on track. *I am a spiritual being protected by my angels and am infinitely loved.* I have found myself repeating these words to help me feel safe, protected, and not alone.

I read somewhere that one of the signs you are moving on with your life is when you start asking yourself, *Am I crazy?* or, *Is it me, or are they crazy?* One never knows what awareness becomes apparent or how long it will take you to crawl out. It works just like that. Many walk through life unaware. It could be denial, survival, fear, shame. Could be, could be.

It's an enormous amount of work finding your truth to live in peace. Just know it will be revealed when you are ready to handle it. That is why it is so important to never judge. Who are we to determine when it is time for someone to be ready to let go of denial? What shoes have they walked in? What is their story? How much pain are they in day in and day out?

I have worked diligently with my affirmations and intentions. I felt then and now that I am living my life with a childlike wonder. I now realize I'm not just waking up. I've been patient and more persevering than ever. I am breaking out of a chrysalis and, perhaps, that negative force just doesn't like it. Get behind me Satan, in Jesus' name. Amen. I am a survivor and a child of God.

In hindsight, the Foreman was an unintended angel. My heartbreaking experience with him helped me proceed in my healing and learn a different way to care for myself on every level. Despite the delays, derailments, and disappointments, I know I am not a quitter.

Quitting was just never an option. It's all getting me to my God-ordained purpose. I have chosen to learn and change, continuing to remind myself what's ahead is all good. All my experiences have strengthened my character. God never wastes an experience. He uses it all for our good and his glory. I am blessed.

Two weeks later, it was the Foreman's birthday. My goal continued to be to disengage even more and to work hard to not slide backwards. I chose to stay with what was best for me. Again, I would say my struggles have made me better, not bitter. Even though clarity showed up more, my emotions were all over the place, ranging from sadness, anger, pity, heartache, compassion, grief, unconditional love, hours and hours of emotional work. I didn't abandon him. I made a healthy statement. I will no longer accept abuse and am not willing to cart around the emotional residue of this old situation. Continually reading the list I made when working with Grace helped me stay strong and centered.

I now see clearly I butted in where I didn't belong. I tried to make the Foreman's lessons easier on him and to move him at my pace. Not wanting to leave him behind, just as much as I didn't want to feel abandoned and unworthy once again. His pretending to cooperate only delayed our pain and growth. I had to eliminate this connection to avoid future triggers.

I now understand I was wrong, though, to try to get him to do anything he wasn't willing to do. His willingness to change and grow is his business, not mine. We all have our own journey and our own free will. I don't know what is best for him or what lessons he has chosen.

I'm worn-out, depleted. I used so much energy trying to reason with him. Believing I was helping, forgetting what I know only so well. We are all exactly where we are supposed to be, each and every moment. Also, that is exactly what gets us to where we are going.

Trusting in God in my own breakthroughs and experiences, I feel something new, wonderful, meaningful emerge constantly.

Every day, I receive an abundance of love: compliments, hugs, gifts, surprises.

I'm still not done processing the physical symptoms of healing—the triggers, the sick stomach, intense fears, headaches, shortness of breath, trembling, sensitivity to loud noises, raised voices, people too close, too tall. In addition to the Foreman's stalking, the never-ending cell phone calls and messages. Dr. Amy, Grace, back and forth, up and down.

Faith Kept Me Alive

I intentionally started to spend more time focusing on gratitude and less in fear, now understanding that every thought is a form of prayer, and those thoughts create a vibration that draws its equal. When I learned to see things in that way, I realized the part I played in keeping the good coming to me. I consciously made an effort to be aware of what or who brought peace, love, or joy to me. I was open to change and now felt free to create the life I longed for—and so deserved.

I take the time now to decide whether I'm on the path that's best for me, a gentle glide forward to my highest good, or if I'm facing some sort of hell, do I need to turn around and run. I've also come to realize my achievements in life are good enough. I now *like* being me.

I'm grateful God made me just as he did, recognizing all he has carried me through. Through his grace, my faith stayed strong and assured me I'm exactly where I'm supposed to be.

I have a good heart and sharp mind. My survival skills gave me the ability to learn and use what I learned to bring a greater understanding and awareness to me and those around me.

This has helped me to continue to escape the messages and the circumstances that limited me all my life. I broke free from following the steps, from repeating the patterns, of many generations before me.

I decided, in a sense, to be a bad student, to stop demonstrating what I was taught.

I have found peace and rest for my soul. All my hard work was worth it. The dark nights helped me grow spiritually. The anxiety that blanketed me and the constant state of uncertainty pushed me forward onto a square of necessary growth.

Some days, I needed to check in hourly with my thoughts and intentions. In time, my life was more peaceful, a little less rocky, less obscured by all the confusion. It changed slowly but surely for the better. More and more moments of peace of mind occurred.

Taking care of me wasn't being selfish. I was learning about self-care and self-love, asking myself what I wanted or needed and listening to my responses. Spiritual love nurtured and healed me every day. I sensed my healing stayed continuous and drew me to people who brought more of the same love and healing to share.

I did my best to stay open to the new and participated to the best of my ability for where I was at that moment. Spirit does show up in unpredictable ways; just know it is always there upon request.

Proud of Myself

Nicholas turned fourteen today. I'm very proud of him, but proud of myself, too. Look at all I've done. I have learned. I've accomplished, grown, healed, and taught. For many years, my divine light may have been dimmed to a mere glimmer, but each week now, I feel like a new me.

I visualize my divine light as a candle burning on the beach on a beautiful summer night. I want to keep it lit for the ambience when the turbulence of life hits and the winds whirl. I know the storms will still come and the winds will still roar, but I am now equipped with a shield to protect my ever-growing light. I have visualized my candle glowing like a bonfire one day very soon.

Just two days after Nicholas's birthday, the demons started playing in my head again, tormenting me. I had plans to attend an out-of-state conference with friends. We were going back to Florida to repeat last year's Hay House You Can Do It weekend. I had saved my money, made arrangements for Nicholas, and was ready to book a flight when the girls informed me they couldn't go. They didn't have enough time to do the other traveling they'd planned *and* attend the conference with me. The cost, the thought of traveling alone, and the anxiety that would bring made it impossible to attend on my own. The "what did I do wrong" demon clung to me for days. *They couldn't do it all, so they chose to drop me rather than their own plans.*

I was so disappointed that I forgot all I had learned. I caught myself on day four. I told myself not to take it personally and that, no, I wasn't to blame. These thoughts did not bring me peace. *Get off this square immediately,* I scolded myself.

I sat for a while, trying to identify what was really going on. It was all fear—fear of abandonment, fear of loss, fear of being manipulated or controlled, fear of withdrawal of love and approval. Had I been left out, excluded? No. Their decisions for their lives had nothing to do with my worth.

Naming these deep, underlying fears was a *huge* step forward. I know these old fears will pop up again. I can only hope that I will recognize them sooner, and they will show up less and less.

That next weekend I went on retreat, the theme, "we walk by faith." I chuckled quietly, intrigued by the possibilities of what this weekend would bring. Some of my notes:

- Walking by faith is learning to dance with life.
- Learn to accept being human when you don't have a map.
- Just hold Jesus' hand and hang on to God's love.
- Our goodness is deeper than our brokenness.

Some other good ones:

- How you see yourself is how you see others.
- Remember, fear blocks you from seeing the truth.
- Leap off that boulder. God's arms are waiting.
- Hold on to your dreams, don't give in to barriers, and don't accept "what is" all the time.
- Remember to plant your seeds and allow Spirit to decide how many flowers will sprout.

That weekend Sr. Mary read a book called *Stitches* by Kevin Morrison, a story about having an imperfection and how far in life you can still go. I cried on that beautiful Sunday morning and every time I've read the book since. I hope someday you take the time to read it, enjoy it, and identify. I believe you will be touched and will move forward in your life. You can do it. You are good enough just as you are, and only the Spirit knows what hall of fame you will land in.

That retreat confirmed that I have walked in faith much of my life. I have done a great job walking through all the darkness and the fears. The degree of loss has caused great agony, but the awareness I have today showed me I am worthy, loving, and blessed. I am not a victim any longer, and I am not living in fear or in fight or flight. I am a survivor!

My ah-ha moment that weekend was that all my traumatic experiences in this life cannot destroy me unless I let them. I have choices. I could stay stuck on the poor-me square or choose to see that I am getting better each moment, with every experience and every step forward, even if it's sideways. If it sounds like I repeat myself, I do. That's exactly what we must do to move forward.

I love the fact I always had an "I'll show you!" attitude. I'm proud of my spunk. Again, I like exactly who I am. I love being me.

As we departed that weekend, a young woman from my group stopped me to thank me for my openness and sharing. She added, "You truly do walk by faith." Her words brought me a sense of pride. I thought, *Oh! This is what recognition and approval feel like.* Her words were an affirmation I am doing just fine.

Through the Eyes of an Eleven-Year-Old

A month has passed since the retreat. Each day I recognize more and more that I have broken the cycle of abuse. I have broken cycle after generational cycle—the dysfunctional systems my parents came from and the fact that broken children grow up to raise more broken children. I may not have done it perfectly by some standards, but I'm doing it. My son does not live in a home with sexual, emotional, or physical abuse. No woman beaters, incest, or addicts. I know I have given him a good base, far better than one coming from a two-parent home filled with chronic distress and domestic violence. The information he has received at his young age is priceless. The tools of the process are the symbols he'll remember for life.

This brings to mind one of my favorite experiences with Nicholas. At church one Sunday when he was around eleven years old, after receiving communion, I began my short after-communion prayer, *Lord, help me become the woman you have created me to be.*

I never got past "Lord" when Nicholas feverishly tapped my shoulder.

I did my best to ignore him, but at his fifth attempt to get my attention, I looked at him and in a very irritated tone, asked a quiet, "Wha-a-a-at?"

Nicholas then leaned into me, and, attempting to speak quietly, exclaimed, "I think you pray *wa-a-a-ay* too much." I turned away, choosing to ignore his inappropriate timing for expressing his observations.

Discontent with no response from me, he leaned back into me and added, "And I'm sure God thinks you're quite annoying."

With widened eyes and a quiet, disgruntled tone, I ordered that he go to the car. Nick didn't budge.

Thankfully for him, by the time I left church, I wasn't annoyed. After contemplating his words, my annoyance turned to pride. Walking to our car, I was able to view the whole experience as a wonderful pat on the back, a job well done. He was really only sharing his observation and his concern that I was annoying to God.

I drove home with a big smile on my face. For eleven, my son was aware, very aware, and quite grown up. With the right perception and awareness, gifts will show up often. The truth is, in every situation there is a gift. It is our job to find it or recognize it.

Always remember, there are no coincidences, no mistakes.

It's Your Job

One of my new tools when I think in a backward way is to picture a beautiful fountain. The sound of the trickling water brings me peace as the clear water quietly releases the past, gently washing it all away. All the pain, hurt, anger, shame, and guilt are gone. I feel I'm a miracle in process. Mother Theresa of Calcutta said it well. "I am a little pencil in the hand of a writing God who is sending a love letter to the world."

At other times, I envision the Blessed Mother walking with me, lovingly and gently cradling me. I believe her love and guidance have assisted me in mothering my own son and helped me accept my own experience with my birth mother. I have been able to let go of all the hurts I experienced from a woman who didn't protect me, who abandoned me. Again, I can only imagine what her story was. It saddens me to think about what she must have endured or what her messages were as she grew up.

It seems we all have messages to delete or something to crawl out from, no matter what type of home we grew up in. Someone will always be unkind. Our job is to do our best to find loving and supportive people to help undo the negative.

An Emphatic "YES!"

The Foreman is back to calling me, fifteen times today. His messages ask me why I told people he didn't satisfy me. He thought our personal life and love were just that, personal. Each message was more delusional, his thoughts more bizarre.

His paranoia had him convinced a male business associate of mine was more than that. The Foreman asked where we met and where we went. "Is he the one you were with the other night?" He repeated the question unendingly.

I ignored every call, knowing only too well it was yet another diversion to sidestep the real problem, his drinking.

On the fifteenth call, I picked up that damned phone. I wanted to make it all stop. I remained as calm as I could when I told him his thoughts were way out of line and absurd. He continued to profess his love.

"I love you, do you hear me? I'll do anything for you. I'll do anything for you."

I responded, "But you didn't. I wish you the best." And click, I hung up the phone.

With every message, he became crazier and crazier. Where he came up with the issue he didn't satisfy me is beyond me. It was never discussed.

Two days later, he was back, accusing and jealous, again asking, "How long have you dated this guy behind my back?"

The Foreman called the cell phone so much, it became a trigger. My body reacted at just the sound of the ring.

He didn't get it. He just wouldn't leave me alone.

I was sure that he was stalking me. No matter what time I went for my daily walk, he drove by me numerous times. If I was at work, he frequented the store next door. If I was home, he used that store.

One Sunday he drove through the back parking lot at my condo. I was out weeding my little garden. I chose not to acknowledge him in any way. I thought he drove away.

About ten minutes later, he came up from behind me, startling me. He rambled on about he knew we should be together. Next breath: "I don't even want to hold you or kiss you." Next breath: "Please go to the movies with me. Let me just hold your hand." He was nervous and shook as he spoke.

My bodily reactions made it clear to me I was still extremely vulnerable. My hands trembled, my heart raced, but my thinking was clear.

"Look. It's the same old game you're playing, just a different angle. Please go away. Leave me alone. I'm tired of telling you that I have chosen not to be friends with someone who is capable of lying and betraying me as you have. It's simple as that."

He did leave, only to return for another attempt. Luckily, I was back inside and I was able to ignore the doorbell and all his other attempts to get my attention.

I had about forty-eight hours of peace. Then, as I pulled out of my driveway to meet a girlfriend for dinner, there he was. He had popped up out of nowhere. I drove thirty minutes out of my way to lose him. I refused to let him follow me or stalk me. I became quite angry, feeling that I was still a hostage.

Of course, the Foreman stayed consistent. The next morning I arrived at work to message after message: "I never thought you would lie to me. Who is he? Where did you go? Who were you with? Please call me."

I hadn't even finished listening to all the voicemails when the business phone rang. It was he, pleading, "Please, let's talk. I love you. I want you. I want to hold you and kiss you. Please."

I told him to please leave me alone. Click. He immediately called me back, asking me to call him at the end of my day.

With my quick "NO," he went into how I have too many boyfriends and I'm too busy for him.

I responded with, "Just stop! Just stop!"

He then asked, "Do you totally want me to leave you alone?"

"YES!" I hung up.

No Band-Aids for Me

About this time, I came across an article describing what happens to the body and how it reacts to fear. The amygdala, an almond-shaped structure in the brain, directs a cascade of changes in the body the moment you recognize a threat so you can respond properly. Your heart beats faster, raising blood pressure to speed circulation. The blood flow to the skin decreases; experts believe this is to minimize blood loss if injured. Your adrenal glands release the stress hormone cortisone that heightens awareness and focus. This gland also generates a hormone called epinephrine that increases the heart rate and signals the liver to release stored energy. It's primarily responsible for governing the body's adaptation to stress of any kind—including to the thyroid.

Hmmm! Was there a connection between all my medical issues and my lifelong experiences with fight or flight? It certainly appeared that way to me.

How the body reacts to fear

AMIGDALA
The moment you recognize a threat, this almond-shaped structure in your brain directs a cascade of changes in your body so that you can respond appropriately.

HEART
It beats faster, raising the blood pressure to speed circulation.

ADRENAL GLANDS
Located just above the kidneys they release the stress hormone cortisol which heightens your awareness and focus. The glands also generate Epinephrine, a hormone that raises heart rate and signals the liver to release stored energy.

SKIN
Blood flow to skin decreases; experts believe this is to minimize blood loss if you are injured.

EYES
Your pupils dilate to let in more light, heightening perception.

LUNGS
You begin breathing more rapidly, infusing blood with oxygen for your muscles.

GUT
Your stomach may clench, and your intestines will slow down or stop activity altogether so that blood can be shunted to major muscles and the brain.

MUSCLES
They tense throughout the body in preparation.

I learned one will breathe more rapidly to infuse the blood with oxygen for muscles. Your pupils dilate to let in more light to heighten perception. The stomach may clench and the intestines will slow down or stop activity altogether so that blood can be shunted to major muscles and the brain.

When I finished the article, I was convinced cause and effect played a major role between all of this and my medical problems—thyroid, high blood pressure, adrenal fatigue, fibromyalgia, and every other medical issue I have experienced.

Learning all this brought me back to Louise Hay's view on medical problems. I looked up some of my problems again.

High blood pressure: longstanding emotional problem not solved

Adrenal problems: defeatism and anxiety

Retaining fluids: What are you afraid of losing?

My thyroid issues are an autoimmune disease. Autoimmune disorders are a process where the immune system attacks one or more parts of the body. Adrenal fatigue greatly enhances autoimmune disorders.

In time, I know the physical issues I have developed from living in fight-or-flight mode and in such a chronic agitated state for so long will slip away one by one. I plan to continue my work with constantly changing my thoughts, shifting my perceptions and intentions when needed. I am moving from adversity into opportunity mode, changing my life one minute, one hour, one day at a time.

Peeling away the blame, the expectations, and the need to fix whomever or whatever has certainly helped me live a healthier life.

Being able to address PTSD and its underlying causes, my symptoms are lessening. I am healing and on the road to recovery without Draconian measures from Western medicine. I don't knock Western medicine. There is a place for it; it's just as important for people to learn the underlying issues that caused dis-ease in the body, not just put a band-aid on it.

Research, read, listen, and learn at your own pace, in your own time. You have to live through the process. Sometimes it will feel like you're going back and forth. Don't despair. The answers will come. You will take actions, and healing will follow.

I must always remember not to let *your* journey get in the way of *my* peace. I constantly remind myself if something or someone robs me of my peace, it's wrong for me. I must get off that square immediately.

The Foreman always told me, "You don't live in the real world. Not everyone is as good as you give them credit for. Not everyone is pure and innocent without an ulterior motive or hidden agenda."

I would always say, "Oh, stop with your negative thoughts about everyone."

I still choose to believe the best of everyone until they prove differently to me. I find joy in looking at life with wonder, with a positive attitude, skipping and singing.

We are all mirrors to each other. Anything you see in another is a reflection of some feature, mannerism, in you. There is really no room for someone to stand in judgment of another human being.

It's May 7. The Foreman isn't getting it. I received another movie invite with a "Let's be friends. Let me call just to say, 'Hi!' Let me be a gentleman. Let's just be together."

I was very tired of him coming at me from so many different angles. The difficult part was seeing glimpses of the man I loved. But nothing had changed in the two years since he admitted he was an alcoholic; he still hadn't started treatment.

I sat with Priscilla one afternoon talking about this book and everything going on with the Foreman. She noted, "Abused children are often hypercompetent little adults, doing everything perfectly to compensate for the other stuff."

I nodded sadly, with a quick glimpse back to my childhood.

I finally talked to Dr. Amy about the Foreman popping up everywhere. Her advice: "Call the police."

The next time he was in my face, I shared her advice with him. He actually stopped in his tracks, shocked. He was speechless.

As soon as I said it, I felt my body shift out of victim mode. I felt empowered; it took a lot of work to allow those self-protecting words to fly out of my mouth.

I have to admit, though, I went from empowered to exhausted rather quickly and struggled to hang on to *I am only taking care of myself.* That's just how healing works.

Just hours later, the empowerment was gone, my words tormenting me, and my thoughts became, *I was mean this morning.* The deleting, reprogramming, the Foreman, Grace, Dr. Amy. I couldn't sleep.

What is normal or right was on my back again.

Adrenal fatigue and Stockholm syndrome, that's what was going on. I wasn't going backwards at all. I just went back to my tools and reread my notes.

On top of all the mess with the Foreman, I was having landlord problems at work that began to harm my business. With all that I had on my plate, I had days I just wanted to lie down. I could go to bed in the early afternoon. I tried to hang on to all that I learned to control my thoughts. It was my responsibility to choose where they went. Dwelling on the past or on the negative would only keep me there.

I still struggled with trusting. It was hard to ask for help. Would I have to pay a price? Would I appear needy or vulnerable? That made giving up old ways of survival or control that didn't work very difficult.

Leaving the Foreman was a perfect example: Healing can take years. The road to recovery is ongoing. The Foreman continued to show up somewhere, sweet talking me, coming up with a new angle to hook me. I did my best not to engage in any way. His was relentless. He chose not to hear I couldn't or wouldn't be around people like him. I couldn't afford to have my immune system triggered to make me sicker.

The next morning, upon arriving at work, I found that the beautiful, expensive pedestal planter I had placed outside my shop door was gone. My landlord's security video showed a truck similar to the Foreman's pulling up. The driver got out, put the planter in the back of the truck, and drove away. I believe the Foreman staged this theft to get me to call him for help.

The Foreman's delirium about my supposed new boyfriend turned into another accusation—I was having an affair. He refused to understand that it was just a business acquaintance, that we were only discussing potentially merging our businesses.

He badgered me that my new "love interest" was a lady's man. He repeated, "I thought you wanted a gentleman." He started to frequent Gary's new location and left me messages about how Gary's staff was all talking about our affair.

At one point, I would have reacted to that. I would have gone to Gary to ask what the Foreman had said or done. Now, though, I knew only too well how good the Foreman was at his game—acting one way with someone and another way with someone else, creating havoc among all, if, indeed, he even approached the first person.

I could only imagine what I would have looked like, running to Gary's place, inquiring about such bizarre and absurd accusations. I would not be sucked in to prove anything; this was only the Foreman's crazy thinking.

Lying or Delusional?

The Foreman's addictive behavior, his feeling not good enough, running from himself, and the reality of losing me were too painful for him. So he decided to invent some ridiculous untruth to try to keep me engaged.

Even though I stayed true to myself, strong and clear, I awoke in the middle of the night, the Foreman's words racing through my mind, keeping me from getting back to sleep.

My thoughts flitted from one thing to another, stopping on the times I worked with Priscilla. Her smiles of approval, her nod of the head for a job well done, helped me calm down. My next thoughts went to the Foreman's ex-wife's words. It was only four months since that Sunday morning after that yoga class when Deborah said, "The Foreman is going to regret losing you." Her words became a tool of validation. She poked a hole into the cloud of confusion I'd found myself in once again.

The more I thought about her words, the more my dimmed light grew. I realized more each day that I absolutely did not resemble the woman the Foreman drew me as since he became aware that I was leaving him. He tried to shift his worth, or lack of worth, onto me to control me.

Ilene Wolf of HEAL had this advice: "They are wound-driven. Bless them and walk away."

I reminded myself that I had nothing to fear. Fear does not come from God.

Days later, I felt intuitively that the vandalism and theft at my salon was just another of the Foreman's ploys. Ilene advised me to call the police and open a case against him. She truly believed he was stalking me. She added that someone who ignores when I say "NO" is potentially dangerous. She ended her conversation with, "He could be another Scott Peterson." Her words frightened me. The police did arrive, took some notes, but there was really nothing they could do. They told me to call them if I had any more problems.

Two days later, the Foreman left more desperate messages to call him. Ignoring the calls only prompted him to walk in on me at work, walking to the back of the salon, looking for me with his "there is nothing wrong" attitude. He told me the building was sold and I would be kicked out; the new owner wanted my space. He acted like he was trying to help, but I knew he was only trying to scare me so I would look to him for help. A sick, mean-spirited move.

I remained calm and asked for the money he owed me, then told him to leave my salon. He looked around, saw bouquets of flowers, and boldly read the notes attached to them before he left. In seconds, he was calling, assuming the flowers were from a gentleman.

"With all those flowers, I guess you've moved on. I won't put up with it. I won't tolerate sharing you. I told you I won't compete." Sick bastard. The irony of it was, I sent those flowers to myself to use up money I had accumulated from a barter exchange. Some lasted longer than others. That day, there must have been three bouquets with messages like "Have a great day!" More affirmations.

At the end of my scheduled appointments, I called the police. I shared with the dispatcher some of the story and Ilene's advice. The dispatcher sent an officer. The police and the Foreman pulled in to the parking lot at the same time. The Foreman walked in only about three or four feet ahead of the officer.

I warned him, saying forcefully, 'You need to leave. You *need* to *leave*." He ignored my words. The front door opened and the police officer walked in. The Foreman looked up and with surprise in his voice, asked, "You here for me?"

The police officer asked his name and immediately said, "Step outside."

They were outside for quite a while, the Foreman's arms flying around as he told his story. I was anxious and curious about what lies he was telling, what he was exaggerating to make me sound or look crazy.

Breathe, I reminded myself. *Breathe*"

In the middle of their conversation, Francine showed up with his checkbook. The Foreman must have called her to bring it, but his underlying reason, I'm sure, was for show—"Look what's she's doing to me now."

Finished with the Foreman, the officer came back inside, telling me not to worry. He said the Foreman told him we were family, we have kids, and he loves me. I responded, "Not together. Besides, he chose alcohol over us."

"Miss, we see this all the time. I told him he absolutely cannot come to your business. He cannot go to your home. Don't call your cell phone or any phone number he has for you."

That day took its toll on me. I was only trying to take care of myself and stay in a safe atmosphere. Again, somewhere inside me, I felt I had done something wrong. I had hurt somebody.

The next morning I felt a little better. That I had taken another step forward. Day by day, the fear-based living and people fell away. I thought that maybe I was starting to become the woman God created me to be. Oh, watch what you pray for; it can be quite a journey.

At that point, all my relationships were loving and harmonious. I was excited about my new friends and adventures. I felt like I was a magnet for miracles and aware of the good in all areas of my life. Each week I moved forward, and each week life got better. My options were improving, along with the peace in my life. The best was on its way, and it was my turn.

I was excited about the future. My clients enjoyed watching me live with a new lightness. I knew I would have to relocate my business. I had no idea where, but I had picked out a beautiful new paint color, expecting that it all would work out perfectly.

That weekend I had a conversation with my dear friend Faith, who also knew the Foreman. That conversation disturbed me. She shared she heard that I had made 911 calls from someone's cell phone, saying I feared for my life as well as my son's. Because of my calls, the police went to the Foreman's house twice, Friday evening around 10:00 p.m. and Saturday morning around 7:00 a.m. Faith must have watched for my reaction, because she immediately said, "By the expression on your face, you're unaware of these goings-on."

"I never did that! That's a lie!"

What in the world was he up to now? Faith then explained she was told the state police were at the Foreman's house until the local police department showed up.

"I never made such a call—not yet anyway."

I started to wonder whether someone was impersonating me, maybe one of the Foreman's ex-wives or girlfriends. I called Ilene. Again she advised, "Call the police."

I actually drove to the local PD and spoke to an officer about my concerns. He went to check things out for me. About an hour later, the officer came back and told me they had no record of being at the Foreman's house in the past year, adding he had only lived there a year.

"Miss, he's making it up."

The next day I called the state police to enquire because the story went that two state cops had been at his door until the local PD showed up. The state police dispatcher told me that they didn't go out on that type of call. She said they were not there because it would automatically be directed to the local police department. So, was the Foreman lying or delusional?

More Alcoholic Crazies

This experience frightened me. What would the Foreman do or say next? Where would he land if he continued on that destructive path? His family refused to look at the problem.

The next week he came up with another bizarre story. I learned from Faith that he told people he was walking by my business when I came running across the street, yelling at him to leave me alone. According to him, he didn't even look at me, just kept walking. He did walk by the salon—often—but the only time I ran across the street screaming at him was in his imagination.

Ilene was very concerned. She feared for my life. I feared for his, especially when he continued to believe he was going to win me back.

Senselessly, I attempted to contact one of his adult sons to make it clear I never did these things. He rudely hung up on me with just the mention of the incidents. It was difficult to be treated like the enemy. How bizarre all of that was. Yet it was just another episode of all the lives affected by the alcoholic crazies.

About this time, Nicholas graduated from eighth grade. My son would be in high school. The Foreman's words came back to me. "If you don't let him grow up, he's going to be in big trouble. He'll never make it." I had changed nothing. I loved and cared for Nicholas as I always had. He was doing great. Another pat on my back.

I have learned not to put my happiness in someone else's hands, because, in reality, they can always take it away. It took me fifty years to learn I can ask myself what I want or what I need. I won't ever give my power away again. The Ping-Pong game is over.

I've also learned that answered prayer is sometimes like a tapestry. It's often not answered instantly, like opening a window blind. It can take immense patience and unwavering faith so God can work miracles. Be grateful now. This moment, look for the good. Find the joy. Be quiet. Listen. God is talking. Learn the language that is true prosperity.

More Big Decisions

I woke up one day and it was like a light bulb turned on. I realized that my work environment was nothing I signed up for, nothing I wanted. I had accepted the status quo for too long.

I realized the situation was abusive. The new landlords made running my business nearly impossible with their stubborn views. The most difficult to deal with was the sudden limited parking. No-parking signs were posted on every tree or vacant spot around three sides of the building. This left the three of us women with only three parking spaces. If all of us worked on the same day, like a Saturday, that meant no parking for our clients. All around me were people with flared tempers, angry words; tow trucks and police were called almost weekly.

The sisters had a three-year agreement with me. When that time came near, they decided to close their business. The stressful situation brought upon us by the landlords was more than they could handle. Under great distress, they decided, *NO MORE!* In just two months, they would be gone.

Their decision left me with more overhead expense than I was willing to carry on my own, but I decided to stay put and fill the empty space. For one year, all my creative, out-of-the-box thinking got squashed interview after interview when the big question came up. "What's up with all the no-parking signs?"

Once again, it was time to look for a place to move my business. This situation really angered me. It brought back all of the past years' frustrations and thoughts of how we spent a lot of money and worked very hard to improve that old, outdated building for it to turn out this way.

At first, all my choices seemed pitiful. The spaces were too big, too small, too old, had stuffy, old-thinking landlords. I thought, *This isn't fair; I'm paying a price for others' bad behavior.*

I called two friends, one who was in the business years back and one who was still working in the beauty industry. They both listened and were very supportive. We met so they could give their view on my choices.

It turned out one of the locations I was hesitant about, they both loved. Seeing things through their eyes helped me move past my own fears to some degree. I wasn't thrilled about the location but was able to move forward thinking, *I'll just make the best of it.* I had no other choice.

Shortly after I decided on that location, I realized one of the issues was the hallway. It frightened me being in the middle of the building with no windows to the outside. It brought me back to when I was young and I hid in the closet until late at night. At first, I thought someone could get me and hurt me and no one would help. I even referred to this space as "the closet."

With my new skills and safe people, I was able to get past that old stuff, release some more, and stopped calling it the closet. My perception has changed 180 degrees. Working through those feelings helped me heal a little more and see things a little differently. It wasn't horrible and I wasn't trapped. My prayer: *Lord, help me be renewed by the transforming of my thoughts. Help me let go of all that no longer serves me. Move me to a new way of thinking. Help me see it as You see it* became a mantra.

Once I realized that I wasn't going to a dark closet, that I no longer needed to hide, things turned around almost immediately. Doors opened. People showed up to help. Workers were on time, gifts arrived in all forms. I stopped focusing on how I thought it should be or should go and started to trust this change would be in my highest good. I stuck close to my supportive friends, the ones who had faith in me, who saw me in the best possible light. I repeated, *All is well!* whenever I needed reassurance.

Out of the fog, I saw myself as a pillar of strength. Many along the way shared: "Look at how well you have done for yourself." I heard it from friends, clients, business associates. But that small voice would whisper, *Didn't get it perfect yet.*

I don't care about getting it perfect anymore. I have always done the best I could for where I was. I am not brainwashed any longer. I've woken up. I am open and willing to go the distance. To experience happiness, peace of mind, and all the things I so deserve in this lifetime.

My Busy Life

My days were very full, running my business, baseball mom, football mom, housekeeper, cook. Nicholas was in high school. Life seemed to swirl all around me. Yet I found myself with a new sense of inner peace like I had never experienced before. Finally, I was living joyfully.

August 24, 2007. It was moving day. In twenty-four hours, another new beginning.

The move went well. Things fell into place, and my new landlord was wonderful. He and his work crew made this move the best business experience I ever encountered. I was less stressed, life was easier. Downsizing the business was the perfect solution to take all that weight off my shoulders.

Even though it was all good at the new salon, I was tired and had to deal with a lot in a short time. I needed to be held, I wanted my hair brushed from my face. I wanted to listen to a peaceful heart beating. All I could think of was, *Lord, hold me; help me through this lonely moment.*

I'd no sooner finished my prayer when a friend showed up with coffee and hand-picked wildflowers. It was a clear, sunny, beautiful morning. He also brought some quotes from Albert Einstein that he felt sounded like they could have been mine:

"There are two ways to live your life. One as though nothing is a miracle. The other as if everything is a miracle."

"Few are those who see with their own eyes and feel with their own hearts."

"The only real valuable thing is intuition."

I was touched by his sweet compliments and thoughtfulness. What do you think? Was God holding me and ever so sweetly brushing the hair from my face? I believe so. It was the perfect gift to remind me that I am not alone and that all is well.

Magnet for Miracles

Right after Labor Day, the Foreman passed me eight times on my walk, pulling to the side of the road each time, trying to speak to me. He started to say he wanted to thank me. I did my best not to listen, to ignore him and stay focused. I got upset and found myself wanting to repeat all that I had already said. The words raced through my head. *You made your choices. You hurt me. You lied, manipulated. You betrayed me.* It was a battle not to let them fly from my lips. My heart raced as I sped up my walk, my body reacting to his craziness.

Remember all you've learned, I repeated to myself. But I weakened and screamed, "You lied!"

Instantly, I pulled myself together. I walked even faster, looking straight ahead. Passersby started to notice his scary, stalking behavior. Someone even stopped to ask if I was okay.

The Foreman had to stop for a red light but quickly caught up with me. This went on for more than a mile. He pulled over one last time. When he realized I was not going to acknowledge him and now more people were around to witness my attempt to ignore him, he sped away.

I got home safely, but I was upset about being so upset. I could hardly unlock my front door, my hands trembled so.

I immediately went to my tools. The first thing I came across was a note from Grace, the synopsis I asked her to write about our work together. I reread her words many times to cling to what she knew. She wrote about how distraught I was over the experiences with the Foreman. She added that I was clearly a gentle and caring person. The note referred to my difficulties with PTSD and how fearful I was much of the time as she explained the complexities of alcoholism. The note helped remind me of all that I had worked through.

She continued with the uphill struggle that I never gave up on. How I now saw my own inner strength and the confidence that I could glean from that strength. I had done all of the homework she had given me and found myself growing and putting new information into practice. "She has become a source of strength for others also." I was able to ride the positive emotional wave and not slide backwards.

I sat for quite a while, thinking about what Grace wrote. Eventually, I was at peace, a calm body, and clear thinking. I made myself a cup of tea and settled down with Doreen Virtue's *Angel Therapy,* where she writes about how the angels channel their view.

> What is the heart of betrayal?... A feeling of being compromised or being unloved. Truly the person who hurts you is betraying him or herself alone. Your focus upon hurt will only serve to further hurt you.
>
> Leave the hurt behind. You need to heal. So cleansing yourself of hurt will both free your consciousness and rid you of the deep and stinging wound of having a dear one disappoint you.

The angels ask you to give them this pain, the loss you feel by this friend's betrayal. The sense of foolishness because you feel you should have known better than to trust this person's sincerity.

That was exactly what infuriated me. I should have known better. Fooled again, more wasted time.

I arrived at work the next morning to more messages on the answering machine. The Foreman began by mentioning he shouldn't be calling me per our local police. Second, he advised me to change my outgoing message to let my clients know of my new location, adding, "Just some business advice from me."

He was so unaware. The very reason my outgoing message didn't mention my new location was so he couldn't find me. So he couldn't just show up. He rambled, telling me he knew I could have him arrested for contacting me, but he was taking the risk because we were meant to be together. He started to choke up and hung up.

His second message was with more controlled emotions and attitude when he referred to our situation "being like the show *Touched by an Angel*," where an angel comes down, picks someone up out of the dirt, dusts them off, points them in the right direction, and they end up falling in love with the angel. Which wasn't meant to be because angels always move on to the next page or project.

He continued, "I want to thank you for all you have done for me"—where he lived, his job, and how I had improved the quality of his life. "Always being there for me. I want to thank you again." He was now stuttering and stumbling through his words and thoughts. "I don't think I was in love with you after all. I was in love with the way you are, who you are, and what you did.

"Thank you for what you have done for me. Congratulations on your new place. I want to be a friend to you. We knew all along the differences between Kathleen and Casey. Kathleen is the angel," and he didn't appreciate being treated the way I, Casey, treated him.

I just kept telling myself, *Let it go. Just let it go. No logic here, no reasoning. Just let it go.*

It felt great to be able to step away and hear clearly how his messages went full circle, ending up once again blaming me for his actions. The cost of loving someone like the Foreman was expensive, way beyond my means, and I was not only speaking just financially.

I told myself that the experience with the Foreman only prepared me for unconditional love—a love where we go together like peanut butter and jelly or milk and cookies. Living in a world with peace and respect that we co-create.

A Beautiful Butterfly

Months passed. Being away from the Foreman did wonders for my emotional well-being. I didn't have conversations with him in my head anymore. I lived a less fear-based life, cognizant of how fear was choking me and causing harm to my body.

I was sitting on the back step when a yellow and black butterfly landed on my shoulder, staying there until I moved.

Back inside, I researched butterflies in *Animal Speak*. When a butterfly shows up, Andrews says, make note of important issues confronting you.

> In early Christianity, the butterfly is a symbol of the soul… To Native Americans, it is a symbol of change, joy, and color… In traditional angelology, [yellow and black are] often associated with Archangel Auriel [who oversees the] activities of the nature spirits. [Butterflies also symbolize new beginnings.] They remind us not to take things quite so seriously. They awaken a sense of lightness and joy… Life is a dance and dance, though powerful, is also a great pleasure… Finding joy within, lighten up… Don't forget that all change is good… Growth and change do not have to be traumatic.

St. Paul says, "Be renewed by the transforming of your mind." This has become yet another mantra. I add to it, *Lord, help me let go of thoughts and ideas that no longer serve me. Move me, Father, to a new way of thinking. Help me allow your spirit to guide and direct me in all I think and do. For the moment, I am at peace with all this change. Amen.*

"Just when the caterpillar thought the world was over, it became a butterfly" were the words on the cup I drank tea from that afternoon.

Funny. I never noticed that cup stuffed way back in the cupboard. What made me decide to reach way back to grab that one?

I sat quietly with my angel cards. The first card that flew out as I shuffled was Butterfly Maiden. Under her name was the word, "Transformation." Under her picture it said "You are experiencing enormous change right now which brings great blessings."

Also under the Butterfly Maiden, it says, "To bring in your desired newness, you must first allow old parts of your life to fall away." I'm doing my best to allow that, trying to remember that "change is to be celebrated, not feared." Once I was able to calm the storms, I could hear and see God speaking and lovingly guiding me. I thank the old for all the lessons and now let it go. *God bless you, Foreman,* I quickly prayed. *I hope someday you will find a more gentle way to cope with your real problems.*

My Sails Were Raised

It has been so freeing to let go and try a new road. Each new day brings a better picture in this huge transition I'm walking through.

Physically, emotionally, professionally, I feel healthier. People, places, and things are showing up all around me. I have been guided through and out of survival mode. I still have a moment here and there when I am angry with the Foreman for not being emotionally available and for not getting sober. But that's yesterday thinking. That's all it is.

Jesus said, "I tell you the truth, if you have faith as small as a mustard seed, you can say to this mountain 'move from here to there' and it will move. Nothing will be impossible for you." (Matthew 17:20) Through my eyes, I have moved mountains on every level and in many areas. What is your mountain and how will you move it?

At Mass this morning our reading, Mark 5:3 and 4: Daughter, your faith has made you well. Go in peace and be healed of your disease.

Spirit was talking. I was still sad about the stream of emotionally unavailable men who were in and out of my life, starting with my birth father. Unfortunately, I never recognized them as such. Of course, how would I? I never knew the difference until now.

A friend told me recently, "Don't let anyone ever tell you you're not a great mom. I've witnessed your interaction with your son."

Clearly, affirmation after affirmation. Two days later, I had dinner with a team from church. Father D. happened to sit next to me. After a wonderful evening of good food and great conversation, Father D. said, "Nicholas is blessed to have a stable mom." At that moment, I felt all of Tony's and the Foreman's hurtful words leave me. As tears welled up, I thanked the Lord for placing these wonderful people in front of me. "What a good boy you have," Father D. continued, followed by a slight giggle. "What do you feed him? He's at least a head taller than his classmates."

Self-doubt was leaving and I was no longer a hostage to misinformation. I was not responsible for what has happened to me, but it was clear I am responsible for how I react to each situation. If I thought I was a victim, I would stay a victim. I would stay trapped and doomed. I now could breathe, become clearer, and choices do show up.

Job 22:21: Agree with God and be at peace. In this way good will come to you.

God had always been my strength. Without His grace, I wouldn't be here today to share with you and, hopefully, give you one word to move you through your deleting and gently wake you up.

Rama Krishna said it well: "The winds of God's grace are always blowing. It is for us to raise our sails."

Don't Take It Personally

I was certainly a product of negative understandings. I often think about how I see people as clouds, crashing into each other as they go about their day. I hang onto Jesus' words. "Forgive them for they know not what they do." The crashing will stop when their healing begins.

Change is the only real constant. It can take time, so be patient with yourself as well as with others. It could take months; it could take years. A prayer from your heart can be just the release you need to bring it about. Just the act to lift you from despair.

Make a point to be around people who make you feel good, people who support you, who see the good in you, who see your potential and tell you so. Learn to ask yourself the important questions, questions that will aid you in learning who you are, what you want, what you need. Learn what works for you and what doesn't.

Try to envision your heart's desires to begin to create your new life. Begin to believe you have all that you need inside of you, the strength, the power, the intelligence.

Expand your thinking. Your thoughts can create your tomorrows. Decide today what they will be.

If that's too difficult, begin with gratitude. Be grateful for what you do have. Perhaps it's a reliable car, good health, a warm, clean bed, and so on. You will notice a shift rather quickly. Hope will creep in little by little, especially if you choose positives rather than negatives. Albert Einstein said, "In the middle of every difficulty lies opportunity."

I pay more attention to my small voice. I sit quietly, practice listening and speaking from a place of peace. I am now surrounded by love and acceptance, by people and friends not focused on finding fault. I am encouraged to see the good in me, and the more I see the good, the more I see that what you give out is what comes back to you.

I learned not to take anything personally. Don Miguel Ruiz says if you take things personally, you are just setting yourself up to suffer. You make yourself easy prey for predators to send emotional poison. What others think is not about me; it's really about them.

If someone in your life doesn't treat you with love and respect, it is *a gift* if they walk away from you or you choose to walk away from them. My gift when I left the Foreman was that I walked away from all the hurt and the pain, stopping the suffering that I surely would have endured for many more years if I continued to believe his words.

Continued Affirmations

I just finished speaking with my brother Ken. He sensed I was having a tough day; his words helped me move off the square of despair.

Ken reminded me that there are not many women like me in this world. He thinks I'm wonderful, often wishing I weren't his sister, always adding, I would make a great wife. Ha ha! He told me once again that I had it all and added that I was the sweetest woman he has ever known. So just for today, I'll try to remember I can be a loving, trusting person and at the same time not allow others to abuse or mistreat me.

I know that I experience the ebb and flow of healing and growing daily. I'm going to hang on. I made these choices trusting I'd move forward, take my power back, and continue to create a better life for myself. It all begins within.

I recently heard Ilene Wolf speak on emotional ambush. I decided to attend the meeting to support her, but I walked away with a list of how to recognize a potential emotional ambusher.

- Is charming
- Often uses romantic strategizing
- Pressures; doesn't listen to your words
- Is self-absorbed
- Sends double messages
- Diminishes your feelings, complaints, etc.
- Ignores your preferences or concerns

- Has double standards
- Is dishonest
- Criticizes you for what he/she does wrong
- Criticizes you when you practice self-care (for example, when the Foreman complained about me attending a meditation at church)
- Is arrogant
- Is patronizing
- Is stingy (financially as well as emotionally)
- Is moody (a common response when they don't get their way)

As I left the building that dreary afternoon, I was grateful that I pushed myself out of the house. Ilene's talk was just what I needed to keep my thinking on track, that little boost forward.

On my drive home, my thoughts seemed to automatically turn to the people who have left my world since I've started to heal. I see how we mirrored each other in our dysfunction, something I no longer needed in my life.

I haven't lost anything, but I have gained so much. I now believe every experience I have ever had and every person who has ever played a role in my life was sent to me for my healing journey. I thank you all. Without you I wouldn't be healthier or more the woman I was created to be. I only hope that I have helped you on your journey as much as you have helped me.

I thank all my loved ones who have loved me unconditionally, and I thank all the others for teaching me what I don't want and what I will no longer tolerate. I continue to work hard to not discount my thoughts and feelings. Spirit is bringing out the best in me.

I was pleased with myself. Pleased to have acknowledged all I have forgiven and how far I have come. Don Miguel Ruiz taught me, "When you can touch a wound and it doesn't hurt, then you know you have truly forgiven." This reality was so empowering, a refreshing feeling.

The Energy of Death

It's September 30, 2007, three months since the wedding of my friend's daughter and one month since I moved my business. It's parade day during our town's annual Apple Festival. Our little town green filled up quickly. Children with painted faces, balloons, music from the kiddie rides, and aromas of the much-desired apple fritters.

I observed for only a short while and decided to go to work. My salon is in walking distance from the parade route, and I wanted to finish unpacking and settling in.

After a while, I could hear less excitement from outside and decided the parade must be over.

I heard the front hallway door squeak slowly open. By now the sound of the front door was a familiar one, but this time it was different. Instantly, I felt cautious. Seconds later, I felt an energy that frightened me. I could feel it coming up the hallway toward my salon.

My heart pounded. I couldn't swallow. My stomach tightened. My hands started to tremble. It felt like death coming toward me.

Thoughts raced through my mind. *Why is the front door unlocked on a Sunday? No one knows I'm here today.*

I felt the presence come closer. I looked up, and walking by the salon window was the Foreman. I turned away not to engage on any level just as he turned his head to look in at me.

My panic was intense. I worried what he would do. Would I have the strength and sense not to engage? I looked away with no acknowledgment, and he just walked by.

I stood there, shaking, not sure what to do or think. Then I panicked again, anxious. *Where was he? What was he doing in the building? Why was he there? Was he hiding? Waiting for me? Watching me? Waiting to corner me?*

I started to talk to myself, telling myself to stop, calm down, and breathe. Repeating over and over, *I am safe. I am safe. Breathe. Don't give your power away.*

The panic and the fear spread like an insidious virus. Still shaking, I decided to just lock up and get out of the building. The long hallway went on forever. Panicked, I expected to find him lurking in every doorway.

The fresh air felt wonderful. As I drove home, I decided a nice, long walk would help me calm down.

As I walked around the park on that beautiful afternoon, I felt great. I had deliberately created a peaceful outcome. I cringed to think what would have been if I had just spoken one word, made eye contact, or acknowledge his presence in any way.

It took all my strength to walk the walk of my new knowledge and awareness. All the old reactions bubbled up inside of me when I saw him in the hallway. I wanted to scream, "What the hell are you doing here? Leave me alone!"

But I had managed to keep that good little girl who received the wrong messages from showing up. This time, all my hard work won. Another step of letting go of the old. Another step toward not letting him violate my boundaries, from detaching.

As I continued to heal, of course, more old childhood pain and abuse resurfaced. In certain instances, it took me years to recognize that these behaviors, too, were not acceptable. I had learned I dismissed them because my broken little being had so many bad, inappropriate experiences that I minimized them all. As I healed, it became clear that nothing of what I once considered minor *was* minor. The hidden, stuffed memories just kept popping up, showing their ugly faces.

I acknowledge now that I am strong enough, brave enough to leave the denial square. I no longer need the tool of stuffing to help me survive.

The Stalker

October 1, 2007. Only days after the Apple Festival parade incident with the Foreman in the hallway, there he was again, but this time, at 5:20 a.m. and at my home.

Just stepping out of my shower, I realized I had forgotten my robe on the end of my bed. As I dashed into my bedroom to get the warm robe, I noticed lights beaming into my bedroom window. At first I wondered, *Is that my neighbor's van, just parked in a different space? Was it there when I went to bed?*

As I put my robe on, the van started to back up, and the more I looked at it, the more it looked like the Foreman's work van. I saw ladders on top as it backed up under the streetlight. I was able to see the back rear panel—dented, just like his.

You bastard, I whispered to myself.

I felt angry, vulnerable, and violated. Buttoning up my robe, I ran downstairs, out my front door, and into the early morning cold air. My intent was to run down my driveway to catch him. I was screaming under my breath, "You son of a bitch, stay away from me! Just stay away from me!"

I stopped, talking to myself. *Your hair is wet. You're half-naked. It's early morning and a very sick man was looking up into your bedroom.*

As I turned around to walk back, the Foreman passed the front of my home, driving very slowly. I could feel his eyes on me. I glared back at him, then walked into my home and locked the door behind me.

It took days for me to stop being so upset over the violation of my privacy, but that anger was growth—for the first time, fright wasn't my initial reaction.

I was at work when a friend stopped by. She commented that I radiated love, peace, and joy, adding, "It's beaming from you."

What a great feeling! A huge gift! Someone saw my light today. I was able to let go of all craziness from the hallway. When I walked through the darkness, I was given opportunities to access my light. Continued digging deep within expanded my capacity, bringing me to a greater awareness, pulling me out of despair and struggle.

I am stronger than any old thoughts, habits, or belief system that no longer serves me. I am free to create, free to choose thoughts to lift and encourage me. I am free to choose a less fear-based life and open to change, expecting the best. As I sat and thought about this reality, gratitude welled up inside me. My life is clearly improving thought by thought, moment by moment, and day by day.

It Wasn't a Closet

It's December. Four and a half short months ago, I was in such discernment, everything seemed so bleak, and yet God knew better. My new business location has helped me heal my way through my old hiding-in-the-closet fears. At a HEAL group, I became aware that my business setting brought me back to when I hid in that closet or dark, cold front hallway to escape my abuser. I finally understood I wasn't frightened by the new salon location after all; I was frightened to bring up that old, horrible memory.

Once that clarity showed up, I realized I have never experienced such a joyous working environment. I am stress-free, no headaches, no miserable neighbors or landlord. I have plenty of new clients, passersby smiling and waving hello. A handful of my new friends often check in on me to chat a minute or two. I often hear compliments about how nice it feels in my salon or that the energy is *great* there. One woman went as far as to say she wished her home felt like that. What a beautiful compliment.

Today I came across a note I wrote to myself years ago that read, "To worry is to doubt every promise of God." Cleaning out my mental closet was lots of hard work; thank goodness I have never been afraid of that.

I'm starting to let my imagination run a little wild, dreaming big. I started to relax and change my thoughts by making one collage after the other of things to dream about—simple, everyday things for most people but treats and extravagances for me. I've found myself engrossed in my new dreams. I've left the past behind. I spend hours cutting and pasting, allowing myself to play for a change.

This playtime has become a great tool for me—a mini-escape, at times like a mini-retreat—quieting my mind and calming me. Now relaxed and open enough to let Spirit surprise me.

A Kiddie-Coaster This Time

It's a new week; here comes the rollercoaster again. I am lonely and angry. The good news is that I ride that coaster better these days.

I picked up the book *The Power of Intention* by Dr. Wayne Dyer and randomly opened it. "Remember, as Gandhi reminds us, 'Divine guidance often comes when the horizon is the blackest.'" It was a wink from God. My present will be a testimony of my past thoughts.

Hang on, I told myself. *It's just a kiddie-coaster this time.*

The more blessings I'm aware of, the more I find. The more love I open my heart to, the more love I have to share.

Still looking for something to fix my thoughts on, I picked another book, *The Language of Letting Go,* a daily mediation by Melody Beattie that I've used for the past sixteen or seventeen years, like a second bible.

I often say there are no coincidences. The page I opened to was about relationships.

> There is a gift for us in each relationship that comes our way. Sometimes the gift is a behavior we're learning to acquire: detachment, self-esteem, being confident enough to set a boundary, or owning our power in another way. Some relationships trigger healing in us, often healing from issues of the past. Or an issue we're facing today. Sometimes we find ourselves learning the most important lessons from the people we least expect to help us.
>
> Relationships may teach us about loving ourselves or someone else. Or maybe we'll learn to let others love us. Sometimes we aren't certain what lesson we are learning, especially while we're in the midst of the process. But we can trust that the lesson and the gift are there. We don't have to control the process. We'll understand when it's time. We can also trust that the gift is precisely what we need.

That is what this daily meditation was for me, a gift. It helped me back onto the happy, grateful-where-I-am square. Perceiving my loneliness as a gift is a much healthier, happier way to think as I move forward on this journey.

After about a week of figuring where my deeper feelings and emotions were coming from, I realized the Foreman's lurking kept me in victim mode. I struggled with "some love is better than no love."

Once again, it was the mistake of remembering only the good and ignoring the bad. It's so easy to forget the hell you have lived when you're trying to forgive.

Looking back on another level, I see some of the confusion with the Foreman and his behavior came from him not physically abusing me like Tony did. The Foreman's abuse was more subtle. His comments made me question my own views and often left me explaining or questioning what I knew.

The realization that I wasted more time on a man who didn't deserve me was difficult. I felt so stupid. How could another one have fooled me so? The battle of what I was taught over what I was learning was a job in itself.

Holiday Gifts

It's wonderful to be able to forgive and forget. And yet I think it could come back to haunt you if you forget too well. With the charmer, you can slip right back onto one of those old dysfunctional squares, forgetting all about yourself, your wants and needs.

I learned years ago not to dwell on the negative and the valuable lesson to stay mindful of my own life, creating peace and joy in my heart and home. One of my favorite verses from the Bible: "Judge not and ye shall not be judged. Condemn not and ye shall not be condemned. Forgive and ye shall be forgiven." (Luke 6:3-7) I also like to remember a quotation from Eckhart Tolle: "All negativity, unhappiness, or suffering come from resistance. Resistance is arguing with what is." I chuckle to myself as I recall often saying to the Foreman, "Calm down. It is what it is."

I also learned that with acceptance comes freedom, allowing our true self to show up or to be revealed. I think some piece of us is continually dying. It takes strength and courage to walk through our fears. And to stop using denial, anger, aggressions, addictions, manipulation, or control to pave our way.

God is available to all of us. Real love is honoring one's own process, not standing in judgment or making lists of mistakes. Loving relationships bring comfort, not stress or anxiety.

Thanksgiving was beautiful. Nicholas and I shared with friends and family. We had lots of good food, good conversation, and, most important, lots of love. It was a glorious, peaceful, fun day, the most pleasant and peaceful, love-filled day in a very long time.

In the early hours of the next morning, my brother called to check in. I told him I was so looking forward to a beautiful Christmas and ending 2007 on the best physical and emotional square I had ever been on. With a childlike giggle, I declared that I was open and ready for the best opportunities and outcomes. Believing they would be more wonderful than I could ever imagine.

Ken's next words, "Don't ever forget. We are really good people, considering what we *crawled out* of," left me speechless.

So many emotions bubbled up inside me. His words were a validation of my feelings and pain. That he felt the same was heartbreaking. It brought me to tears. As we hung up, I realized what a gift he and I just shared. Truly, a gift that cannot be bought, a closeness that comes only from years of having each other's back. A closeness even distance can't deny.

To add to my joy, my daily reading happened to be "Therefore encourage one another and build up each other as indeed you are doing." (Thessalonians 5:11)

I sat for a while reflecting on where I have been in my life. I know not all of my decisions have been easy or felt great. I do know that I have always done my best, or, as Louise Hay puts it, "with the knowledge, understanding, and awareness I had at the time." And I trust it's the same for everyone. I don't believe anyone of us ever wakes up in the morning and says, "Let me make bad decisions to intentionally add to my misery," or, "I'm going to be an asshole today."

Learning this has been a tremendous welcoming gift for me. It has helped me move forward by leaps and bounds on the forgiveness square. Again, when I knew more, I did things differently. I am grateful each day for my clear thinking, for my not taking others' behaviors personally, and the light that showed me the way to crawl out and land on healthy ground.

My right-hand men and women have been the authors I have chosen to learn from. Another gift from Louise: "Blame is the surest way to stay in a problem. Once we learn to stop the blame, we learn to aid in our healing."

No one escapes childhood without some scar or sabotaging messages—some worse than others. Nor is becoming the person God intended us to be without scars or bruises. We are healed by using the dark times for good. If we don't have tough dark times, how would we ever recognize the light of God's blessings when they appear?

It's December 2. As the holiday season got into full swing, I occasionally struggled with what I came from, with what some family members have chosen or not chosen to do. In my old awareness or perception, I'd have said, "How sad. How sad Nicholas has no idea who these people are." Even today, I still think, perhaps, how sad, but oh how blessed. Hopefully, he will have less work to do in the message-deleting department.

My thought for today, "What you're aware of, you're in control of, and what you're not aware of is in control of you." So today, I am doing great! And quite content with what is.

Today at the doctor's office, I read a quotation: "You have found true balance when you are grateful for who you are."

No coincidences, I say.

I also received a phone call from my friend Noreen, who offered to take Nicholas shopping for a Christmas gift for me. After their shopping experience, she called to tell me, "You have a really good boy. No, he's quite a wonderful young man."

She said that he was quite mature and a great conversationalist. Adding they even discussed me leaving the Foreman. She told Nick she was proud of me. She knew it was a difficult decision for me but the right thing to do.

To my surprise, Nicholas told Noreen he was glad as well because Danielle had shared a lot about her dad. Noreen didn't go into his actual conversation but said most of it was not very complimentary. I never knew Nicholas and Danielle had that type of conversation. So Nick was watching what I was going to do with this guy the whole time. Wow!

Later that evening, Noreen called back. She had forgotten to tell me about another conversation Nick and she had.

Nicholas said, "You know, my mom didn't have it easy when she was little. And look how successful she is. And she did it all by herself."

Tears welled up. Did I dare think that my fourteen-year-old had a good start on this thing called awareness?

As his mother, every ounce of despair or struggle I experienced will be worth it to see him grow up to be a healthy, aware, loving, nonjudgmental, free, and peaceful human being. Do I dare start to believe I have broken the cycle?

Christmas Joy

Christmas is getting closer. I'm feeling exceptionally well. My whole being is content with exactly what is. I don't long for anything or anyone. I appreciate the joys that fill my days. I still enjoy the Nicholas Christmas story, sharing it with a few close friends. My heart fills with pride as I watch their expressions of approval or "Good job!" pats on the back.

Looking forward to celebrating the birth of our savior as well as welcoming in the New Year, I feel like life is just beginning for me. My darkest times have been transformed with the help of my silent partner. The seed of peace has sprouted and now I feel that new-life vitality. "With God, all things are possible." (Matthew 19:26)

I have become a magnet, attracting many who treat me with love and respect. I smile, knowing I weathered the storms quite well. I feel magnificent, not carrying someone else's guilt or shame.

Christmas week was wonderful. Not a moment of feeling overwhelmed or rushed. I simply prioritized each day and sailed through, celebrating, loving, and laughing with friends and loved ones. I had the best time with my son, just loving him and sharing that he is truly a wonderful and fun young man.

New Year's Eve is tomorrow. As usual, I am spending time thinking about my year. I also went around the house gathering some of my affirmations. I love this habit. I can't even keep track of how many times one of them caught my eye throughout the year and immediately brought a smile to my face. Some of them:

- Miracles are on their way this very day.
- If you do the work, He will furnish the bricks. [Joyce Meyer]
- Clarity is the state of seeing clearly, seeing things in a new light, like applying Windex to your soul. (Cherie Carter-Scott)
- True peace is found within.
- They are wound driven; bless them and walk away. (Ilene Wolf)
- Today is a brand-new day, one you have never seen before.
- The ego urges you to accomplish, while the soul merely asks you to enjoy the process.

I end my year knowing that life is a matter of what we listen for. By staying in tune with my inner self, I will experience joy and fulfillment, a sense of true peace, not just a bunch of temporary escapes.

I have unlimited potential. I can't overcome years of conditioning with only one prayer or one therapy session or one whatever. I'm just ecstatic that I was willing to do the work. It's true. Change your thoughts, habits, old beliefs, and patterns, and watch your life transform.

Louise Hay says, "If we belittle ourselves, our life will mean very little. If we love and appreciate ourselves, life can be a wonderful present."

I gave these words a lot of thought. One new belief at a time has shaped a new life for me and my son. I have forgiven many, but, more important, I have forgiven myself.

It was "there" that got me "here." I appreciate all that I am and continue to work on becoming the woman God created me to be. As I live with more richness in my moments, I look back at all the storms that got in the way as if they were someone else's life. I feel like a toddler growing and exploring this wonderful world I was born in. Only this time around, with no abuse.

I believe every person who crosses our path is fighting some kind of battle, some just more evident than others. Be kinder than you need to be; you could make a world of difference to someone today.

No shame or blame can hold you back. We all have the power we need to create whatever our heart's desires may be. The power is within you this very moment. You must find the tools you need to ground yourself so you can begin to take charge of what you want or need to take the next step.

Begin with spending as little time as possible with negative people, places, or things. Refuse to become immobile out of fear. Refuse to be drawn into the turbulence of others' drama. Stop seeing yourself as a victim. Find something or someone to be grateful for. It will immediately raise your spirit out of the depths of despair and contribute toward your own well-being. Even if it's just one new thought a day.

Remember that suffering is a sign something is out of line. Suffering is like a sticky note reading, "This needs to change." Or you need to grow or transform, etc. When you change the way you look at things, the things you look at change. There are no quick fixes for anyone. I refuse to let what I came from define who I am today.

Adversity has been my greatest teacher, and my faith has given me the breath I needed to make it to the next moment. I understand now that I was a courageous, resilient child who has grown and transformed into a whole, healthy, authentic, powerful, playful, confident, free woman living a more mindful life. Some friends have called it inner strength and determination along with a relentless and unflappable spirit. Others have added nonjudgmental, compassionate, humble, a giving angel. A true survivor. Ken calls me "the Rock."

Want to Know What I Know?

These days I am surrounded with a righteous support team, people who love and lift me up.

February 6, 2010. Four years ago today, I first decided to leave the Foreman. For a moment today, I thought about how he used to insinuate that I didn't live in the real world. His words were sharp and his voice, condescending and ridiculing. He referred to my "positive outlook" and "evident expectation" of the best from everyone or every situation, when, in hindsight, I was very much on track. It was my job to find my way and my joy. We must continually ask ourselves:

- What do I need?
- What do I want?
- Is this situation bringing me peace?
- Am I loved and respected?
- Which part of my mind rules me today, the old negative, stuffed subconscious or the new, positive conscious?

I believe life is a process of learning and teaching. That the enduring lessons I learned have come through the power of perseverance—don't stop, just keep moving forward. There was a time I thought, *If I could only teach the Foreman one thing, it would be worth it.* But in the end, I was the student who learned from yet another alcoholic what I will no longer tolerate.

I broke the cycle of what I came from. Today I stand as a survivor! Is it your turn to start your journey of *crawling out?* Please join me. I'll be waiting for you.

Epilogue

Much has happened since I finished this book.

My son is a fine, upstanding young man, finishing his third year of college, majoring in criminal justice. I was brought to tears by a sentence in his college entry essay: "I want to be the one who is called on to help women and children." Tears over no matter how hard I tried to protect him, he still suffered and, on some level, he knew there was nobody protecting us. *He gets it* and wants to make a difference. I am extremely proud of him, and, together, we have broken the cycle and will continue to raise awareness of domestic violence.

I understand that Teddy died of cancer in the mid-1970s, only two years after running away with and marrying my mother's best friend. Tony passed away at the very young age of fifty-nine in 2009. The Foreman, according to mutual friends, has not altered from the path he was on.

In the six years since my last session with Dr. Amy, I have become strong and clear on what I will or will not accept, and I *don't* step backwards. Fear and confusion no longer dictate my every thought or move. My battle with my subconscious gets easier by the day. I am healthier than I have ever been, prescription-free, and my physical issues slipped away one by one, just as I thought they would.

Leaving home at sixteen with an I'll-show-you attitude clouded the fact I also carried within me the fear of making a mistake. I turned to unavailable people for love and support, something I learned as a small child. In hindsight, the mistakes taught me what works and what doesn't.

I worked very hard to break the cycle of denial, to learn the steps, to be treated as a human being. Victims of abuse are so unclear about what is acceptable and what is not. Every person is what he or she has learned. Please don't stand in judgment while we work to figure out what's right. Don't judge our process or how long it takes. Sadly, for most of us, it is a lifetime of work.

The most important decision you can make is to decide today to let go of your old story. Know it is only the result of the wrong messages you internalized in your childhood. Then, seek out a supportive circle to help you reprogram and heal.

I'll say it again. When you remember that you're exactly where you're supposed to be at any given moment, no matter what's going on, it takes the anxiety and, perhaps, the overwhelmed feelings away, giving you permission to calm down and just let things go. It's all in the plan.

Writing my story was a cathartic journey, a big release of toxicity on all levels, with an ocean of tears shed along the way. I am proud of who I am and proud of where my history has brought me. No more shame or blame. I live my life with empathy but keep myself safe at the same time.

As *a survivor*, I honor myself and my present with pride. I cherish who I am. Statistics predict someone with my history usually has a devastating ending.

I am enchanted by life, inspired and guided by Spirit every step of the way. I am not simply surviving—I am now *thriving*. It is exciting to be clear and to see the doors opening and the next steps revealed. I do my part each minute of every day to be the best I can be with my understanding at that moment to create an exceptional, peace-filled life.

I stand tall with an open heart to give and receive, knowing my outcome is nothing but a miracle—by the grace of God. Amen.

I hope my story will move you to empowerment and that you will join me on the survivor square!

Dear Reader

Has my story touched you, moved you in any way? I'd love to hear your comments, reactions, personal stories, or any feedback you'd like to share. I always say, "We're either the teacher or the student," even though we don't necessarily know which we are until hindsight shows us. You can email me at casey@caseymorley.com.

Please join me in my mission and share my website with your friends and contacts. Remember, one statistic shows that one in three women is abused by an intimate partner. That means if you have ninety women contacts, thirty of them suffer from some form of domestic abuse. Similarly, one out of nine men are victims of domestic abuse. If that same list contains ninety *male* contacts, eleven of them endure abuse. Help me nudge people to a new awareness, one person at a time.

If you'd like to stay up-to-date with my mission to increase awareness of and help reduce domestic violence statistics, please go to caseymorley.com. While there, submit your name and email address. You will receive a what's-been-happening newsletter every other month.

Resources

CRISIS INTERVENTION

The Twenty-Four-Hour National Domestic Violence Hotline

1-800-799-7233

If You Need Immediate Emergency Assistance

Dial 9-1-1

Break the Cycle
    www.breakthecycle.org
Casa de Esperanza (Linea de crisis 24-horas)
    www.casadeesperanza.org
Child Abuse Hotline
    800-422-4453
Covenant House Hotline/Youth Nine Line
    800-999-9999
CT Child Abuse and Neglect Hotline
    800-842-2288
CT Coalition Against Domestic Violence
    www.ctcadv.org
CT Dept of Children and Families
    www.ct.gov/dcf
CT Sexual Assault Crisis Services
    www.connsacs.org
    Hotline 888-999-5545

Futures Without Violence
    www.FuturesWithoutViolence.org
HEAL [Healing Emotionally Abused Lives]
    www.emotionalheal.org
Just for Kids Hotline
    888-422-4453
Kid Save Line
    800-543-7283
Love Is Respect
    www.loveisrespect.org
National Child Abuse Hotline
    800-792-5200
National Coalition Against Domestic Violence
    www.ncadv.org
National Dating Abuse Hotline
    866-331-9474
National Domestic Violence Hotline
    800-799- SAFE
National Resource Center on Domestic Violence
    www.nrcdv.org
National Runaway Hotline
    800-621-4000
National Sexual Violence Resource Center
    www.nsvrc.org
National Youth Crisis Hotline
    800-442-HOPE (4673)
No More
    www.nomore.org
Prevent Child Abuse America
    312-663-3520

Rape Abuse Incest National Network [RAINN]

www.rainn.org

800-656-4673

Safe Horizon's Domestic Violence Hotline

800-621-HOPE (4673)

Safe Horizon's Rape, Sexual Assault & Incest Hotline

1-212-227-3000

Safe Place

512-440-7273

Suicide Prevention Hotline

800-827-7571

SELF-HELP RESOURCES

Al-Anon/Alateen

800-4AL-ANON

Alcoholics Anonymous

212-870-3400

CBC National AIDS Hotline

800-342-2437

Co-Dependents Anonymous

602-277-7991

Cocaine Anonymous National Referral Line

800-347-8998

Future Point (empowering teens)

www.futurepoint.com

Grief Recovery Institute

323-650-1234

www.grief-recovery.com

National Center for Post-Traumatic Stress Disorder

www.dartmouth.edu

National Health Information Center

800-336-4797

National Institute of Drug Abuse

800-662-4357

Planned Parenthood

212-541-7800

www.plannedparenthood.org

Spanish HIV/STD/AIDS

Hotline 800-243-7889

Teen Outreach

www.teenoutreach.com

www.teencentral.net

End Matter

FYI

Adrenal Fatigue

Adrenal fatigue, also referred to as hypoadrenia, a deficiency in the functioning of the adrenal glands, part of the endocrine system. In *Adrenal Fatigue: The 21st Century Stress Syndrome,* James L. Wilson, N.D., D.C., Ph.D., states that the adrenal glands typically release a precise and balanced amount of steroid hormones into the body. Because the adrenal glands are designed to respond to changes in the body's inner physical, emotional, and psychological environment, many things can interfere with this balance. Meaning too much physical, emotional, and psychological stress can deplete your adrenal glands.

Modern medicine does not recognize hypoadrenia as a distinct syndrome; nevertheless, it can wreak havoc with your life and well-being. In more serious cases, gland activity is reduced so much a person may have difficulty getting out of bed and staying up for more than a few hours a day. Each incremental reduction in adrenal function profoundly affects every organ and system in the body.

Fatigue is a universal symptom of adrenal fatigue, but it is such a common complaint—that rundown feeling or an inability to keep up with life's daily demands—that physicians rarely consider a diagnosis of adrenal fatigue.

This syndrome, along with its signs and symptoms, is not readily identifiable. People with adrenal fatigue often look and act relatively normal, may not have obvious signs of physical illness, yet live with grey feelings and a general sense of unwellness. Hypoadrenia sufferers tend to experience allergies, arthritic pain. Women can have more premenstrual tension, as well as increased difficulty during menopause.

People with the syndrome can also show a tendency toward increased fears, anxiety, and depression, including intervals of confusion and difficulty with concentration. Tolerance levels may decrease and frustration levels increase. Insomnia may result from imbalance. If this condition worsens, seemingly unrelated conditions may appear, including asthma, allergies, fibromyalgia, hypoglycemia, adult-onset diabetes, autoimmune disorders, and alcoholism.

Sufferers must drive themselves much harder merely to accomplish everyday duties, because when small stresses occur simultaneously, accumulate, or become chronic, the adrenals do not have time to fully recover, and, most likely, the result will be adrenal fatigue. Perfectionists, a driven person, anyone who does not get enough rest, one who is under constant pressure or feels *trapped* or *helpless*, who feels *overwhelmed* by continuous difficulties, one who has experienced severe or chronic emotional or physical traumas may suffer from this syndrome.

Battered Woman Syndrome

This condition results from domestic abuse and relates to the physical, emotional, and psychological effects of that abuse. The four stages of the syndrome include

- The victim's *denial* of trouble within the relationship
- *Guilt/self-blame* that occurs when the victim finally admits the abuse to herself and others but believes "she deserves it"
- *Enlightenment* that takes place when the victim realizes she is not responsible for the abuse and does not deserve it; she may

stay in the relationship out of fear that her partner may seriously harm or kill her or her children

- *Responsibility* that arises when the victim knows she cannot change her abuser and she must leave the abusive relationship for her sake and that of her children

Domestic abuse occurs in cycles of violence. The partner, typically but not always male, begins with verbal abuse—insults and criticism—then escalates to slaps and shoves. These then become physical assaults and batterings.

Between cycles, the abusive partner apologizes, promising never to abuse the victim again. The victim relents, allowing the perpetrator to remain in her home, and the cycle soon begins again, over time increasing in severity.

Domestic abuse can lead to a cascade of other symptoms and illnesses, including, but not limited to, withdrawal (because of bruising, fear of reprisal for being away from home, etc.), nervousness when interacting with others, distrust of others, depression, posttraumatic stress disorder (PTSD). Recent research has shown that chronic stress, which unleashes damaging fight-or-flight hormones, can have as negative an effect on the body as bad nutrition.

Borderline Personality Disorder

In my many readings, I came across the book, *Skills Training Manual for Treating Borderline Personality Disorder*, by Marcia M. Linehan. She states that many suffer from something known as borderline personality disorder (BPD). Basically, BPD is a combination of an emotional response system that is oversensitive and overactive and an inability to modulate strong emotions and reactions. So one gets stuck in the extremes of emotions, unable to move to calmness.

Experience has taught me that centering yourself in this process rather than living at the extremes requires awareness and a lot of hard work. But, the outcome is a validation of where you've been—the abuse—and where you're going or want to be—your abuse-free future. It also requires that you recognize your transition as you make your journey.

You must learn to become comfortable with change. Emotional disregulation comes from an *invalidating environment* and is damaging, especially to a child. I wrote earlier about saying, "I'm thirsty" but hearing "No, you're not. You just had a drink." Or, "I have a headache" vs. "No, you don't. You're too young to have a headache." "I did my best." "No, you didn't."

How can a child discriminate whether his or her own feelings and other emotions are real when always receiving such conflicting information? The parents or family are the problem by invalidating the child's feelings or needs. Many parents are unaware of the damage they cause—the confusion that occurs with the discrepancies between the child's private experience and how others respond.

As a child, many of my painful experiences were trivialized and attributed to negative traits—"You can't because you're a baby." "You're lazy." Or even, "You can't because you're a girl." I would have to guess that this was the start of me learning to not trust my own thoughts or emotions.

According to Linehan, "One of the most traumatic invalidating experiences a child can go through is sexual abuse. Researchers have estimated that up to 75% of individuals with BPD have experienced some sort of sexual abuse in childhood." I certainly fit this category.

Posttraumatic Stress Disorder

Virtually any event that is life-threatening or that severely compromises the emotional well-being of an individual may cause posttraumatic stress disorder (PTSD). Examples of such events include natural disasters like floods and earthquakes, combat, serious accidents, physical or sexual abuse as an adult or in childhood. PTSD may be manifested immediately after the event, or years later.

PTSD/anxiety disorder is defined as a constellation of changes in personality and behavior that begin after such an experience and persist for more than a month. Typically, a person who experiences such an event feels like the everyday world is no longer real and that she/he is in a dream state. Some may feel that their minds are detached from their emotions as well as from their physical bodies, a condition referred to as dissociation. In some cases, "psychic numbing," or "emotional anesthesia," occurs when the sufferer exhibits feelings of being detached from other people, from the outside world, or from activities that used to be enjoyable. Other sufferers have difficulty falling asleep or staying asleep. Many suffer from heightened startle response. Some may have trouble concentrating, have blackouts, have difficulty remembering things, be hypervigilant to threats, or have phobias of places or people or of an experience that reminds the sufferer of the trauma.

People suffering from PTSD may feel scared, confused, angry, edgy, and irritable, constantly on guard. These symptoms can disrupt life, making it hard to continue everyday activities. Some people tend to reexperience the event in flashbacks, dreams, or nightmares. Symptoms can worsen for people who find themselves in situations that resemble the original trauma; most anything in everyday life can be a trigger to the past trauma.

Anxiety and depression are very common among PTSD sufferers. Guilt can play a major role, causing those with this disorder to turn to alcohol or drugs to escape the pain; others may become self-defeating or suicidal.

This emotional deadness and distancing of oneself makes it very difficult for sufferers to see good in their future, difficult to make plans.

It becomes a battle trying to regulate feelings and control explosive anger.

Victims of abuse feel helpless at the hands of their all-powerful abusers. This helplessness becomes a reminder to PTSD sufferers of their inability to protect themselves, and many are convinced that the world is unjust or evil.

Stockholm Syndrome

Stockholm syndrome is a phenomenon in which kidnap victims form an emotional bond with their kidnappers. It gained much press attention during the kidnappings of Patricia Hearst and Elizabeth Smart.

Research has suggested that Stockholm syndrome also helps explain certain behaviors of survivors of more commonplace types of abusive relationships—battered wives, incest survivors, and physically or emotionally abused children.

References

Al-Anon Family Groups, Inc. *Courage to Change: One Day at a Time in Al-Anon II.* New York: Al-Anon Family Group Headquarters, Inc., 1992.

American Heritage Medical Dictionary Online. Houghton Mifflin Company, 2007. Accessed June 2013.

Andrews, Ted. *Animal Speak.* St. Paul, MN: Andrews: Llewllyn Publications, 1993.

Beattie, Melody. *The Language of Letting Go.* New York: Harper Collins Publishing, 1990.

Dyer, Dr. Wayne. *The Power of Intention.* Carlsbad, CA: Hay House, Inc., 2004.

Foundation of Inner Peace. *A Course in Miracles.* New York: Viking, 1996.

Hay, Louise L. *Heal Your Body A–Z.* Carlsbad, CA: Hay House, Inc., 1998.

———. *You Can Heal Your Life.* Carlsbad, CA: Hay House, Inc., 1999.

Holmes, Ernest. *Science of Mind: A Guild for Spiritual Living.* New York: Tarcher Putnam, 1966.

Lineham, Marcia M. *Skills Training Manual for Treating Borderline Personality Disorder.* New York: The Guilford Press, 1993.

Morrison, Kevin. *Stitches.* Worcester, MA: Ambassador Books, 2003.

Northrup, M.D., Christine. *The Dr. Christine Northrup Newsletter.* Premier issue. Carlsbad, CA: Hay House, Inc., 5; 1(1).

Richo, David. *When Love Meets Fear.* New York: Paulist Press, 1977.

Ridha, M.D., Arem. *The Thyroid Solution.* Emmaus, PA: Rodale/Ballantine, 2008.

Ruiz, Don Miguel. *The Four Agreements.* San Rafael, CA: Amber-Allen Publishing, 1997.

Science of the Mind Newsletter, 11:06; 79(11).

Soul Retrieval. Accessed October 29, 2012.

Soul Retrieval. Wikipedia. Wikipedia Foundation. Accessed September 5, 2012.

Virtue, Ph.D., Doreen. *Divine Prescriptions.* New York: St. Martin's Press, 2000.

———. *Guidance for the Goddess, Guidance Oracle Cards.* Carlsbad, CA: Hay House, Inc., 2004.

———. *Healing with the Angels Oracle Cards.* Carlsbad, CA: Hay House, Inc., 1999.

WebMD, "Posttraumatic Stress Disorder (PTSD)." WebMD, n.d. Accessed October 2012.

Wilson, N.D., D.C., Ph.D., James L. *Adrenal Fatigue: The 21st Century Stress Syndrome.* Petaluma, CA: Smart Publications, 2001.

Wolf, Ilene. (Ambusher). Abuse facilitator, HEAL. Naugatuck, CT: EmotionalHeal.org